Cases in International Finance

Second Edition

CASES IN INTERNATIONAL FINANCE

Second Edition

Gunter Dufey
The University of Michigan

Ian H. Giddy
New York University

With Contributions by
Edgar Barrett • Frederick Choi • Thomas Hofstedt
Roy Smith • Arthur Stonehill • Raymond Vernon
Ingo Walter • Christine Weisfelder

ADDISON-WESLEY PUBLISHING COMPANY
Reading, Massachusetts • Menlo Park, California • New York
Don Mills, Ontario • Wokingham, England • Amsterdam • Bonn
Sydney • Singapore • Tokyo • Madrid • San Juan • Milan • Paris

Sponsoring Editor: Mac Mendelsohn
Assistant Editor: Kim Kramer
Production Supervisor: Peggy McMahon
Senior Marketing Manager: David Theisen
Senior Manufacturing Coordinator: Judy Sullivan
Cover Designer: Absolute Design
Editorial/Production Services: PC&F, Inc.

Library of Congress Cataloging-in-Publication Data

Cases in international finance / [edited by] Gunter Dufey, Ian H.
  Giddy.—2nd ed.
        p. cm.
    Rev. ed. of: 50 cases in international finance. c1987.
    Includes bibliographical references.
    ISBN 0-201-51307-2
    1. International finance—Case studies.   I. Dufey, Gunter.
  II. Giddy, Ian H.   III. 50 cases in international finance.
  HG3881.A125   1992
  332'.042—dc20   92-23755
                                                      CIP

ISBN 0-201-51307-2

2 3 4 5 6 7 8 9 10-AL-959493

Preface

International finance continues to be a dynamic area of study: its importance is growing and the field is evolving rapidly—in practice as well as theory. More and more business firms find themselves confronted by international competition, know-how and financial capital is becoming available on a global basis. As a consequence, firms are increasingly affected by shifts in real exchange rates, are affected by relative borrowing costs and (perhaps) differing costs of capital. In spite of the more extensive integration of markets for real as well as financial assets, markets remain partially segmented giving rise to arbitrage profits to those that are "swift of foot and keen of mind." New risks are becoming apparent but, by the same token, tools and techniques evolve for firms to mitigate their effects.

All this requires new mindsets and skills and this collection of cases represents our modest contribution to this end.

In response to market demands and the advice of friends and colleagues at many institutions we have slightly reduced the number of cases to keep the price down and leave more time for the teaching of theory and concepts. We have updated many cases and added 22 new ones, cases developed for use in our classes and seminars that reflect the revolution in international financial markets, institutions and techniques.

Equally important, we completely recast the sequence and structure of this collection: beginning with three cases designed to allow for a quick and efficient understanding of the International Monetary System, we follow what we believe is a logical sequence dealing with issues of international investment, funding the capital structure, and a special section on corporate foreign exchange risk management, reflecting the importance of this topic in international corporate finance. Twelve cases that focus on the instruments and techniques available in international financial markets complement the corporate finance sequence. We conclude the book with a series of cases on special topics, organized around the issues of (a) taxation, control and reporting, (b) international banking including the exciting area of privatization, and (c) two comprehensive cases dealing with organizational issues of finance in multinational corporations and a comprehensive financing case.

We have tried to maintain a balance of traditional, full length cases that challenge the students' ability to sort out the relevant data, as well as mini cases that lend themselves to flexible use by the instructor, ranging from use as quasi-problems to the basis for rich discussion with practitioners when unstated assumptions and conditions are elicited in the case discussion. The casenotes for all of the cases are available upon request from the publisher.

As in the first edition, we can attest to the fact that all cases have been successfully tested with MBA students and/or with executives. The authors are indebted to all these unnamed "guinea pigs," as well as to many colleagues and friends for helpful suggestions, without implicating them in remaining, or new, "bugs." In a field as dynamic as international finance, one remains an eternal student and we repeat our plea from the first edition: "write to us," directly or through our publisher.

Ann Arbor, Michigan   G.D.
New York, New York   I.H.G.

Contents

II *International Investment Decisions* 33

IV *Foreign Exchange Risk Analysis and Management*   131

V *Instruments and Techniques*   181

VI *Special Issues: Taxation, Control and Reporting*   223

VII *International Banking* 259

VIII *Integrated Financing and Organization Decisions*   307

I

The International Monetary System

Ian H. Giddy

Case 1

Fun in Finland

Richard Artschwager was looking forward to having fun in Finland in the summer of 1990. In a few days he was due to fly to Vaasa, on the Gulf of Bothnia. August, he had heard, was wonderful: one could stay up all night with barely a few hours of darkness. All at the expense of the London branch of Westdeutsche Landesbank, which had hired Artschwager straight out of university, where he had majored in art and economics. The bank was seeking to develop stronger relationships with companies in the northern rim of Europe, namely Norway, Sweden and Finland, countries that were making noises about wanting to join the European community.

Before he and his senior colleague went over, however, they had to prepare. Their department manager had given them some statistics on the country's international transactions, for the bank wanted to understand conditions in a country before getting involved. In particular the bank was concerned about what might happen to capital flows and the currency, the Finnish markka, as Finland readied itself for possible membership in the European Monetary System. The tables, shown as Exhibit 1 and Exhibit 2, gave summary information about Finland's balance of payments.

What is this, a test already? Artschwager wondered. Nevertheless he was determined to give a credible showing of his answers to the questions.

Richard and Hans, please examine the attached figures on Finland's balance of payments for 1989, and tell me the following:

1. *Did Finland have a **trade** surplus or deficit? What is the trend?*
2. *Was Finland's **current account** in surplus or deficit?*
3. *What is the implication of your answer to the previous question for Finland's **capital account?***
4. *Did Finland have a **capital account** surplus or deficit?*
5. *Did Finland have an overall balance of payments surplus or deficit?*
6. *Compare the country's overall balance of payments surplus or deficit with its change in official reserves.*
7. *Given that Finland had a fixed exchange rate in 1989, what is the implication of your answers to the last two questions for conditions in the domestic money market?*

Exhibit 1 *Finland's current account*
Current Account, MILL FIM

During period	Exports of goods, f.o.b.	Transport receipts	Travel receipts	Other services receipts	Services receipts, total (2+3+4)	Exports of goods and services (1+5)	Investment income	Transfers and other income	Current account receipts (6+7+8)	Imports of goods, c.i.f.	Transport expenditure	Travel expenditure	Other services expenditure
	1	2	3	4	5	6	7	8	9	10	11	12	13
1985	82 475	6 216	3 258	6 224	15 698	98 173	5 847	3 791	107 811	80 764	2 545	5 031	6 554
1986	81 066	5 757	3 195	5 616	14 568	95 634	4 510	3 609	103 752	76 736	2 160	5 587	5 415
1987	83 826	6 370	3 736	6 099	16 204	100 030	5 075	3 231	108 336	81 867	2 610	6 811	6 488
1988	91 313	7 026	4 280	6 132	17 438	108 750	7 836	4 415	121 002	91 232	3 338	7 907	7 390
1989	98 265	7 662	4 497	6 277	18 436	116 701	10 646	3 652	130 999	104 400	3 869	8 969	8 759
1988													
I	20 516	1 623	776	1 583	3 982	24 498	1 863	1 083	27 443	19 684	671	1 829	2 011
II	22 569	1 752	1 041	1 379	4 172	26 740	1 890	1 119	29 750	23 184	780	1 916	1 730
III	21 621	1 880	1 486	1 264	4 631	26 251	1 978	1 188	29 360	23 767	940	2 210	1 789
IV	26 608	1 771	977	1 905	4 653	31 261	2 105	1 080	34 446	24 597	944	1 951	1 860
1989													
I	24 944	1 853	869	1 322	4 044	28 988	2 057	851	31 896	24 292	820	1 922	2 170
II	23 370	1 948	1 078	1 376	4 401	27 771	2 793	930	31 494	24 762	947	2 170	2 234
III	22 534	1 982	1 421	1 466	4 869	27 403	2 476	927	30 806	25 637	1 022	2 431	2 070
IV	27 418	1 879	1 129	2 114	5 122	32 540	3 320	944	36 803	29 708	1 080	2 446	2 285
1990													
I	24 418	2 053	806	1 515	4 374	28 792	3 056	820	32 667	24 697	968	2 461	2 288
II	26 480	2 142	1 145	1 290	4 576	31 057	3 332	967	35 356	27 572	1 060	2 697	2 292

Exhibit 1 (*Cont.*)

During period	Services expendi- ture, total (11+12 +13)	Imports of goods and services (10+14)	Invest- ment ex- pendi- ture	Trans- fers and other ex- pendi- ture	Current account expen- diture (15+16 +17)	Trade account (1–10)	Trans- port (2–11)	Travel (3–12)	Other services (4–13)	Services account (20–21 +22)	Goods and services account (19+23)	Invest- ment income, net (7–16)	Trans- fers and others, net (8–17)	Current account (24+25 +26)= (9–18)
	14	15	16	17	18	19	20	21	22	23	24	25	26	27
1985	14 130	94 893	12 134	5 300	112 327	1 711	3 671	−1 773	−330	1 568	3 279	−6 287	−1 509	−4 517
1986	13 162	89 898	11 719	5 964	107 580	4 329	3 597	−2 392	201	1 406	5 735	−7 209	−2 355	−3 828
1987	15 909	97 775	12 617	5 860	116 251	1 960	3 760	−3 075	−390	296	2 255	−7 542	−2 629	−7 915
1988	18 634	109 866	15 769	6 975	132 610	80	3 689	−3 627	−1 258	−1 196	−1 116	−7 933	−2 560	−11 608
1989	21 596	125 996	21 099	7 561	154 656	−6 134	3 793	−4 471	−2 482	−3 160	−9 294	−10 453	−3 910	−23 657
1988														
I	4 510	24 194	3 882	1 974	30 050	832	952	−1 053	−428	−529	303	−2 019	−891	−2 606
II	4 426	27 610	3 863	1 556	33 029	−616	972	−875	−351	−254	−870	−1 972	−437	−3 279
III	4 942	28 709	3 511	1 558	33 778	−2 146	937	−723	−525	−311	−2 457	−1 533	−424	−4 415
IV	4 756	29 353	4 514	1 888	35 754	2 010	827	−975	45	−102	1 908	−2 409	−808	−1 308
1989														
I	4 911	29 203	4 169	2 120	35 492	652	1 034	−1 053	−848	−867	−215	−2 112	−1 269	−3 596
II	5 351	30 114	5 691	1 884	37 689	−1 393	1 001	−1 092	−858	−950	−2 343	−2 898	−954	−6 195
III	5 522	31 160	5 137	1 730	38 027	−3 103	960	−1 010	−604	−654	−3 757	−2 661	−804	−7 221
IV	5 811	35 519	6 102	1 827	43 448	−2 291	799	−1 316	−171	−689	−2 980	−2 782	−883	−6 645
1990														
I	5 717	30 414	5 895	1 927	38 236	−279	1 085	−1 655	−774	−1 343	−1 622	−2 839	−1 107	−5 569
II	6 049	33 621	6 974	2 235	42 830	−1 092	1 082	−1 553	−1 002	−1 473	−2 565	−3 642	−1 268	−7 475

6

***Exhibit 2** Finland's capital account*
Capital Account, MILL FIM

During period	Direct investment in Finland	Portfolio investment in Finland	Long-term credits				Imports of other long-term capital	Imports of long-term capital (1+2+6+7)	Direct investment abroad	Portfolio investment abroad	Long-term export credits	Exports of other long-term capital	Exports of long-term capital (9+10+11+12)	Long-term capital account (8–13)
			Central government	Author-ized banks	Others	Total (3+4+5)								
	1	2	3	4	5	6	7	8	9	10	11	12	13	14
1985	392	9 507	–66	–12	–1 678	–1 756	140	8 283	2 073	1 329	–1 313	1 026	3 115	5 168
1986	1 627	9 301	–240	31	–3 056	–3 265	87	7 750	3 641	2 592	–381	457	6 309	1 441
1987	424	9 319	–556	1 823	103	1 370	91	11 204	3 741	3 029	158	2 508	9 436	1 768
1988	1 164	14 457	–1 892	2 304	2 548	2 960	85	18 666	7 935	2 492	1 369	753	12 550	6 117
1989	1 353	14 756	–1 638	4 152	6 094	8 608	79	24 796	11 793	887	2 934	78	15 692	9 104
1988														
I	63	2 080	–422	355	1 069	1 002	89	3 234	1 113	1 200	8	272	2 593	642
II	313	5 204	–310	139	–219	–390	–42	5 085	2 972	439	218	132	3 761	1 324
III	107	1 274	–382	950	503	1 074	–19	2 436	1 677	415	67	134	2 293	143
IV	681	5 899	–778	857	1 195	1 274	57	7 911	2 173	438	1 076	215	3 902	4 009
1989														
I	–165	7 696	–761	1 033	456	728	42	8 301	3 173	328	1 395	357	5 253	3 048
II	176	1 415	–403	397	1 082	1 076	–22	2 645	1 785	430	543	160	2 918	–273
III	484	2 841	–113	563	1 031	1 481	–16	4 790	3 237	333	225	158	3 953	837
IV	858	2 804	–361	2 159	3 525	5 323	75	9 060	3 598	–204	771	–597	3 568	5 492
1990														
I	563	6 709	–310	2 125	10 482	12 297	126	19 695	2 285	295	101	357	3 038	16 657
II	531	2 646	–234	449	1 647	1 862	–34	5 005	2 910	–342	–1	–163	2 404	2 601

Exhibit 2 *(Cont.)*

During period	Basic balance	Short-term capital imports of authorized banks	Import liabilities and prepayments related to exports	Imports of short-term capital (16+17)	Short-term capital exports of authorized banks	Export receivables and prepayments related to imports	Exports of short-term capital (19+20)	Other short-term capital incl. errors and omissions	Short-term capital account (18-21+22)	Overall balance excl. reserve movements (15+23)	Change in central bank's foreign exchange reserves (26+27)	Of which: Convertible reserves	Of which: Tied reserves
	15	16	17	18	19	20	21	22	23	24	25	26	27
1985	651	6 890	350	7 240	323	1 732	2 055	−2 092	3 093	3 744	−3 744	−3 729	−15
1986	−2 387	6 019	−3 796	2 222	9 933	−92	9 841	2 075	−5 544	−7 930	7 930	11 678	−3 748
1987	−6 147	19 324	−665	18 659	−7 343	−183	−7 526	−4 302	21 883	15 736	−15 736	−17 817	2 081
1988	−5 492	10 950	−399	10 551	5 970	644	6 614	1 737	5 674	183	−183	−517	334
1989	−14 553	4 284	1 627	5 912	2 641	475	3 116	5 796	8 592	−5 961	5 961	4 455	1 506
1988													
I	−1 965	6 244	−1 632	4 612	2 966	−692	2 274	1 968	4 305	2 341	−2 341	−1 295	−1 046
II	−1 955	13 610	484	14 094	4 363	−692	3 671	−3 750	6 673	4 718	−4 718	−4 662	−57
III	−4 272	−142	1 411	1 269	3 405	1 014	4 419	334	−2 816	−7 088	7 088	6 337	751
IV	2 700	−8 761	−663	−9 424	−4 764	1 014	−3 750	3 185	−2 488	212	−212	−897	685
1989													
I	−548	5 699	−287	5 412	4 685	214	4 899	1 855	2 368	1 820	−1 820	−1 372	−449
II	−6 468	10 761	−2 108	8 653	4 648	214	4 861	1 502	5 293	−1 174	1 174	152	1 022
III	−6 384	4 244	1 107	5 351	4 747	24	4 771	2 818	3 398	−2 987	2 987	1 802	1 185
IV	−1 153	−16 419	2 915	−13 505	−11 439	24	−11 415	−378	−2 467	−3 620	3 620	3 873	−253
1990													
I	11 088	18 613	782	19 394	11 407	−593	10 814	−8 822	−242	10 847	−10 847	−11 254	408
II	−4 874	9 581	793	10 374	5 901	−593	5 309	582	5 648	774	−774	−873	100

Ian H. Giddy

Case 2

Le Serpent

Shortly after his arrival in Paris (late in 1992), Geoffrey Harrington was faced with a problem. He had recently joined the financial management staff of his company's French subsidiary. Glancing at a memo that he had just received from the subsidiary's manager, Pierre Le Cheffe, he reflected that it was proving tough to gain the confidence of the subsidiary's management. They were naturally suspicious of a young British newcomer, even a graduate of le business school, INSEAD.

Perhaps, he thought, this memo will give me a chance to prove the value of a B-school education. But what can I tell Le Cheffe? He reread the memo carefully:

To: Geoffrey Harrington
From: M. Le Cheffe

According to the financial press, Italy's weak export performance, high inflation and dwindling reserves are leading people to believe that Italy

9

might demand a realignment — in other words, break out of the European "snake" limits and allow the lira to devalue. Could this happen under the rules of the European Monetary System? What are Italy's alternatives?

I would value your opinion of the possible consequences of this for our affiliate in Milan. In particular, could you give me a concise assessment of the effect of such an event on
(a) cost and prices, and the outlook for sales; and
(b) interest rates, including the prospects for monetary policy following the exchange rate change.

If it's any help to you, I have attached a table showing Italy's position in the EMS and some interest rates in the European Community countries. I note that Italy's is the weakest currency, except for the pound, which (like Portugal) is presently permitted a 6 percent movement against any other currency. Italy's maximum move is 2¼ percent.

What would *your* answer be?

Exhibit 1 The European monetary system

	Ecu Central Rates	Currency Amounts Vs. Ecu Sep 14	% Change from Central Rate	% Spread Vs. Weakest Currency	Divergence Indicator	Official Interest Rates	Euro-currency Interest Rates
Portuguese Escudo	178.735	173.588	-2.88	6.11	47	-	13⅜
Spanish Peseta	133.631	129.992	-2.72	5.94	46	8.5	9⅜
Belgian Franc	42.4032	42.0440	-0.85	3.94	28	8.75	9⅜
German mark	2.05586	2.04111	-0.72	3.80	29	8.5	9¹¹⁄₁₆
Dutch Guilder	2.31643	2.30134	-0.65	3.73	19	-	-
Irish Punt	0.76742	0.76742	-0.14	3.20	-5	10.25	10⅜
French Franc	6.89509	6.89298	-0.03	3.09	-13	9.5	11
Danish Krone	7.84195	7.85106	0.12	2.94	-17	13.75	15⅝
Italian Lira	1538.24	1541.57	0.22	2.83	-23	-	10⅝
Sterling	0.69690	0.71820	3.06	0.00	-60	-	10¹¹⁄₁₆

Ecu central rates were set by the European Community at the time of the last EMS realignment. Currencies listed in descending strength. Percentage changes from central rate are for Ecu: a positive change denotes a weak currency. Divergence shows the percentage difference between two spreads: the % change of the actual market rate from the Ecu central rate, and the maximum percentage deviation of the currency's market rate from its Ecu central rate. Bank rate refers to central bank discount rate, where quoted. Eurocurrency rates are offered rates in the interbank market.

Ian H. Giddy

Case 3

Turkey

As the Air France jumbo jet bound for Istanbul left the ground, Sykes Wilford slipped off his seat belt and reached into his briefcase for the materials on Turkey that he had brought with him. Surrey Machinery, Wilford's employer, had decided to find out for themselves the prospects of getting the local currency they had earned out of the country without suffering too serious a loss from a declining currency — or worse, one that was blocked.

He paged through the papers, looking for clues to the present and future state of the Turkish lira. First, he examined the data he had saved in a Lotus spreadsheet on his laptop computer. Looking at a plot of the exchange rate over time, he wondered about the difference between the kind of exchange rate policy the country had had in the late 1970s compared to the late 1980s. At one time, he recalled, the Turkish lira had been fixed against the U.S. dollar. What had happened, and why? Perhaps the other data in the spreadsheet would provide a clue.

Next, he turned to the summary economic data contained in the few pages copied from *International Financial Statistics,* published monthly by the International Monetary Fund. There he hoped to see what had happened to the Turkish government's foreign exchange reserves and to the balance of trade.

For commentary on the current state of Turkey's economy and present policies, he had brought along key pages from The Economist Intelligence Unit's *Quarterly Economic Review* of Turkey. He intended to use this to look for any evidence of current and future inflation, including the government budget and wage pressures.

Finally he browsed through an article on the black market in Istanbul, hoping to find a way to stretch the meager per diem that Surrey provided its travelling troubleshooters.

Exhibit 1 *Turkey: Graphs of exchange rate and consumer price index*

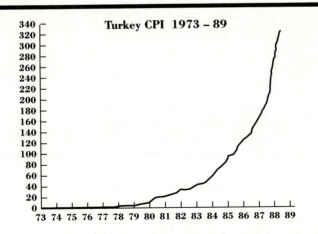

Exhibit 1 *(Cont.)*

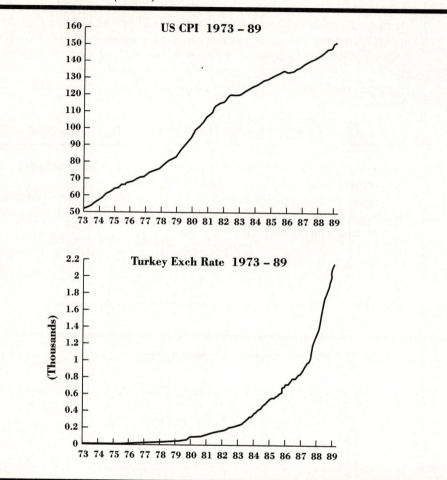

Exhibit 2 Turkey: Excerpts from International Financial Statistics

186

Exchange Rates — Liras per SDR: End of Period (aa); Liras per US Dollar: End of Period (ae), Period Average (rf). Fund Position — Millions of SDRs: End of Period. International Liquidity — Millions of US Dollars Unless Otherwise Indicated: End of Period. Monetary Authorities — Billions of Liras: End of Period.

Turkey	1982	1983	1984	1985	1986	1987	1988	1986 I	1986 II	1986 III	1986 IV	1987 I	1987 II	1987 III	1987 IV
Exchange Rates															
Market Rate .....aa	206.0	296.1	435.9	633.6	926.9	1,448.3	2,442.2	756.8	803.2	848.0	926.9	1,000.1	1,089.4	1,194.8	1,448.3
Market Rate .....ae	186.8	282.8	444.7	576.9	757.8	1,020.9	1,814.8	664.8	682.1	698.9	757.8	777.9	852.4	933.7	1,020.9
Market Rate .....rf	162.6	225.5	366.7	522.0	674.5	857.2	1,422.3	603.6	673.1	683.7	737.6	763.0	810.7	889.3	965.9
Fund Position															
Quota 2f.s	300	429	429	429	429	429	429	429	429	429	429	429	429	429	429
SDRs 1b.s	—	1	1	—	—	—	—	1	1	1	—	1	1	1	—
Reserve Position in the Fund 1c.s	—	32	32	32	32	32	32	32	32	32	32	32	32	32	32
Use of Fund Credit: Gen. Dept. 2e.s	1,319	1,497	1,455	1,208	887	543	222	1,133	1,073	966	887	789	711	613	543
incl.: Comp. Financing Facility .....2 dus	90	45	9	—	—	—	—	—	—	—	—	—	—	—	—
Oil Facility 2dzs	11	—	—	—	—	—	—	—	—	—	—	—	—	—	—
Credit Tranche: Ordinary 2ees	137	130	244	225	211	162	63	225	225	218	211	204	197	183	162
Credit Tranche: SFF 2dds	1,080	1,323	1,203	983	676	381	159	908	848	748	676	586	514	430	381
International Liquidity															
Total Reserves minus Gold 1l.d	1,080	1,288	1,271	1,056	1,412	1,776	2,344	1,195	1,418	1,375	1,412	1,551	1,356	1,324	1,776
SDRs 1b.d	—	1	1	—	—	—	—	2	2	2	—	2	2	2	—
Reserve Position in the Fund 1c.d	—	34	32	35	39	46	43	37	38	39	39	42	41	41	46
Foreign Exchange 1d.d	1,080	1,253	1,239	1,020	1,372	1,730	2,301	1,157	1,379	1,335	1,372	1,508	1,314	1,282	1,730
Gold (Million Fine Troy Ounces) 1ad	3,769	3,775	3,800	3,858	3,840	3,831	3,822	3,850	3,819	3,810	3,840	3,812	3,824	3,832	3,831
Gold (National Valuation) .....1 and	155	155	823	1,069	1,275	1,584	1,580	1,067	1,058	1,055	1,275	1,266	1,270	1,272	1,584
Monetary Authorities: Other Liab. .....4..d	6,047	7,084	7,440	9,507	11,786	16,388	15,013	9,847	10,505	11,322	11,786	12,914	13,252	13,252	16,388
Deposit Money Banks: Assets 7a.d	950	992	2,076	1,994	2,178	2,425	3,280	1,421	1,560	2,013	2,178	1,843	1,561	2,024	2,425
Liabilities 7b.d	343	446	1,693	2,507	3,990	6,184	6,274	2,782	3,346	3,877	3,990	4,594	4,692	5,389	6,184
Other Banking Insts.: Liabilities 7l.d	504	439	492	551	366	398	671	312	355	359	366	333	350	343	398
Monetary Authorities															
Foreign Assets 11	808	1,404	1,662	2,241	3,545	7,365	13,811	2,532	2,921	3,106	3,545	3,793	3,895	4,051	7,365
Claims on Central Government 12a	1,349	1,803	4,441	6,668	9,599	14,660	22,690	7,617	7,553	8,513	9,599	10,836	11,174	12,360	14,660
Claims on Official Entities 12bx	261	256	41	122	213	763	1,082	52	52	134	213	200	210	133	763
Claims on Deposit Money Banks 12e	377	629	307	369	512	1,126	1,796	264	378	385	512	456	530	620	1,126
Claims on Other Financial Insts. 12f	67	76	37	50	84	145	478	56	59	73	84	89	102	121	145
Reserve money 14	1,011	1,397	2,101	2,900	3,681	5,284	9,457	2,820	3,089	3,427	3,681	3,793	4,222	4,533	5,284
of which: Currency Outside DMBs 14a	412	548	736	1,011	1,415	2,275	3,426	1,092	1,270	1,527	1,415	1,591	1,810	2,250	2,275
Quasi-Monetary Liabilities 15	3	4	2	5	6	12	31	8	8	4	6	5	5	6	12
Restricted Deposits 16b	73	61	90	72	153	394	840	86	74	148	153	178	210	221	394
Foreign Liabilities 16c	1,401	2,447	3,943	6,249	9,754	17,517	27,788	7,404	8,027	8,732	9,754	10,836	11,481	11,481	17,517
Central Government Deposits 16d	301	191	37	120	101	124	377	96	93	143	101	174	194	234	124
Central Govt. Lending Funds 16f	11	16	10	30	30	55	78	176	60	31	30	23	120	120	55
Capital Accounts 17a	39	55	75	103	158	246	448	115	121	126	158	155	169	180	246
Other Items (Net) 17r	23	-3	230	-30	70	428	840	-212	-505	-399	70	-322	-552	-772	428

Exhibit 2 *(Cont.)*

Turkey

186

Billions of Liras: End of Period (quarterly columns under 1986 and 1987)

	1982	1983	1984	1985	1986	1987	1988	1986 I	1986 II	1986 III	1986 IV	1987 I	1987 II	1987 III	1987 IV
Deposit Money Banks															
Reserves............20	592	827	1,299	1,834	2,205	2,806	5,635	1,633	1,760	1,785	2,205	2,112	2,266	2,191	2,806
Central Bank Bonds............20r	73	61	90	72	153	394	840	86	74	148	153	178	210	221	394
Foreign Assets............21	177	281	923	1,150	1,651	2,475	5,953	944	1,064	1,407	1,651	1,434	1,725	2,134	2,475
Claims on Central Government............22a	384	376	915	2,030	2,845	5,165	8,556	2,097	2,216	2,143	2,845	2,430	3,115	3,854	5,165
Claims on Official Entities............22bx	156	199	174	439	1,347	2,249	3,425	571	677	638	1,347	1,438	1,350	1,807	2,249
Claims on Private Sector............22d	1,814	2,708	3,625	5,725	8,993	13,992	20,072	5,800	6,891	7,567	8,993	9,424	10,525	11,380	13,992
Claims on Other Financial Insts............22f	12	17	26	32	55	118	287	34	43	35	55	50	59	70	118
Demand Deposits............24	924	1,371	1,491	2,191	3,615	6,063	*8,134	1,748	1,928	2,005	3,615	2,878	3,132	3,586	6,063
Time and Savings Deposits............25	1,217	1,353	2,926	4,937	6,627	8,228	*15,895	5,592	5,841	6,063	6,627	7,007	7,203	7,946	8,228
Bonds............26ab	7	12	9	7	7	7	55	7	7	7	7	7	7	7	7
Restricted Deposits............26b	181	379	512	550	456	904	1,353	686	754	1,020	456	1,180	1,134	1,480	904
Foreign Liabilities............26c	64	126	753	885	3,023	6,314	11,386	1,850	2,282	2,709	3,023	3,574	4,000	5,032	6,314
Central Government Deposits............26d	218	362	569	576	1,321	2,232	*1,481	1,131	1,369	1,437	1,321	1,239	1,601	1,652	2,232
Central Govt. Lending Funds............26f	218	268	376	369	1,731	2,860	4,093	738	784	1,481	1,731	2,201	2,103	2,821	2,860
Credit from Monetary Authorities............26g	377	629	307		512	1,126	1,796	264	378	385	512	456	530	921	1,126
Credit from Other Financial Insts............26i	2	1	2	4											
Capital Accounts............27a	174	291	455	676	997	1,854	3,689	781	832	876	994	1,247	1,441	1,523	1,854
Other Items (Net)............27r	−175	−323	−347	−359	−1,041	−2,388	−3,116	−1,632	−1,450	−2,261	−1,041	−2,723	−1,900	−3,309	−2,388
Monetary Survey															
Foreign Assets (Net)............31n	−480	−889	−2,111	−4,304	−7,581	−13,990	−19,411	−5,777	−6,324	−6,928	−7,581	−9,081	−10,134	−11,953	−13,990
Domestic Credit............32	3,523	4,883	8,651	14,062	21,715	34,736	54,732	14,972	16,030	17,523	21,715	22,419	24,732	28,327	34,736
Claims on Central Govt. (Net)............32an	1,214	1,626	4,749	7,694	11,023	17,469	29,388	8,488	8,308	9,076	11,023	11,287	12,494	14,328	17,469
Claims on Official Entities............32bx	417	456	215	561	1,560	3,012	4,507	594	728	772	1,560	1,571	1,550	2,427	3,012
Claims on Private Sector............32d	1,814	2,708	3,625	5,725	8,993	13,992	20,072	5,800	6,891	7,567	8,993	9,424	10,525	11,380	13,992
Claims on Other Financial Insts............32f	79	93	62	82	139	264	765	90	102	108	139	138	162	191	264
Money............34	1,343	1,941	2,292	3,256	5,091	8,541	11,956	2,936	3,257	3,647	5,091	4,558	5,088	5,927	8,541
Quasi-Money............35	1,220	1,357	2,928	4,942	6,634	8,299	15,925	5,600	5,845	6,067	6,634	7,012	7,208	7,952	8,299
Central Govt. Lending Funds............36f	229	284	386	606	1,761	2,915	4,171	913	845	1,512	1,761	2,224	2,223	3,165	2,915
Other Items (Net)............37r	251	412	935	953	648	1,051	3,269	−253	−240	−630	648	−456	78	−670	1,051
Money, Seasonally Adjusted............34..b	1,146	1,642	1,928	2,725	4,250	7,129	9,980	3,042	3,361	3,655	4,250	4,714	5,240	5,930	7,129
Other Banking Institutions															
Reserves............40	3	4	10	14	37	84	303	29	17	10	37	29	25	44	84
Foreign Assets............41	2	3	4	9	10	31	63	13	18	13	10	19	36	35	31
Claims on Central Government............42a	4	4	35	32	42	54	108	34	31	42	42	113	67	66	54
Claims on Official Entities............42bx	260	323	364	503	512	613	1,341	344	373	454	512	637	555	560	613
Claims on Private Sector............42d	126	179	301	390	583	909	1,770	407	452	484	583	621	663	720	909
Claims on Deposit Money Banks............42e	2	1	2	4											
Bonds............46ab	71	121	103	147	238	446	1,136	191	233	227	238	351	369	381	446
Long-Term Foreign Liabilities............46cl	94	124	219	318	278	406	1,218	207	242	251	278	259	298	321	406

Exhibit 2 (Cont.)

Turkey
186

	1982	1983	1984	1985	1986	1987	1988	1986 I	1986 II	1986 III	1986 IV	1987 I	1987 II	1987 III	1987 IV
Other Banking Institutions															*Billions of Liras: End of Period*
Central Govt. Lending Funds 46f	75	70	99	127	202	212	305	125	152	178	202	149	141	192	212
Credit from Monetary Authorities.... 46g	67	76	37	50	84	145	478	56	59	73	84	89	102	121	145
Credit from Deposit Money Banks.. 46h	7	9	18	16	10	9	2	14	18	10	10	—	—	—	9
Capital Accounts 47a	64	79	189	227	280	315	404	237	242	246	280	292	301	302	315
Other Items (Net) 47r	20	35	53	67	94	159	43	-4	-54	18	94	180	135	108	159
Banking Survey															*Billions of Liras: End of Period*
Foreign Assets (Net)........ 51n	-478	-885	-2,106	-4,295	-7,571	-13,959	-19,347	-5,764	-6,306	-6,915	-7,571	-9,062	-10,098	-11,918	-13,959
Domestic Credit........ 52	3,834	5,296	9,289	14,906	22,714	36,049	57,186	15,667	16,784	18,395	22,714	23,552	25,855	29,482	36,049
Claims on Central Govt. (Net) 52an	1,218	1,631	4,784	7,725	11,065	17,522	29,496	8,522	8,339	9,119	11,065	11,400	12,562	14,394	17,522
Claims on Official Entities 52bx	677	779	579	1,065	2,072	3,625	5,848	938	1,102	1,226	2,072	2,107	2,106	2,987	3,625
Claims on Private Sector 52d	1,939	2,887	3,926	6,116	9,576	14,901	21,842	6,207	7,343	8,051	9,576	10,045	11,188	12,101	14,901
Liquid Liabilities........ 55l	2,560	3,294	5,210	8,185	11,687	16,696	27,578	8,506	9,084	9,704	11,687	11,541	12,272	13,835	16,696
Bonds........ 56ab	78	133	112	154	245	453	1,190	198	240	234	245	358	376	388	453
Long-Term Foreign Liabilities.... 56cl	94	124	219	318	278	406	1,218	207	242	251	278	259	298	321	406
Central Govt. Lending Funds 56f	304	354	484	734	1,962	3,127	4,476	1,039	996	1,690	1,962	2,373	2,363	3,357	3,127
Other Items (Net) 57r	320	506	1,158	1,220	970	1,408	3,376	-47	-85	-399	970	-41	448	-337	1,408
Interest Rates															*Percent Per Annum*
Discount Rate (*End of Period*)...... 60	31.50	48.50	52.00	52.00	48.00	45.00	54.00	52.00	52.00	52.00	48.00	45.00	45.00	45.00	45.00
Deposit Rate........ 601	45.0	51.9	54.3	49.2	41.9	35.4	....	46.7	43.5	41.2	36.2	35.4	35.4	35.4	35.4
Lending Rate........ 60p	36.00	35.50	52.33	53.50	52.63	50.00	....	53.50	53.50	53.50	50.00	50.00	50.00	50.00	50.00
Prices															*Index Numbers (1985 = 100): Period Averages*
Wholesale Prices (A) 63a	*35.6	46.4	69.8	100.0	129.6	171.1	287.9	*120.7	126.8	130.9	139.8	150.3	164.3	174.6	195.1
Wholesale Prices (B) 63b	37.6	48.2	70.6	100.0	127.5	177.6	....	117.3	122.1	127.2	140.3	....	....	....	....
Consumer Prices........ 64	*35.4	46.5	69.0	100.0	134.6	186.9	327.8	123.5	128.4	135.5	151.1	163.3	177.9	188.0	218.4
International Transactions															*Billions of Liras*
Exports........ 70	937.3	1,298.9	2,608.3	4,152.9	5,012.0	8,844.0	16,809.2	1,123.3	1,124.4	1,123.7	1,640.9	1,513.7	1,802.3	2,335.9	3,192.4
Imports, cif........ 71	1,453.3	2,114.0	3,999.8	5,959.2	7,708.0	12,353.0	20,470.6	1,710.1	1,794.5	1,827.3	2,229.2	2,172.6	2,455.6	3,122.6	4,602.2
															Millions of U.S. Dollars
Exports........ 70..d	5,746	5,728	7,134	7,958	7,466	10,190	11,662	1,878	1,688	1,660	2,230	1,989	2,244	2,636	3,322
Imports, cif........ 71..d	8,794	9,179	10,663	11,275	11,020	14,158	14,335	2,812	2,640	2,647	3,006	2,840	3,038	3,517	4,663
Imports, fob........ 71..vd	8,359	8,708	10,048	10,667	10,426	13,394	13,562	2,660	2,498	2,504	2,844	2,687	2,874	3,327	4,412
															1980 = 100: Indexes of Unit Values in US Dollars
Unit Value of Exports........ 74..d	82.9	73.2	74.4	....	....	....	....	....	....	....	....	....	....	....	....
Unit Value of Imports........ 75..d	95.0	85.4	77.4	....	....	....	....	....	....	....	....	....	....	....	....
Balance of Payments															*Millions of US Dollars: Minus Sign Indicates Debit*
Current Account, nie........ 77a.d	-935	-1,898	-1,407	-1,030	-1,528	-982	1,503	-709	-378	-282	-159	-563	5	308	-732
Merchandise: Exports fob........ 77aad	5,890	5,905	7,389	8,255	7,583	10,322	11,846	1,959	1,716	1,669	2,239	2,010	2,281	2,659	3,372
Merchandise: Imports fob........ 77abd	-8,518	-8,895	-10,331	-11,230	-10,664	-13,551	-13,646	-2,767	-2,523	-2,513	-2,861	-2,695	-2,908	-3,365	-4,583
Trade Bal., 77aad–77abd........ 77acd	-2,628	-2,990	-2,942	-2,975	-3,081	-3,229	-1,800	-808	-807	-844	-622	-685	-627	-706	-1,211
Other Goods, Serv. & Income: Cre.. 77add	2,038	2,041	2,366	3,132	3,250	4,111	5,945	733	808	877	832	699	1,071	1,342	1,029

Exhibit 2 (Cont.)

Turkey
186

Balance of Payments

Annual and quarterly figures — *Millions of US Dollars: Minus Sign Indicates Debit*

Line	Code	1982	1983	1984	1985	1986	1987	1988	1986 I	1986 II	1986 III	1986 IV	1987 I	1987 II	1987 III	1987 IV
Other Goods, Serv. & Income: Deb..	77aed	-2,639	-2,734	-2,945	-3,185	-3,646	-4,282	-4,812	-938	-772	-938	-998	-972	-1,041	-1,093	-1,176
Private Unrequited Transfers......	77afd	2,189	1,549	1,885	1,762	1,703	2,066	1,806	284	347	594	478	348	514	682	522
Official Unrequited Trans., nie	77agd	105	236	229	236	246	352	364	20	46	29	151	77	88	83	104
Direct Investment..................	77bad	55	46	113	99	125	110	352	31	44	24	26	16	73	21	—
Portfolio Investment, nie	77bbd	—	—	—	—	—	-29	-4	—	—	—	—	-16	—	-13	—
Other Long-Term Capital, nie........	77bcd	127	-319	44	-700	525	1,573	930	-184	528	-1	182	205	455	106	807
Total, 77a.d+77bad–77bcd...........	77c.d	-753	-2,171	-1,250	-1,631	-878	672	2,781	-862	194	-259	49	-358	533	422	75
Other Short-Term Capital, nie	77d.d	81	1,033	36	1,649	1,478	356	-1,979	1,166	114	342	-144	675	-352	-224	257
Net Errors and Omissions............	77e.d	-76	506	317	-792	-65	-457	346	-130	-76	-73	214	-141	-240	-67	-9
Total, lines 77.cd–77e.d............	77f.d	-748	-632	-897	-774	535	571	1,148	174	232	10	119	176	-59	131	323
C'part to Mon./Demon. of Gold	78a.d	—	—	—	—	201	—	—	—	—	—	201	—	—	—	—
Counterpart to SDR Allocation	78b.d	—	—	—	—	—	—	—	—	—	—	—	—	—	—	—
C'part to Valuation Changes........	78c.d	14	162	-823	-6	57	100	-113	—	9	35	13	25	-23	-43	140
Total, lines 77f.d–78e.d...........	78d.d	-733	-470	-1,726	-781	793	670	1,035	174	241	45	333	201	-82	88	463
Exceptional Financing..............	79a.d	902	622	1,002	676	—	—	—	—	—	—	—	—	—	—	—
Liab. Const. Fgn. Author. Reserves ...	79b.d	—	—	—	—	—	—	—	—	—	—	—	—	—	—	—
Total Change in Reserves	79c.d	-169	-152	724	105	-793	-670	-1,035	-174	-241	-45	-333	-201	82	-88	-463
Govt. Finance-National Accts																
Population	99z	46.31	47.28	48.27	49.27	50.30	51.35	52.42	….				….			99z

See page for Tanzania
Millions: Mid-Year Estimates

Govt. Finance-National Accounts
Population   99z

Date of Fund membership: March 11, 1947

Standard Sources:

B: Central Bank, *Monthly Statistical and Evaluation Bulletin* and *Quarterly Bulletin*

S: National Institute of Statistics, *Monthly Bulletin of Statistics*

Exchange Rates: *Market Rate (End of Period and Period Average)*: Official midpoint rate.

International Liquidity: *Gold (National Valuation)* (*line 1ad*) is equal to *Gold in Million Fine Troy Ounces* (*line 1ad*) valued at U.S. dollars 42.2222 per fine troy ounce from February 1973 through November 1984 and revalued annually as follows: U.S. dollars 216.65 from December 31, 1984 through December 30, 1985: U.S. dollars 277 from December 31, 1985 through December 30, 1986: U.S. dollars 332 from December 31, 1986 through December 30, 1987: and U.S. dollars 413.50 thereafter.

Monetary Authorities: Consolidates the Central Bank of Turkey and monetary functions undertaken by the central government. The contra-entry to Treasury IMF accounts, SDR holdings, and currency issues is included in *line 12a*.

Restricted Deposits (*line 16b*): Comprises required import deposits and other restricted deposits.

Deposit Money Banks: Consolidates commercial banks and other banks engaged primarily in mortgage and other long-term lending, while having some commercial banking functions. Of the latter the most important are the state-owned Etibank and Sumerbank, which also control large industrial enterprises. As far as possible, only their banking operations are reported here.

Central Bank Bonds (*line 20n*): Counterpart to *line 16b* in section 10.

Beginning 1988, demand, time and government deposits reflect an improved sectoral classification.

Exhibit 2 *(Cont.)*

Turkey 186

	1988 I	1988 II	1988 III	1988 IV	1989 I	1989 II	1989 III	1989 Mar	1989 Apr	1989 May	1989 June	1989 July	1989 Aug	1989 Sept	1989 Oct
Exchange Rates															
Market Rate ...... aa *(Liras per SDR: End of Period)*	1,697.7	1,820.9	2,130.0	2,442.2	2,620.9	2,667.5	2,856.2	2,620.9	2,691.0	2,607.5	2,667.5	2,771.8	2,760.8	2,865.2	2,937.3
Market Rate ...... ae *(Liras per US Dollar: End of Period)*	1,223.8	1,389.3	1,650.7	1,814.8	2,027.5	2,140.2	2,238.8	2,027.5	2,076.9	2,096.7	2,140.2	2,152.8	2,214.8	2,238.8	2,298.7
Market Rate ...... rf *(Period Average)*	1,144.1	1,297.7	1,502.3	1,745.3	1,913.1	2,081.4	2,190.7	1,978.2	2,056.6	2,069.4	2,118.1	2,141.6	2,187.8	2,242.8	2,278.0
Fund Position															
Quota ...... 2f.s *(Millions of SDRs: End of Period)*	429	429	429	429	429	429	429	429	429	429	429	429	429	429	429
SDRs 1b.s	—	—	—	—	—	—	3	—	3	—	—	3	—	3	3
Reserve Position in the Fund 1c.s	32	32	32	32	32	32	32	32	32	32	32	32	32	32	32
Use of Fund Credit: Gen. Dept. 2e.s	440	363	279	222	151	106	55	151	131	106	106	94	67	55	55
incl.: Comp. Financing Facility ...... 2 dus	—	—	—	—	—	—	—	—	—	—	—	—	—	—	—
Oil Facility 2dzs	—	—	—	—	—	—	—	—	—	—	—	—	—	—	—
Credit Tranche: Ordinary 2ees	134	105	84	63	42	21	7	42	35	21	21	21	7	7	7
Credit Tranche: SFF 2dds	306	258	195	159	109	85	48	109	96	85	85	73	60	48	48
International Liquidity *(Millions of US Dollars Unless Otherwise Indicated: End of Period)*															
Total Reserves minus Gold 1l.d	1,708	1,745	1,985	2,344	2,060	2,672	3,715	2,060	2,375	2,246	2,672	2,983	3,146	3,715	...
SDRs 1b.d	1	1	1	4	4	4	4	4	4	4	4	4	4	4	...
Reserve Position in the Fund 1c.d	45	42	42	43	42	40	41	42	42	40	40	42	40	41	...
Foreign Exchange 1d.d	1,663	1,702	1,943	2,301	2,018	2,632	3,673	2,018	2,329	2,206	2,632	2,938	3,105	3,673	...
Gold (Million Fine Troy Ounces) 1ad	3,830	3,820	3,827	3,822	3,865	3,785	3,792	3,865	3,867	3,791	3,785	3,785	3,786	3,792	...
Gold (National Valuation) ...... 1 and	1,584	1,580	1,582	1,580	1,598	1,565	1,568	1,598	1,599	1,567	1,565	1,565	1,566	1,568	...
Monetary Authorities: Other Liab. ...... 4..d	16,344	15,491	15,184	15,013	13,999	12,908	...	13,999	13,578	12,577	12,908	...	...	...	...
Deposit Money Banks: Assets 7a.d	2,103	2,368	2,655	3,280	3,231	2,904	...	3,231	3,535	3,014	2,904	...	...	...	...
Liabilities 7b.d	5,969	5,893	6,185	6,274	5,885	5,926	...	5,885	5,887	5,829	5,926	...	...	...	...
Other Banking Insts.: Liabilities 7f.d	438	592	520	671	583	550	...	583	455	450	550	...	...	...	...
Monetary Authorities *(Billions of Liras: End of Period)*															
Foreign Assets 11	8,740	10,205	12,434	13,811	14,574	13,569	...	14,574	13,161	12,844	13,569	...	...	...	...
Claims on Central Government 12a	17,415	18,119	20,703	22,690	24,135	25,150	...	24,135	26,212	24,490	25,150	...	...	...	...
Claims on Official Entities 12bx	756	752	1,023	1,082	979	912	...	979	913	913	912	...	...	...	...
Claims on Deposit Money Banks 12e	1,136	1,162	1,205	1,796	1,744	1,742	...	1,744	1,723	1,924	1,742	...	...	...	...
Claims on Other Financial Insts. 12f	159	234	335	478	576	672	...	576	581	594	672	...	...	...	...
Reserve Money 14	6,023	6,868	8,510	9,457	10,777	12,396	...	10,777	11,348	11,551	12,396	...	...	...	...
of which: Currency Outside DMBs 14a	2,501	2,929	3,907	3,426	4,229	5,222	...	4,229	4,611	4,701	5,222	...	...	...	...
Quasi-Monetary Liabilities 15	5	13	14	31	20	11	...	20	15	14	11	...	...	...	...
Restricted Deposits 16b	434	446	409	840	707	300	...	707	541	375	300	...	...	...	...
Foreign Liabilities 16c	20,748	22,184	25,658	27,788	28,778	27,909	...	28,778	28,555	26,646	27,909	...	...	...	...
Central Govt. Deposits 16d	163	466	506	377	474	349	...	474	483	536	349	...	...	...	...
Central Govt. Lending Funds 16f	348	211	229	78	80	1,187	...	80	196	1,588	1,187	...	...	...	...
Capital Accounts 17a	251	272	306	448	412	435	...	412	438	428	435	...	...	...	...
Other Items (Net) 17r	234	12	69	840	761	-541	...	761	1,018	-375	-541	...	...	...	...

19

Exhibit 2 (Cont.)

Turkey
186

Billions of Liras: End of Period

	1988				1989										
	I	II	III	IV	I	II	III	Mar	Apr	May	June	July	Aug	Sept	Oct
Deposit Money Banks															
Reserves 20	3,294	3,524	4,188	5,635	6,070	6,597		6,070	6,228	6,345	6,597				
Central Bank Bonds 20r	434	446	409	840	707	300		707	541	375	300				
Foreign Assets 21	2,574	3,290	4,383	5,953	6,552	6,215		6,552	7,342	6,319	6,215				
Claims on Central Government 22a	5,620	7,113	6,582	8,556	9,311	10,923		9,311	9,378	10,590	10,923				
Claims on Official Entities 22bx	2,296	2,051	3,953	3,425	2,350	2,401		2,350	2,216	2,572	2,401				
Claims on Private Sector 22d	15,127	15,638	15,425	20,072	22,515	23,893		22,515	22,939	22,117	23,893				
Claims on Other Financial Insts. 22f	119	161	152	287	397	401		397	334	331	401				
Demand Deposits. 24	*4,479	4,721	5,280	8,134	6,104	7,198		6,104	6,706	7,214	7,198				
Time and Savings Deposits 25	*10,011	10,584	11,915	15,895	19,240	20,739		19,240	19,826	20,289	20,739				
Bonds 26ab	6	6	5	55	61	64		61	62	63	64				
Restricted Deposits 26b	2,164	2,149	2,861	1,353	3,274	3,360		3,274	3,587	3,653	3,360				
Foreign Liabilities 26c	7,304	8,187	10,210	11,386	11,932	12,683		11,932	12,226	12,222	12,683				
Central Government Deposits 26d	*1,232	1,402	1,631	1,481	1,543	1,984		1,543	1,608	1,529	1,984				
Central Govt. Lending Funds 26f	3,481	4,148	4,077	4,093	4,382	5,210		4,382	4,532	4,917	5,210				
Credit from Monetary Authorities 26g	1,136	1,162	1,205	1,796	1,744	1,742		1,744	1,723	1,924	1,742				
Credit from Other Financial Insts. 26i	—	—	—	—	—	1		—	—	—	1				
Capital Accounts 27a	2,355	2,721	2,801	3,689	4,844	5,100		4,844	4,913	4,953	5,100				
Other Items (Net) 27r	-2,703	-2,856	-4,943	-3,116	-5,223	-7,353		-5,223	-6,206	-8,115	-7,353				
Monetary Survey															
Foreign Assets (Net) 31n	-16,738	-16,876	-19,051	-19,411	-19,585	-20,808		-19,585	-20,278	-19,705	-20,808				
Domestic Credit 32	40,098	42,202	45,986	54,732	58,246	62,019		58,246	60,483	59,542	62,019				
Claims on Central Govt. (Net) 32an	21,641	23,365	25,099	29,388	31,429	33,740		31,429	33,500	33,015	33,740				
Claims on Official Entities 32bx	3,052	2,802	4,976	4,507	3,329	3,313		3,329	3,129	3,484	3,313				
Claims on Private Sector 32d	15,127	15,638	15,425	20,072	22,515	23,893		22,515	22,939	22,117	23,893				
Claims on Other Financial Insts. 32f	278	396	487	765	973	1,073		973	915	926	1,073				
Money 34	7,208	8,065	9,601	11,956	10,811	12,997		10,811	11,826	12,420	12,997				
Quasi-Money 35	10,016	10,597	11,929	15,925	19,261	20,749		19,261	19,841	20,304	20,749				
Central Govt. Lending Funds 36f	3,828	4,359	4,305	4,171	4,462	6,397		4,462	4,727	6,506	6,397				
Other Items (Net) 37r	1,108	2,304	1,099	3,269	4,128	1,067		4,128	3,812	608	1,067				
Money, Seasonally Adjusted ....34..b	7,454	8,298	9,611	9,980	11,180	13,372		11,180	12,488	12,583	13,372				
Other Banking Institutions															
Reserves 40	63	52	39	303	119	138		119	117	69	138				
Foreign Assets 41	34	37	53	63	158	265		158	193	253	256				
Claims on Central Government 42a	81	121	90	108	163	172		163	152	159	172				
Claims on Official Entities 42bx	655	730	870	1,341	1,490	1,858		1,490	1,596	1,728	1,858				
Claims on Private Sector 42d	1,021	1,198	1,472	1,770	1,942	2,120		1,942	1,981	2,026	2,120				
Claims on Deposit Money Banks 42e	—	—	—	—	—	1		—	—	—	1				
Bonds 46ab	652	819	960	1,136	1,318	1,297		1,318	1,325	1,251	1,297				
Long-Term Foreign Liabilities 46cl	537	822	858	1,218	1,182	1,177		1,182	945	943	1,177				

Billions of Liras: End of Period

Billions of Liras: End of Period

Exhibit 2 *(Cont.)*

		1988				1989			1989							
		I	II	III	IV	I	II	III	Mar	Apr	May	June	July	Aug	Sept	Oct
Other Banking Institutions																*Billions of Liras: End of Period*
Central Govt. Lending Funds	46f	230	250	271	305	313	325	....	313	329	329	325	....	....	....	....
Credit from Monetary Authorities.......	46g	159	234	335	478	576	672	....	576	581	594	672	....	....	....	....
Credit From Deposit Money Banks......	46h	4	2	—	2	57	78	....	57	64	80	78	....	....	....	....
Capital Accounts	47a	332	336	369	404	422	505	....	422	436	477	505	....	....	....	....
Other Items (Net)	47r	-50	-326	-269	43	4	489	....	4	358	560	489	....	....	....	....
Banking Survey																*Billions of Liras: End of Period*
Foreign Assets (Net)...........	51n	-16,704	-16,839	-18,998	-19,347	-19,427	-20,552	....	-19,427	-20,084	-19,453	-20,552	....	....	....	....
Domestic Credit...........	52	41,577	43,855	47,932	57,186	60,868	65,096	....	60,868	63,297	62,529	65,096	....	....	....	....
Claims on Central Govt. (Net)	52an	21,722	23,487	25,189	29,496	31,592	33,913	....	31,592	33,651	33,174	33,913	....	....	....	....
Claims on Official Entities	52bx	3,707	3,533	5,846	5,848	4,819	5,171	....	4,819	4,725	5,212	5,171	....	....	....	....
Claims on Private Sector	52d	16,148	16,835	16,897	21,842	24,457	26,013	....	24,457	24,921	24,143	26,013	....	....	....	....
Liquid Liabilities...........	551	17,161	18,610	21,491	27,578	29,952	33,609	....	29,952	31,550	32,655	33,609	....	....	....	....
Bonds...........	56ab	658	825	965	1,190	1,378	1,361	....	1,378	1,388	1,314	1,361	....	....	....	....
Long-Term Foreign Liabilities...........	56cl	537	822	858	1,218	1,182	1,177	....	1,182	945	943	1,177	....	....	....	....
Central Govt. Lending Funds...........	56f	4,059	4,609	4,577	4,476	4,775	6,722	....	4,775	5,056	6,834	6,722	....	....	....	....
Other Items (Net)...........	57r	2,458	2,150	1,043	3,376	4,153	1,674	....	4,153	4,274	1,330	1,674	....	....	....	....
Interest Rates																*Percent Per Annum*
Discount Rate *(End of Period)*...........	60	54.00	54.00	54.00	54.00	54.00	54.00	....	54.00	54.00	54.00	54.00	....	....	....	....
Deposit Rate...........	60l	....	....	....	....	....	....	....	....	....	....	....	....	....	....	....
Lending Rate...........	60p	....	....	....	....	....	....	....	....	....	....	....	....	....	....	....
Prices															*Index Numbers (1985 = 100): Period Averages*	
Wholesale Prices (A)	63a	239.8	274.0	296.3	341.6	400.9	452.7	....	413.7	432.5	448.7	476.9	....	....	....	....
Wholesale Prices (B)	63b	239.4	272.2	....	....	457.5	505.6	....	471.6	488.6	501.0	527.2	....	....	....	....
Consumer Prices	64	268.7	307.6	335.8	399.0	....	....	....	....	....	....	....	....	....	....	....
International Transactions																*Billions of Liras*
Exports...........	70	3,194.0	3,512.7	3,899.1	6,203.4	5,427.7	....	....	2,183.1	2,013.5	....	....	....	....	....	....
Imports, cif...........	71	4,005.7	4,901.8	4,913.6	6,649.5	6,364.3	....	....	2,393.3	2,624.0	....	....	....	....	....	....
																Millions of US Dollars
Exports...........	70..d	2,803	2,725	2,592	3,542	2,830	....	....	1,105	982	....	....	....	....	....	....
Imports, cif...........	71..d	3,494	3,802	3,245	3,795	3,317	....	....	1,209	1,275	....	....	....	....	....	....
Imports, fob...........	71.vd	3,305	3,596	3,070	3,591	3,139	....	....	1,144	1,207	....	....	....	....	....	....
										1980 = 100: Indexes of Unit Values in US Dollars						
Unit Value of Exports...........	74..d	....	....	....	....	....	....	....	....	....	....	....	....	....	....	....
Unit Value of Imports...........	75..d	....	....	....	....	....	....	....	....	....	....	....	....	....	....	....
Balance of Payments											*Millions of US Dollars: Minus Sign Indicates Debit*					
Current Account, nie...........	77a.d	-440	72	836	1,035	323	-194	....	111	5	-220	21	....	....	....	....
Merchandise: Exports fob...........	77aad	2,851	2,819	2,624	3,552	2,865	2,607	....	1,095	987	712	908	....	....	....	....
Merchandise: Imports fob...........	77abd	-3,341	-3,641	-3,094	-3,570	-3,167	-3,794	....	-1,149	-1,232	-1,200	-1,362	....	....	....	....
Trade Bal., 77aad+77abd...........	77acd	-490	-822	-470	-18	-302	-1,187	....	-54	-245	-488	-454	....	....	....	....

Exhibit 2 *(Cont.)*

Millions of US Dollars: Minus Sign Indicates Debit

Turkey 186		1988 I	1988 II	1988 III	1988 IV	1989 I	1989 II	1989 III	1989 Mar	1989 Apr	1989 May	1989 June	1989 July	1989 Aug	1989 Sept	1989 Oct
Balance of Payments																
Other Goods, Serv. & Income: Cre..	77add	978	1,514	1,991	1,462	1,238	1,718	…	458	468	594	656	…	…	…	…
Other Goods, Serv. & Income: Deb...	77aed	−1,240	−1,157	−1,355	−1,060	−1,302	−1,354	…	−490	−407	−524	−423	…	…	…	…
Private Unrequited Transfers	77afd	286	424	564	532	555	563	…	168	163	168	232	…	…	…	…
Official Unrequited Trans., nie	77agd	26	113	106	119	134	66	…	29	26	30	10	…	…	…	…
Direct Investment	77bad	31	49	120	152	64	119	…	38	25	36	58	…	…	…	…
Portfolio Investment, nie	77bbd	—	—	—	−4	—		…					…	…	…	…
Other Long-Term Capital, nie	77bcd	259	248	−152	575	−300	436	…	−313	276	−43	203	…	…	…	…
Total, 77a.d+77bad−77bed	77c.d	−150	369	804	1,758	87	361	…	−164	306	−227	282	…	…	…	…
Other Short-Term Capital, nie	77d.d	216	−278	−723	−1,194	−506	26	…	−133	−268	168	126	…	…	…	…
Net Errors and Omissions	77e.d	7	458	92	−212	337	290	…	−50	298	39	−47	…	…	…	…
Total, lines 77c.d−77e.d	77f.d	73	549	173	352	−82	677	…	−347	336	−20	361	…	…	…	…
C'part of Mon./Demon. of Gold	78ad	—	—	—	—	—	—	…	—	—	—	—	…	…	…	…
C'part to SDR Allocation	78b.d	—	—	—	—	—	—	…	—	—	—	—	…	…	…	…
C'part to Valuation Changes	78c.d	19	−382	184	65	−81	−31	…	−64	6	−99	63	…	…	…	…
Total, lines 77f.d−78c.d	79a.d	93	167	358	418	−163	646	…	−412	342	−119	424	…	…	…	…
Exceptional Financing...............	79a.d	—	—	—	—	—	—	…	—	—	—	—	…	…	…	…
Liab. Const. Fgn. Author, Reserves ...	79b.d	—	—	—	—	—	—	…	—	—	—	—	…	…	…	…
Total Change in Reserves	79c.d	−93	−167	−358	−418	163	−646	…	412	−342	119	−424	…	…	…	…

Monetary Survey: *IFS line 34* differs from the source B measure on money supply and sight savings deposits, as given in the table "Consolidated Statement of the Banking System," in that *IFS* includes the deposits of official entities and government enterprises at the central bank which source B reports in quasi-money.

IFS line 35 differs from the source B measure on quasi-monetary liabilities, as given in the table "Consolidated Statement of the Banking System," in that source B includes (1) the time deposits of the government which *IFS* nets in *line 32an*, (2) deposits of official entities and government which *IFS* includes in money, (3) counterpart funds which *IFS* reports separately, and (4) blocked deposits and deposits of international organizations which *IFS* includes in *line 37r*.

Other Banking Institutions: Comprises other investment and development banks.

Interest Rates: Discount Rate (End of Period): Source B.

Deposit Rate: Data refer to the rate on three-month time deposits denominated in Turkish lira.

Lending Rate: Data refer to banks' short-term loans to the general public.

Prices: Wholesale Prices (A): Source B general wholesale price index calculated by the Department of Economic Analysis, Ministry of Commerce, base 1963. *Wholesale Prices (B)*: Source B general wholesale price index calculated by the Istanbul Chamber of Commerce, base 1963. *Consumer Prices*: Source S general index of cost of living calculated by the State Institute of Statistics, base 1978/79.

International Transactions: All trade value data are from source B. *Imports f.o.b.* are calculated from *Imports, c.i.f.* by applying a freight and insurance factor derived from the *Balance of Payments Statistics*.

Unit Value of Exports: Source B index of unit value, base 1973. *Unit Value of Imports*: Source S index of unit value, base 1973.

Government Finance: Data are derived from the *Budget Revenues Yearbook* and the *Monthly Economic Indicators* published by the Ministry of Finance. *Expenditure (line 82)* includes domestic and foreign amortization payments because such payments cannot be separately identified. *Fiscal year beginning March 1 through 1981; year ending December 31 after 1981.

National Accounts: *Line 99a.p.* is based on national data at 1968 prices.

Source: *International Financial Statistics*, December 1989, pp. 532–535.
Reprinted with permission of International Monetary Fund.

Exhibit 3 *Turkey: Excerpts from Economist Intelligence Unit*

EIU COUNTRY REPORT NO. 4 1989*   TURKEY

The increase in tax revenue is intended to come from a better system of tax collection, helped by more tax officers. The bottom income tax band will actually be reduced by 2–3 percent from its current 25 percent. There is considerable scope to reduce tax evasion at the level of income tax and corporation tax and this objective has become a major political plank of the SHP economic programme recently.

The government has to increase tax revenue to reduce the budget deficit since there is little scope to cut expenditure and many demands for increased spending. The biggest four slices of budget expenditure have gone to the Treasury, with a 55 percent increase to TL17,600 bn, the Ministry of Customs and Finance with its allocation raised 84 percent to TL17,300 bn, the Ministry of Education with its spending raised by 187 percent to TL8,500 bn, and the Ministry of Defence which fell to fourth place although its spending was raised 100 percent to TL7,800 bn. The government seems to be pursuing its promises to raise spending in the education and health sectors. Divided another way, TL20,000 bn will go to personnel payments and TL27,000 bn to transfer payments. TL9,000 bn will be allocated to public investments, but many of these investments are "off-budget."

A budget deficit of TL9,404 bn is projected. The stock of internal domestic debt had reached TL18,900 bn at the end of 1988, equivalent to 20 percent of GDP.

World Bank-IMF warnings on the budget deficit and internal debt

According to Osman Ulagay, a respected economic journalist for the Turkish daily *Cumhuriyet,* World Bank and IMF circles are worried about Turkey's public sector debt. In a question session Brian Stuart — the head of stand-by programmes at the IMF — and World Bank economist Swenden Winjbergen, indicated that Turkey's public sector accounts were difficult to interpret given the large sums now collected and spent through the special funds. Locating the main source of inflation as being in the public sector, they recommended a thorough reform of the State Economic Enterprises — not necessarily only through their privatisation. Turkish officials are reported to be discussing the possibility of an IMF stand-by loan for Turkey in 1990.

*Source: Excerpted from EIU Country Report No. 4 1989
Turkey, The Economist Intelligence Unit. Reprinted with permission.

Tariffs reduced —

At the end of August radical reductions in import tariffs were made on a number of durable goods, as well as on automobiles and textiles. Phased reductions, which have brought protective tariffs from above 50 percent to around 25 percent or less, were aimed to reduce cost pressures on many sectors of industry and slow inflation. They are also designed to bring Turkey's tariff regime closer into line with the EC.

— but other taxes on imported goods rise

However, as a result of various duties, taxes and fund levies also imposed on sales of goods which are mainly imported, the effective duty on imports fell by much less. A study conducted in Bilkent University immediately after the first phase of the tariff reductions showed that effective tariffs on a selected basket of intermediate and manufactured goods had been only reduced from a weighted average of 65 percent to 58 percent. Widely quoted average rates of protection for Turkish industry are 10 percent for raw materials, 10–30 percent for intermediate goods, and over 50 percent for finished manufactures.

Also in a protectionist vein, in October new anti-dumping regulations were brought in, aiming particularly at goods from Comecon and pharmaceuticals from the Far East.

Exchange and capital controls relaxed

Also in August a new exchange control regime was defined by Law 32 for the protection of the Turkish lira. The new law facilitates further the convertibility of the lira by lifting all controls on the import of foreign exchange; raising to $3,000 the upper limit for the purchase of foreign exchange and to $1,000 the limit for the sale of foreign exchange in banks with no administrative requirements; exporters can keep in foreign exchange 30 percent of earnings brought into the country within 90 days of sale; allowance for capital exports abroad has been raised to $25 mn; gold and precious stones imports and exports have been liberalised; and the transfer of funds relating to portfolio investments in Turkish or foreign stock markets has been liberalised.

Another major change in exchange rate policies this year, already mentioned in previous reports, is the slowdown in the rate of depreciation of the Turkish lira. By the end of October the lira had reached TL2,300=$1 and TL238=DM1, depreciating by 27 percent against the dollar and by 24 percent against the Deutschemark since October 1988. During the same period Turkish prices have increased by over 60 percent while German and U.S. prices rose by 3–4 percent. A run on the lira in October was feared by a number of pundits because of the maturing of high interest (75–80 percent) one year deposits in banks as well as the effect of the new measures further easing convertibility. But this did not materialise as most savers simply rolled over their deposits — despite lower interest rates. There could be some speeding up of the rate of depreciation of the lira in the last months of 1989, however, as the government mops up the foreign exchange in the market to pay foreign debt service and there is a seasonal peaking of imports.

Second thoughts on privatisation?

The government's privatisation plans have come under considerable criticism lately and there are signs that there may be a reassessment of the overall programme. Criticism has focused on privatisation of the petrochemicals giant, Petkim. The opposition is wide, encompassing a range of organisations from the SHP to the Chambers of Commerce, which are accusing the government of selling "the family silver to foreigners." The progress on privatisation has not been exactly breathtaking. So far the government has sold off its shares in private concerns; there was a not very successful (share prices fell along with the drop in the stock market) public flotation of Teletas; the sale of Usas, the airline service company, to SAS; and the sale of the cement plants of Citosan to a French firm.

The Petkim sale is particularly contentious because of its size and the fact that the government wants to sell it to a single buyer. Given the inadequacy of domestic capital sources this means another sale to a foreign firm of what is perceived as a strategic industry. There is also the problem of creating private sector monopolies through the privatisation process. Some of the smaller state owned banks were also being prepared for privatisation (Töbank, Caybank, Denizcilik Bank) but it is reported that these plans have been shelved for the time being.

THE DOMESTIC ECONOMY

Decline in industrial output halts

The index of manufacturing output prepared by the Istanbul Chamber of Commerce (ICC), which showed a fall of 13.7 percent in the first quarter of 1989 over the same period in 1988, registered zero growth in the second quarter this year. This partial recovery had already been noted by the Central Bank industrial production index, which showed positive growth in March 1989 over the same month in 1988. On the other hand, in a survey conducted by the State Planning Organisation of 108 basic industrial goods producing sectors, 56 registered significant drops in output in the January-June 1989 period over the first half of 1988. The most reliable of these indicators is likely to be the ICC index, on which the EIU will base its estimates for 1989.

Of the main manufacturing sectors, the ICC index shows continued declines in the first half of this year in the metals and machinery, paper and printing, and textiles, leather and shoes sectors. In a separate survey of production trends in the three major automotive sector firms of Tofas, Otosan and Oyak-Renault, production rose 2.8 percent for the first time this year in September over the same month in 1988.

Agricultural output suffers from drought —
According to the State Institute of Statistics (SIS) provisional estimates released in September, agricultural production will be down 10.4 percent in 1989. Various other sources show that, contrary to earlier expectations, cotton production was 10 percent down on last year; wheat production fell to 11.5 mn tons from the bumper crop in 1988 of 15 mn tons and barley production was down 40 percent. On the other hand it was a good year for hazelnuts and tobacco production. So far the major impact of the drought — which mainly hit the south east and central Anatolia — is in higher than average increases in agricultural goods' prices and a decline in hydroelectric production.

Given these trends, real GDP growth estimates for 1989 have been revised down to around 2 percent.

— helping to keep inflation over 70 percent in the third quarter
Despite the decline in domestic demand there seems to have been little progress made in reducing inflation. Agricultural price increases are clearly

Retail price movements
%

| | 1988 | | 1989 | |
	Monthly	Annual	Monthly	Annual
Jan	6.0	59.6	5.5	74.3
Feb	5.4	63.8	4.3	72.6
Mar	7.6	69.8	2.5	56.1
Apr	4.9	74.5	3.6	62.5
May	2.4	70.0	2.5	62.8
Jun	2.2	74.1	5.2	67.6
Jul	2.8	75.5	5.7	72.4
Aug	3.4	78.4	4.0	73.3
Sep	4.8	81.8	4.7	73.1
Oct	7.5	86.7	7.6	73.2
Nov	6.9	87.5		
Dec	3.9	75.2		

one factor. Monthly inflation in July–September stayed high at between 4–5 percent, giving an average increase on a year earlier of 73 percent in the third quarter for retail price inflation, according to the SIS index for urban areas. In October the monthly rate even accelerated above 7 percent. Although the rate should ease a little in November and December, the increase on twelve months earlier is likely to be still over 70 percent at year end.

Interest rates decline

According to a survey of banks conducted by the financial daily *Dunya* at the end of September, bank lending rates — taking into account the various additional charges — which had risen to 127.8 percent in 1988 had fallen to 79 percent by end September. Interest rates on one year deposits had also fallen from around 80 percent last year to around 60 percent. This rate is of course below the rate of current inflation, but it is a good indication of expectations concerning inflation in the year October 1989–October 1990.

FOREIGN TRADE AND PAYMENTS

Current account reverts to deficit in second quarter of 1989 —
In April–June 1989 the current account registered a $346 mn deficit; in the same quarter in 1988 there had been a small $72 mn surplus. Compared with the second quarter of last year, lower exports resulted in the trade deficit rising by $361 mn to $1,183 mn; invisibles outgoings rose slightly but credits remained level while transfers showed a rise.

However, the cumulative current account in the first seven months showed a $71 mn surplus compared with a $25 mn deficit in the same period of 1988. Again the trade deficit shows a continued widening over last year due to the decline in exports. But tourism revenues were not as low as feared earlier, rising by 2 percent to $1,207 mn; the saviour of the 1989 current account has been transfers, which rose 21 percent to $2,240 mn. Over the seven months to July foreign debt interest payments came to $1,703 mn, a rise of 4 percent.

Turning to the capital account, direct investment rose to $111 mn in the first half of 1989 compared with $49 mn in 1988; and there was a $445 surplus in net errors and omissions compared with the $449 mn surplus in the first half of 1988. Also on the positive side is the further build-up of foreign reserves, by $625 mn in the second quarter compared with a drawdown of $175 mn in the first quarter of 1989.

Exhibit 4 Turkey: *Financial Times articles**

A LONG AND DIFFICULT ROAD

THE PATHWAY TO FULL CONVERTIBILITY
OF THE TURKISH LIRA

The Turkish authorities have an ambitious long-term aim: to establish the full convertibility of the Turkish lira. They see it clearly in the context in which all the reforms and restructuring of the economy in recent years have been set the internal and external liberalisation that will induce market fed growth and closer integration, especially with the European Community.

It is a long road to travel for a currency with such a small stock of credibility, undermined by years of restrictions, controls, local market distortions and, of course, inflation. But the path has been set and this year has seen the introduction of a number of measures intended by the Government as a significant step in the direction of convertibility.

These measures, many of them part of a package produced in August, include:

- Allowing Turks to buy on demand up to $3,000 from banks, a three-fold increase;
- Lifting restrictions on the import of gold and other precious metals (there is very heavy demand for gold in Turkey, mainly as a personal savings investment);
- Allowing banks to buy and sell foreign exchange on credit;
- Allowing exporters greater freedom to utilise their foreign exchange earnings;
- Allowing foreign investment in Turkish securities, with guaranteed repatriation of proceeds, and allowing Turks to invest capital abroad up to $25m, including investments in the main international stock markets.

The timing of the introduction of what was, certainly by the standards of not many years ago, a radical set of liberalising measures appears to have been well chosen by the Government.

This year, the steep depreciation of the TL, at least in line with inflation which had previously been the typical pattern, slowed markedly and the TL strengthened relatively against the big currencies. The differential between the domestic inflation rate and the rate of depreciation this year has been around 40 percent.

*Source: Financial Times, Fall 1989. Reprinted with permission.

At the same time there has been an impressive accumulation of foreign currency in the system. Between them, the commercial banks and the Central Bank were this autumn holding around $6bn in foreign currency, with the Central Bank hoarding a further $1.4bn-worth of gold.

The reason for this flush of foreign exchange lies in several factors. This year the lack of growth has cut the flow of imports and hence demand for foreign currency to finance them. Tourism receipts and remittances by Turkish workers overseas have been strong.

The result has been a sharp decline in demand for foreign currency, reinforced by the perception of a relatively stronger TL in which it is still possible to get good returns on deposit.

Such is the situation that the liberalising measures caused barely a ripple in the system. Indeed, the Central Bank says it has had to intervene in the markets against the TL to stop it strengthening still further.

Sceptics — especially among the foreign banking community — tend to scoff at the notion that the TL is suddenly approaching full convertibility as a result of recent measures. They say it will be a long time before you can walk into a bank in Frankfurt with a case full of TL and get a decent rate of exchange, or — more seriously — set contracts with foreign companies in TL.

Then there is the question of how sustainable the TL's current position may be. Some foreign bankers regard it as being some 20 percent overvalued, engineered there by the authorities (despite protestations to the contrary by the Central Bank).

Holding it there may become difficult, especially as the influential and important export sector is already complaining loudly about the consequent squeeze it has felt this year. Some bankers fear a sudden turnaround in which a run on the TL, stoked by the new foreign exchange rules, could put great pressure on the Government.

Officials take a much less pessimistic view. They point to the large currency reserves as a sufficient buffer against any such switch in demand away from the TL. They point also to October 1988 when a speculative run on the TL was halted abruptly, burning many an Istanbul foreign exchange dealer, by heavy intervention by the Central Bank buying up the local currency.

"Outsiders are still suspicious about how sustainable this whole thing is," says Mr. Ercan Kumcu, vice-governor of the Central Bank. "That is pur task now. To convince them that it is and that where we want to go is attainable — the Turkish lira as a means of exchange in international markets."

Hugh Carnegy

BRISK BUSINESS

THOMAS GOLTZ DESCRIBES THE CURRENCY
BLACK MARKET

As they jump and shout and thrust their fingers in the air, the knots of men seem almost threatening to the casual tourist on the fringes of Istanbul's Grand Bazaar.

Some of them are elderly, others are only youths, but most are young adventurers with a taste for big money.

"Cerek, cerek — Makarna, makarna — Tam, tam — Cikolata, cikolata," goes their weird refrain, unintelligible even in Turkish unless one is an initiate.

These are not beggars or touts, but seasoned veterans of Turkey's semi-legal currency black-market, Tahtakale — named after the district of Istanbul in which it is centred.

Although they may look scruffy, hundreds of thousands of dollars pass through their hands every day. One estimate is that they handle a third of Turkey's over-the-counter foreign exchange dealing.

"These are the runners," said Pepsi (Vehbi), a private dealer, whose main interest is in the relatively small flow of tourist dollars and Deutsche Marks. "The big boys keep their heads low in dummy store fronts in the area. Any time you see a gold shop with no gold in the window, that's where the big money is."

Whether private dealer, lowly runner, or boy, the code-words are the same: "cerek," or quarter, refers to the D-Mark; "tam" (full) is the dollar; "kralice" (queen) is sterling; "cikolata" (chocolate) is the Swiss franc; and "makarna" (macaroni) is the Italian lira, which sees a surprising volume of trade.

In stark contrast to the Istanbul Stock Exchange, on the far side of the Golden Horn, with its floor of colour-coded dealers, Tahtakale's brokers still roam the narrow streets around the Kiliccilar, Kapisi, or Sword Makers' Gate, of the bazaar. The huddles of dealers shift, according to the presence of the police, who break up the trading sessions when they present an obstacle to pedestrian traffic.

"We have to move them on perhaps 50 times a day," said a police officer in the area. "But our concern is because they block the street, and not because of the trade in currencies."

What will happen to Tahtakale in the light of recent moves by the Government to make the lira more freely convertible is debatable. The liberalisation of gold-trading in the spring, by the introduction of a central bank gold-dealing room, has effectively destroyed speculation in the yellow metal. This has driven former dealers to try their luck on futures at the exchange; helping to sustain a first-half bull market in stocks and shares.

The early word is that the currency dealers in the streets of Tahtakale will not only survive, but thrive.

"We work on fractions of percentage points, while the banks work on fixed commissions," said Ihsa, who entered the market a year ago with a trading capital of about DM50,000. "Until there is real full convertibility, we will be in business, and after that — well, we too will move to the exchange."

At least one foreign banker regards Tahtakale as an unhealthy parasite on the economy — made worse by the convertibility moves. "What the Government has done in many respects, is almost to legitimise the black market," he says.

"You come to my counter, I'll charge you a fee. My overheads are much higher. Tahtakale doesn't have to shoulder these. It doesn't pay tax. Why does the Government allow that? What they've permitted to open is a foreign exchange window that's out of control."

II

International Investment Decisions

Gunter Dufey

Case 4

All-World Investment Management

Janet Smith was the executive assistant to the treasurer of a large domestic manufacturing corporation. The treasurer had been recently appointed to this position, and consequently all areas of treasury operations were being reviewed, including the appointments of (external) managers of the company's pension funds.

As part of this review, the company had solicited proposals on investment strategy from both current investment advisers as well as organizations whose services have not been used in the past.

One of the proposals in particular attracted the attention of the treasurer. It had been submitted by All-World Investment Management, Ltd., a joint venture whose prestigious parents comprise an old line Banque d'Affairs in Paris and a British merchant bank with a long history in international finance. The proposal purported to show a superior past performance record in terms of returns (higher) and risk (lower) than any of the usual comprehensive yardsticks for performance in equity markets such as the S & P 500.

The treasurer told Janet to look into this matter, having been particularly impressed by the performance record of the investment adviser. He reasoned that the superior portfolio performance would easily compensate for the investment adviser's fees, which were almost three times those charged by managers of domestic portfolios.

INVESTMENT PERFORMANCE: U.S. CLIENTS' TAX-EXEMPT PORTFOLIOS

This document sets out the total returns for the portfolios managed by All-World Investment Management Ltd. (AWIM) for its tax-free U.S. clients. These portfolios are permitted to invest both in equities and in bonds and are valued in U.S. dollars. Returns are given for portfolios invested outside the U.S. securities markets and are computed from the data for a "global fund" consisting of all the U.S. client's funds invested outside the United States.

TABLE 1 Rates of return, annualized

	Cumulative annual returns through Sept 31, 1991 in percent						
	3rd Qtr	YTD	1 year	3 years	5 years	7 years	10 years
Funds under management by AWIM invested outside U.S. securities markets	9.03	19.93	15.85	6.00	6.10	20.00	16.90
Indices							
MSCI EAFE*	8.58	10.28	21.89	2.58	9.12	22.51	19.10
S & P 500	5.35	20.38	31.17	16.55	14.76	17.01	17.43

*The Morgan Stanley Capital International.(MSCI) Index for Europe, Australia and the Far East is based on over 700 shares listed on the Stock Exchanges of all major European countries, Australia and the Far East. It is adjusted to reflect foreign exchange fluctuations of the various currencies relative to the U.S. dollar. The returns include reinvested dividends.

The Standard & Poor's Composite Index of 500 Stocks includes reinvested dividends.

TABLE 2 *Annual rates of return in percent*

	76	77	78	79	80	81	82	83	84	85	86	87	88	89	90
Funds under management by AWIM invested outside U.S. securities markets	11.7	23.5	30.8	11.7	28.4	-3.7	-2.1	29.4	-2.7	60.5	60.1	11.2	12.5	17.9	-17.6
Indices															
MSCI EAFE	3.7	19.2	33.9	6.0	24.4	-1.0	-0.5	24.9	8.2	56.8	70.1	24.9	28.9	11.0	-23.0
S & P 500	23.5	-7.4	6.5	18.3	32.5	-4.9	21.5	22.5	6.2	31.6	17.5	3.8	15.3	31.6	-3.2

Notes:

1. The data given are historical information, and it cannot be inferred that similar results will be obtained in the future. These results have been affected by variations in the rate of exchange of the U.S. dollar against the currencies of various foreign countries, and such variations may not occur in a similar way in the future.
2. The returns, where applicable, have been computed after the impact of withholding taxes and commissions. No allowance for withholding taxes or commissions has been deducted from the returns of the Capital International Index or the Standard and Poor's Index.
3. The returns have been computed after certain but not all custody fees have been charged, most of which have been paid directly by clients.
4. These returns have been computed after certain but not all of AWIM's investment management fees have been charged. Most of such fees have been paid directly by clients.

Ian H. Giddy

Case 5

Thoughts While in a Sauna

Klaus Groenbarj, finance director of Wartsila Oy, was sweating in the sauna outside his family cottage on a birch-clad island in the Gulf of Finland, when suddenly he remembered that the next day, Monday, was when Wartsila USA would make an $80 million repayment of an intercompany loan. Groenbarj had insisted on this repayment because he felt that the U. S. sub should be able to stand on its own two feet by now, and the money was needed for a forthcoming acquisition in Britain. The purchase price of £60 million would have to be paid to the British seller in three months.

What should we do with the money in the meantime? Groenbarj muttered to himself. Hey! Maybe we could buy one of those floating rate notes that Arvo keeps telling me about. (Arvo was his old buddy from their days in the Finnish military, who had since made a career with a UK merchant bank in securities sales.) Buy one that has a coupon-fixing date three months from now, and if nothing goes wrong, sell it at par on the coupon refixing date and collect the coupon — a whole six months' worth.

Groenbarj thought for a minute. Then, leaping out of the sauna, he ran across the lawn and into the cottage. Totally oblivious of his wife's guests, he rummaged through his briefcase until he found copies of the *International Herald Tribune* and the London *Financial Times*. He rushed back into the sauna.

Groenbarj tore out the section that lists floating rate notes and looked for a note whose next coupon date was early in September. Hmm, let's see. I wonder what my return would be if I bought one of these things? I guess we would have to pay the stated price plus accrued interest. I'll assume we could sell the notes at par. Doesn't that make sense?

Of course, he muttered, it's sterling we need. Maybe I should look for a sterling note, or perhaps a Eurodeposit. If I buy a dollar FRN, we'd have to hedge it into sterling. I wonder what the cost of hedging would be? Look, here are the spot and forward rates. Wait, here are also some prices of currency futures! We've never used those before, but Arvo keeps talking about them. Could that be a cheaper way to hedge? I'd better work out what it would cost compared to a forward contract.

Or how about a Eurodollar deposit hedged with futures? Or hedged with a forward contract? But it's too hot to think. I'll go for a swim — let that new MBA recruit work this out tomorrow, see what he has learned in that program.

Yet Groenbarj was not able to get the FRN problem out of his mind. He recalled Arvo telling him that many FRN investors use a measure called the "discount margin" to evaluate the return on floating rate instruments. After the long drive back to his home in Espoo that Sunday evening, he went through the pile of technical papers and memos in his study. Here it is! he thought, finding the book entitled *Global Financial Markets* that Arvo had urged him to read. Turning to the chapter on Instruments of the International Money Market, he found a couple of paragraphs on the subject (Exhibit 4).

I'll ask that youngster to explain how FRNs can be compared to other money market instruments, he thought.

Study Questions

1. Can one estimate the price at which a FRN will trade at its **next coupon reset** date?
2. If you knew the price at which a FRN would trade at its next coupon date, could you compare it to other money market instruments? Try applying this to a FRN from Exhibit 4.
3. Which would be better: **forward contracts** or **futures** to hedge the FRN's return?
4. Explain to Groenbarj why the **discount margin** measure would, or would not, be helpful to him in comparing FRNs.

Exhibit 1 Floating rate notes

Floating Rate Notes

Issuer & Mat	Price	Crt. Cpn.
Dollars		
Alb Perp	81½	5.25
Alb Perp	77½	4.63
Alaska Finance Jul 01	99	4.41
American s & l 96	99¾	4.28
Amex Bk Dec 97	94¼	4.50
Amex Bk Mar 99	93¼	4.38
Anz Perp	74½	4.46
Autopistas Jun 93	100	5.00
Bankers Trust Mar 00	96¾	5.00
Bankers Trust May 96	99	5.25
Barclays Perp Old	83	4.38
Barclays Perp Ser 1	82¼	4.38
Barclays Perp Ser 2	82¼	4.44
Bco Santo Spirito 93	99⅞	4.50
Bear Stearns Sep 94	99	4.56
Belgium Jul 96	99⅞	4.19
Belgium a Jan 96	100⅜	4.00
Belgium Dec 99	100	4.38
Belgium Nov 96	99½	4.00
Belgium Oct 94	100	4.13
Bergen Bk Perp	65	4.56
Bfce Nov 96	100⅛	4.92
Bfg 92	100	4.44
Bk America Sep 96	97½	5.25
Bk America Mar 97	96½	5.00
Bk Boston Aug 98	88	4.30
Bk Boston Feb 01	85	5.00
Bk Boston Sep 00	90	6.00
Bk Ireland Perp	73½	4.63
Bk Nova Scotia Aug 85	69	4.56
Bk of Ny Dec 97	96⅝	5.25
Bk of Ny Jan 96	97⅜	5.25
Bk Scotland Perp	79½	5.31
Bk Tokyo Oct 93	100	5.50
Bkamerica Feb 97	99⅛	4.56
Bnp Perp	85½	4.70
Bnp Feb 95	101¾	5.25
Boa Jul 96	96½	4.13
Boa Oct 99 (Pp)	99½	5.44
Bq Parlbas Perp 1	95	4.69
Bq Parlbas Perp 2	85¼	4.50
Calxa Geral May 94	100	5.25
Cba Perp New	98⅜	4.44
Cba Perp Old	98½	4.15
Ccf Feb 94	99½	4.48
Ccf Oct 92	99¾	4.30
Cepme Jun 95	100	5.25
Chase Corp Dec 09	84½	5.25

Issuer & Mat	Price	Crt. Cpn.
Chase Corp Dec 09	84½	5.25
Chase Corp May 00	92	5.00
Chase Corp Nov 97	94	4.50
Chase Corp Nov 97	94	4.50
Chase Man o/s Jul 93	99¾	5.25
Chem Sept 96 (Wkly)	97	5.25
Chemical Nov 99	96½	5.25
Chemical Feb 97	96¾	5.25
Chemical Oct 97	96⅜	5.25
Christiania Perp	66	4.31
Chrysler Fin Apr 94	82	4.13
Chrysler Fin Sept 92	98	5.38
Cibc 2085	69	4.44
Cibc 2084	84	4.56
Citicorp Nov 35w	69	5.09
Citicorp Nov 35x	69	5.00
Citicorp Aug 11	78	4.38
Citicorp Aug 96 (wkly)	93½	5.25
Citicorp Jan 97	93¾	5.25
Citicorp Jan 98	92	5.00
Citicorp Jul 97	93	5.25
Citicorp Mar 94	99¾	6.00
Citicorp May 98	91¼	4.38
Citicorp Nov 35	69	5.00
Citicorp Oct 05	84½	5.00
Citicorp Oct 96	94	5.25
Citicorp Perp 1	99	4.00
Citicorp Perp 2	73¾	4.63
Citicorp Sep 96	94	5.25
Citizens Mar 96	99⅝	5.00
Columboa s&l Redeemd	99½	4.19
Comalco Dec 93	100⅛	5.00
Comerica Jun 97	97¼	5.25
Commerzbk Aug 93	99⅞	4.06
Commerzbk Feb 93	99⅞	4.06
Cont Ill Jun 94	97½	5.25
Council of Europe 93	99¾	4.25
Cr Foncier Oct 98	100¼	5.00
Credlop Jul 93	99½	4.25
Crossland Dec 97	99⅞	4.38
Csfb Perp	76½	4.56
Den Danske Bank Perp	84	4.38
Denmark Aug 96	99¾	4.20
Dle Erste Oest 92/94	99¾	5.25
Dnc Perp New	65	4.59
Dnc Perp Old	66	5.25
Do Not Use 19	99¾	4.15
Dresdner Fin Aug 92	100⅜	5.25
Dresdner Fin Oct 93	100½	5.25
Eab 92 Called 30/8	99	5.00
Eab Dec 93	98½	5.00

Exhibit 1 *(Cont.)*

Issuer & Mat	Price	Crt. Cpn.
East River Aug 93	99¾	4.30
Enl Mar 93	100	4.00
Equit Dho Dec-00	93	4.93
Equitable Corp Apr 94	48	5.25
Ferrovie Feb 94	101	4.44
Ferrovie May 97	100	4.44
Fidelity Fed Oct 92	99⅞	4.25
First Bk Syst May 97	97¼	5.25
First Bk Syst Nov 10	95¾	5.25
First Bk Syst Nov 96	97⅜	5.25
First Boston Nov 94	99¼	5.25
First Chicago Aug 94	98½	5.25
First Chicago Dec 96	96¼	4.50
First Chicao Feb 97	96¼	5.25
First Chicago May 92	99⅞	5.25
First City Texas 95	12	5.25
First Inter Jul 94	98¼	4.32
First Inter Dec 95	97	5.25
First Union Nov 96	97	4.31
Fleet Fincl Jun 98	94	4.10
Great Lakes Dec 97	99⅞	4.69
Grindlays 92	99½	5.25
Grindlays 94	98	5.25
Gt Amer'n 1st Sav 92	99⅞	4.25
Gt Western 89/94	99½	5.25
Gt Western Fin 03/95	99½	4.13
Gzb Perp	90	5.38
Hill Samuel Perp	78	5.25
Hong Kong Perp 1	72	5.00
Hong Kong Perp 2	71¾	5.00
Hong Kong Perp 3	70½	4.38
Hydro Perp	90½	4.56
Ibf Frn Mar 94	99¾	5.25
Ibm Cred Corp Dec 95	75	5.06
Ireland Jun 98	99¾	4.46
Isveimer (Pp) Feb 95	98	4.19
Italy Dec 00	101¼	4.50
Jp Morgan Dec 97	99¾	5.25
Jp Morgan Rdmp 28.92	99½	5.25
Kleinwort Perp	69	5.31
Lloyds Perp 1	79½	4.81
Lloyds Perp 2	79	4.44
Lloyds Perp 3	79	4.54
Man Han 30Sept 92	99⅞	5.25
Man Han Corp Apr 98	95¾	5.00
Man Han Corp Jul 97	96½	5.25
Man Han Corp Nov 97	96¼	5.00
Man Han Corp 08/96 w	96½	4.06
Man Han Trust Apr 97	95¾	5.25
Man Nall Sept 96	96¾	4.38

Issuer & Mat	Price	Crt. Cpn.
Mar Mid Dec 00	92	5.25
Mar Mld Dec 00	92	5.25
Mar Mld Dec 09	84½	5.25
Mar Mld Mar 99	92½	4.25
Mar Mld Sep 96	96	5.25
Mar Mld Oct 94	98½	5.25
Mcorp Nov 97	24	5.25
Mellon Bk Nov 96	97½	5.25
Mellon Corp Jul 94	99	4.32
Mgn Grenfell Perp	89	4.81
Midland Int 92	99⅞	5.25
Midland Perp 1	73	5.00
Midland Perp 2	74¼	5.00
Midland Perp 3	72	4.60
Mitsul Fin Jul 97	99⅞	5.25
Morgan Stanley 07/93	99½	4.38
Muirfield Fndg a	5	3.88
Muirfield Fndg b	5	3.88
Nab Perp	75	4.53
Nat Bk Canada 2087	68	4.56
Nat Bk Detroit 12/05	96½	5.25
Nat West Fin Pp Old	84	5.00
Nat West Perp (a)	82	4.19
Nat West Perp (b)	82	4.25
Nat West Perp (c)	81	4.38
New Zealand Aug 93	99⅞	4.25
New Zealand Jun 96	100¼	4.81
Norwest Cor Apr 98	97½	5.25
Nwide Anglia Nov 95	99½	4.34
Paine Webber Sept 93	99	5.00
Pnc 97 Mar 97	97⅜	5.25
Quebec Oct 2001	96¼	4.13
R fleming Perp	68	5.44
Rbs Perp	84½	4.69
Renfe Nov 98	99⅞	4.00
Rep Bk Dallas Feb 97	5	4.13
Rep Ny Dec 09	93½	4.13
Rep Ny Jul 10	93½	5.25
Rep Ny Perp	91	4.56
Rhone-poulenc Perp	89	5.06
Ribwa Perp	97½	4.79
Riggs 1/4 Sept 96	76	5.25
Riggs 3/16 Sept 96	76	5.25
Rio Nov 94	99⅞	5.00
Rothschilds Perp	67	4.94
Royal Bk Canada 2085	84	4.56
Royal Trust 2085	61	4.65
Sabre III Ltd 92	99⅞	4.38
Santa b Aug 96 Redeem	99	4.06
Santa Barbara Redeem	99	4.06

Exhibit 1 *(Cont.)*

Issuer & Mat	Price	Crt. Cpn.
Sanwa Intl Jan 93	99⅞	4.41
Sec Paci Feb 97	97	
3.75Shawmut Corp Feb 97	90	5.00
Shearson Oct 96	95¼	4.38
Soc Gen Sept 96	99⅞	4.56
Soc Gen Perp	85½	5.01
Southeast Bk Dec 96	2	4.25
Southeast Bk Nov 97	2	5.25
St Bk Victoria Perp	90	4.31
St Of Victoria 99/04	98¾	4.36
Stand Chart Perp1	65½	4.19
Stand Chart Perp2	66	4.38
Stand Chart Perp3	65½	4.96
Stand Chart Perp4	65½	4.28
Ste Bk Nsw Feb 98	99½	4.25
Talyo 92/04	100⅛	5.25
Texas Commerce 11/97	97¼	5.25
Uk Govt Sept 96	100	4.06
Union Oil 96	98½	5.13
Wells Fargo Apr 00	92	5.25
Wells Fargo Feb 97	95¾	5.25
Wells Fargo Jul 97	94½	4.25
Wells Fargo Jul 98	93¾	4.13
Wells Fargo Oct 92	99¾	5.00
Wells Fargo Sep 94	98½	5.25

Issuer & Mat	Crt. Price	Cpn.
Wells Fargo Sep 97	94¾	
5.00Wells Fargo Sep 97	94¾	5.00
Westpac Perp	78¾	4.71
Woodside Aldc Jul 97	99¾	5.25
Woodside lbl Feb 97	99½	5.25
Ecus		
Bca Agricoltur Jun 93	99¾	10.50
Belgium Apr 00	99⅞	10.16
Belgium May 99	100	10.19
Bk Greece Apr 97	99⅜	10.88
Bnp Aug 96	99¾	10.25
Ccce Feb 06	99⅞	9.86
Cff Apr 96 (Ecu)	100⅛	10.18
Chel & Glo Frn Xeu 95	99⅝	10.34
Elb Aug 01	101¾	10.06
Elb Feb 2002 Frn	100½	9.63
Ireland Redeem 10/91	99⅞	10.31
Isvelmer Nov 95	99	10.15
Italy 30-oct-05	100⅝	10.10
Lavoro Bc Naz Apr 00	98¾	10.30
Ppcorp 19Sept 97	97⅞	10.50
Renfe 91/94 (Ecu)	99⅞	10.50
St-gobain Perp	90	10.50
Woolwich Frn Apr 96	99¼	10.40

Source: *The International Herald Tribune*, June 8, 1992, p. 8. © by International Herald Tribune. Distributed by New York Times Syndication Sales.

Exhibit 2 *Foreign exchange and interest rates*

Currency Rates

Jun 5	Bank * rate %	Special † Drawing Rights	European ‡ Currency Unit
Sterling.....................	—	0.767934	0.703386
U.S. Dollar	3.50	1.40340	1.28699
Canadian $..............	6.62	1.67369	1.54014
Austrian Sch	7.50	15.7616	14.4284
Belgian Franc	8.50	46.0841	43.1970
Danish Krone	9.50	N/A	7.91728
D—Mark	8.00	2.23786	2.05017
Dutch Guilder	8.50	2.51812	2.30924
French Franc	10¼	7.53766	6.90486
Italian Lira	12	1691.13	1551.14
Japanese Yen............	3.75	178.653	163.602
Norway Krone	—	8.74599	8.00827
Spanish Peseta........	—	N/A	129.067
Swedish Krona.........	10.00	8.08499	7.40248
Swiss Franc..............	7.00	2.04546	1.87321
Greek Drach	19	N/A	247.294
Irish Punt.................	—	N/A	0.768946

* Bank rate refers to central bank discount rates. These are not quoted by the UK, Spain and Ireland.
‡ European Commission Calculations.
† All SDR rates are for June 5

Other Currencies

Jun 8	£	$
Argentina.......................	1.8150 –1.8180	0.9900 – 0.9910
Australia..........................	2.3970 – 2.3990	1.3075 – 1.3085
Brazil...............................	5461.45 – 5464.80	2978.70 – 2978.90
Finland............................	7.9410 –7.9640	4.3250 – 4.3280
Greece.............................	348.650 –354.200	190.620 – 193.670
Hong Kong	14.1830 – 14.1965	7.7350 – 7.7360
Iran..................................	2625.00*	1425.00*
Korea (Sth).....................	1432.30 – 1455.40	783.00 – 792.40
Kuwait	0.53320 – 0.53400	0.29080 – 0.29120
Luxembourg...................	59.95 – 60.05	32.65 – 32.75
Malaysia..........................	4.6110 – 4.6230	2.5200 – 2.5210
Mexico	5535.65 – 5549.35	3112.50 – 3113.50
N. Zealand	3.3885 – 3.3930	1.8470 – 1.8495
Saudi Ar	6.8170 – 6.8940	3.7495 – 3.7505
Singapore.......................	2.9805 – 2.9875	1.6265 – 1.6275
S.Af (Cm).......................	5.1750 – 5.1870	2.8165 – 2.8180
S.Af (Fn)	6.3815 – 6.4145	3.4785 – 3.4965
Taiwan.............................	45.60 – 45.75	24.85 – 24.95
U.A.E................................	6.6750 – 6.7520	3.6715 – 3.6735

*Floating rate. Iran Official rate: £119.10 $65.50

Exhibit 2 (Cont.)

Dollar Spot – Forward Against the Dollar

Jun 8	Day's spread	Close	One month	% p.a.	Three months	% p.a.
UK†	1.8305 – 1.8355	1.8335 – 1.8345	0.09–0.88cpm	5.82	2.71–2.68pm	5.88
Ireland †	1.6725 – 1.6790	1.6770 – 1.6780	0.83–0.80cpm	5.83	2.50–2.43pm	5.88
Canada	1.1905 – 1.1945	1.1930 – 1.1940	0.20–0.22cdis	–2.11	0.58–0.62dis	–2.01
Netherlands	1.7880 – 1.7935	1.7900 – 1.7910	0.84–0.86cdis	–5.70	2.54–2.57dis	–5.71
Belgium	32.65 – 32.80	32.65 – 32.75	14.00–16.00cdis	–5.50	45.00–48.00dis	–5.69
Denmark	6.1325 – 6.1575	6.1375 – 6.1475	3.50–3.88oredis	–7.13	9.95–10.65dis	–6.71
Germany	1.5860 – 1.5950	1.5890 – 1.5900	0.75–0.76pfdis	–5.70	2.32–2.35dis	–5.89
Portugal	132.45 – 132.85	132.50 – 132.60	163–175cdis	–15.30	440–465dis	–13.66
Spain	100.00 – 100.75	100.45 – 100.55	69.72cdis	–8.42	214–220dis	–8.64
Italy	1200.00 – 1205.75	1202.75 – 1203.25	9.00–9.50liredis	–9.23	26.80–27.80dis	–9.08
Norway	6.2025 – 6.2250	6.2050 – 6.2100	3.10–3.45oredis	–6.33	9.60–10.30dis	–6.41
France	5.3450 – 5.3700	5.3550 – 5.3600	2.75–2.80cdis	–6.22	8.34–8.44dis	–6.26
Sweden	5.7350 – 5.7525	5.7350 – 5.7400	3.45–3.75oredis	–7.53	10.45–20.00dis	–10.61
Japan	126.90 – 127.30	127.05 – 127.15	0.07–0.08ydis	–0.71	0.21–0.23dis	–0.69
Austria	11.1750 – 11.2075	11.1875 – 11.1975	5.10–5.45grodis	–5.66	15.40–16.40dis	–5.68
Switzerland	1.4475– 1.4550	1.4515 – 1.4525	0.66–0.68cdis	–5.54	1.95–1.97dis	–5.40
Ecu	1.2840 –1.2905	1.2875 – 1.2885	0.71–0.68cpm	6.48	1.95–1.97pm	6.09

Commercial rates taken towards the end of London trading. † UK, Ireland and ECU are quoted in U.S. currency. Forward premiums and discounts apply to the U.S. dollar and not to the individual currency.

Euro-Currency Interest Rates

Jun 8	Short term	7 Days notice	One Month	Three Months	Six Months	One Year
Sterling	9 7/8 – 9 5/8	9 1/4 – 9	9 7/8 – 9 3/4	9 13/16 – 9 29/32	10 – 9 7/8	10 – 9 7/8
US Dollar	3 7/8 – 3 3/4	3 15/16 – 3 13/16	3 15/16 – 3 13/16	4 – 3 7/8	4 1/8 – 4	4 5/8 – 4 1/2
Can. Dollar	5 7/8 – 5 3/4	6 1/16 – 5 15/16	6 – 5 7/8	5 15/16 – 5 13/16	5 7/8 – 5 3/4	6 1/4 – 6 1/8
Dutch Guilder	9 9/16 – 9 7/16	9 9/16 – 9 7/16	9 9/16 – 9 7/16	9 9/16 – 9 7/16	9 1/2 – 9 3/8	9 1/2 – 9 3/8
Swiss Franc	9 1/2 – 9 1/4	9 1/2 – 9 1/4	9 1/2 – 9 3/8	9 5/16 – 9 3/16	9 1/8 – 9	8 7/8 – 8 3/4
D-Mark	9 11/16 – 9 9/16	9 5/8 – 9 1/2	9 11/16 – 9 9/16	9 3/4 – 9 5/8	9 3/4 – 9 5/8	9 11/16 – 9 9/16
French Franc	10 1/8 – 10	10 1/8 – 10	10 1/8 – 10	10 1/8 – 10	10 1/8 – 10	10 1/16 – 9 15/16
Italian Lira	12 – 10	13 1/8 – 12 7/8	13 – 12 1/2	13 – 12 1/2	13 – 12 5/8	13 1/4 – 13
Belgian Franc	9 5/8 – 9 1/2	9 5/8 – 9 1/2	9 5/8 – 9 1/2	9 5/8 – 9 1/2	9 5/8 – 9 1/2	9 5/8 – 9 1/2
Yen	4 3/4 – 4 11/16	4 3/4 – 4 11/16	4 3/4 – 4 11/16	4 11/16 – 4 5/8	4 19/32 – 4 17/32	4 5/8 – 4 9/16
Danish Krone	10 3/4 – 10 1/2	10 7/8 – 10 5/8	10 3/4 – 10 1/2	10 5/8 – 10 3/8	10 1/2 – 10 1/4	10 3/8 – 10 1/8
Asian $Sing	2 11/16 – 2 9/16	2 13/16 – 2 11/16	3 1/8 – 3	3 1/8 – 3	3 5/16 – 3 3/16	3 3/4 – 3 5/8
Spanish Peseta	12 7/16 – 12 5/16	12 7/16 – 12 5/16	12 1/2 – 12 3/8	12 9/16 – 12 7/16	12 9/16 – 12 7/16	12 9/16 – 12 7/16

Long term Eurodollars: two years 5 9/16 – 5 7/16 per cent; three years 6 1/8 – 6 per cent; four years 6 5/8 – 6 1/2 per cent; five years 7 – 6 7/8 per cent nominal. Short term rates are call for U.S. Dollars and Japanese Yen; others, two days' notice.

Exhibit 2 *(Cont.)*

Exchange Cross Rate

Jun 8	£	$	DM	Yen	F Fr.	S Fr.	N. Fl.	Lira	C$	B Fr.	Pta.	Ecu
£	1	1.834	2.915	233.0	9.825	2.662	3.285	2206	2.189	60.00	184.0	1.423
$	0.545	1	1.589	127.0	5.357	1.451	1.791	1203	1.194	32.72	100.3	0.776
DM	0.343	0.629	1	79.93	3.370	0.913	1.127	756.8	0.751	20.58	63.12	0.488
YEN	4.292	7.871	12.51	1000.	42.17	11.42	14.10	9468	9.395	257.5	789.7	6.107
F Fr.	1.018	1.867	2.967	237.2	10.	2.709	3.344	2245	2.228	61.07	187.3	1.448
S Fr.	0.376	0.689	1.095	87.53	3.691	1	1.234	828.7	0.822	22.54	69.12	0.535
N Fl.	0.304	0.558	0.887	70.93	2.991	0.810	1	671.5	0.666	18.26	56.01	0.433
Lira	0.453	0.831	1.321	105.6	4.454	1.207	1.489	1000.	0.992	27.20	83.41	0.645
C $	0.457	0.838	1.332	106.4	4.488	1.216	1.501	1008	1	27.41	84.06	0.650
B Fr.	1.667	3.057	4.858	388.3	16.38	4.437	5.475	3677	3.648	100.	306.7	2.372
Pta	0.543	0.997	1.584	126.6	5.340	1.447	1.785	1199	1.190	32.61	100.	0.773
Ecu	0.703	1.289	2.048	163.7	6.904	1.871	2.309	1550	1.538	42.16	129.3	1.

Yen per 1,000: French Fr. per 10: Lira per 1,000: Belgian Fr. per 100: Peseta per 100.

Source: *Financial Times,* June 9, 1992, p.34. Reprinted with permission.

Exhibit 3 *Futures and Options Prices*

Financial Futures and Options

Liffe Long Gilt Futures Options
£50,000 64ths of 100%

Strike Price	Calls-settlements Sep	Dec	Puts-settlements Sep	Dec
94	3–58	4–15	0–12	0–25
95	3–02	3–29	0–20	0–39
96	2–16	2–48	0–34	0–58
97	1–37	2–08	0–55	1–18
98	1–03	1–38	1–21	1–48
99	0–42	1–11	1–60	2–21
100	0–24	0–53	2–42	2–63
101	0–14	0–37	3–32	3–47

Estimated volume total, Calls 2197 Puts 2745
Previous day's open int. Calls 30915 Puts 24110

Liffe Bund Futures Options
DM250,000m points of 100%

Strike Price	Calls-settlements Sep	Dec	Puts-settlements Sep	Dec
8650	1.79	2.31	0.08	0.21
8700	1.36	1.91	0.15	0.31
8750	0.97	1.54	0.26	0.44
8800	0.65	1.21	0.44	0.61
8850	0.42	0.93	0.71	0.83
8900	0.27	0.69	1.06	1.09
8950	0.15	0.50	1.44	1.40
9000	0.09	0.36	1.88	1.76

Estimated volume total, Calls 9035 Puts 1146
Previous day's open int. Calls 59588 Puts 55766

Liffe US Treasury Bond Futures Options
$100,000 64ths of 100%

Strike Price	Calls-settlements Sep	Dec	Puts-settlements Sep	Dec
96	4–03	3–44	0–27	1–10
97	3–16	3–03	0–40	1–33
98	2–34	2–31	0–58	1–61
99	1–58	2–00	1–18	2–30
100	1–25	1–37	1–49	3–03
101	0–62	1–14	2–22	3–44
102	0–41	0–60	3–01	4–26
103	0–27	0–45	3–51	5–11

Estimated volume total, Calls 0 Puts 0
Previous day's open int. Calls 474 Puts 895

Liffe Euromark Options
DM1m points of 100%

Strike Price	Calls-settlements Jun	Sep	Puts-settlements Jun	Sep
8950	0.76	1.00	0	0
8975	0.51	0.76	0	0.01
9000	0.27	0.53	0.01	0.03
9025	0.03	0.33	0.02	0.08
9050	0	0.17	0.24	0.17
9075	0	0.08	0.49	0.33
9100	0	0.03	0.74	0.53
9125	0	0.01	0.99	0.76

Estimated volume total, Calls 942 Puts 861
Previous day's open int. Calls 130095 Puts 83854

Exhibit 3 (Cont.)

Liffe Italian Govt. Bond (BTP) Futures Options
Lira 200m 100ths of 100%

Strike Price	Calls-settlements		Puts-settlements	
	Sep	Dec	Sep	Dec
9400	1.97	2.25	0.44	0.57
9450	1.62	1.91	0.59	0.73
9500	1.31	1.61	0.78	0.93
9550	1.04	1.33	1.01	1.15
9600	0.81	1.09	1.28	1.41
9650	0.61	0.88	1.58	1.70
9700	0.45	0.70	1.92	2.02
9750	0.34	0.55	2.31	2.37

Estimated volume total, Calls 1766 Puts 1857
Previous day's open int. Calls 9392 Puts 11505

Liffe Short Sterling Options
£500,000 points of 100%

Strike Price	Calls-settlements		Puts-settlements	
	Jun	Sep	Jun	Sep
8900	0.96	1.18	0	0
8925	0.71	0.94	0	0.01
8950	0.46	0.71	0	0.03
8975	0.22	0.49	0.01	0.06
9000	0.02	0.30	0.06	0.12
9025	0	0.16	0.29	0.23
9050	0	0.08	0.54	0.40
9075	0	0.04	0.79	0.61

Estimated volume total, Calls 586 Puts 780
Previous day's open int. Calls 115692 Puts 98895

London (LIFFE)

20-Year 9% Notional Gilt
£50,000 32nds of 100%

	Close	High	Low	Prev.
Jun	97-15	97-20	97-15	97-30
Sep	97-23	98-00	97-19	98-06

Estimated volume 33559 (59209)
Previous day's open int. 68628 (69034)

9% Notional Ecu Bond
Ecu 200,000 100ths of 100%

	Close	High	Low	Prev.
Sep	99.52			99.15
Dec				

Estimated volume 0 (0)
Previous day's open int. 0 (0)

US Treasury Bonds 8%
$100,000 32nds of 100%

	Close	High	Low	Prev.
Jun	100-24	100-25	100-25	100-31
Sep	99-20	99-24	99-17	99-27

Estimated volume 615 (801)
Previous day's open int. 1944 (1900)

12% Notional Italian Govt. Bond (BTP)
Lira 200M 100ths of 100%

	Close	High	Low	Prev.
Sep	95.53	96.20	95.38	96.42
Dec	95.68			96.55

Estimated volume 22213 (34060)
Previous day's open int. 38841 (40549)

6% Notional German Govt. Bond
DM250,000 100ths of 100%

	Close	High	Low	Prev.
Sep	88.21	88.22	88.02	88.06
Dec	88.60			88.45

Estimated volume 10117 (48847)
Previous day's open int. 96606 (95211)

Three Month Sterling
£500,000 points of 100%

	Close	High	Low	Prev.
Jun	89.96	89.98	89.93	89.95
Sep	90.18	90.18	90.15	

6% Notional Long Term Japanese Govt. Bond
Y100m 100ths of 100%

	Close	High	Low
Jun	102.19	102.19	102.19
Sep	101.75	101.82	101.75

Estimated volume 902 (1317)
Traded exclusively on APT

Exhibit 3 *(Cont.)*

Chicago

U.S. Treasury Bonds (CBT) 8%
$100,000 32nds of 100%

	Close	High	Low	Prev.
Jun	100–26	100–27	100–19	100–25
Sep	99–23	99–24	99–15	99–22
Dec	98–19	98–21	98–12	98–18
Mar	97–19	97–19	97–13	97–18
Jun	96–21	96–21	96–20	96–20
Sep	95–26	95–26	95–21	95–25
Dec	95–01			95–00
Mar	94–10			94–09
Jun	93–21			93–20
Sep	93–02			93–01

U.S. Treasury Bills (IMM)
$1m points of 100%

	Close	High	Low	Prev.
Jun	96.29	96.31	96.29	96.31
Sep	96.14	96.15	96.11	96.14
Dec	95.70	95.71	95.67	95.70
Mar	95.56		95.53	95.56

British Pound (IMM)
$s per £

	Close	High	Low	Prev.
Jun	1.8320	1.8344	1.8280	1.8310
Sep	1.8058	1.8080	1.8020	1.8046
Dec	1.7818	1.7826	1.7800	1.7806

Swiss Franc (IMM)
SFr 125,000 $ per SFr

	Close	High	Low	Prev.
Jun	0.6892	0.6895	0.6863	0.6878
Sep	0.6803	0.6808	0.6773	0.6790
Dec	0.6728	0.6725	0.6714	0.6715

Japanese Yen (IMM)
Y12.5m $ per Y100

	Close	High	Low	Prev.
Jun	0.7862	0.7873	0.7856	0.7885
Sep	0.7850	0.7861	0.7845	0.7873
Dec	0.7847	0.7855	0.7845	0.7871
Mar	0.7855			0.7879

Deutsche Mark (IMM)
DM125,000 $ per DM

	Close	High	Low	Prev.
Jun	0.6290	0.6293	0.6276	0.6281
Sep	0.6200	0.6203	0.6185	0.6192
Dec	0.6121	0.6125	0.6115	0.6114
Mar	0.6055			0.6048

Three-Month Eurodollar (IMM)
$1m points of 100%

	Close	High	Low	Prev.
Jun	96.01	96.03	96.00	96.01
Sep	95.74	95.75	95.71	95.72
Dec	95.11	95.12	95.07	95.10
Mar	94.98	94.99	94.93	94.96
Jun	94.53	94.54	94.48	94.51
Sep	94.10	94.11	94.04	94.07
Dec	93.41	93.42	93.35	93.52
Mar	93.41	93.13	93.08	93.38

Standard & Poors 500 Index
$500 times index

	Close	High	Low	Prev.
Jun	413.60	414.15	412.35	414.30
Sep	414.60	415.10	413.40	415.30
Dec	415.90	416.00	414.80	416.50
Mar	417.60			418.50

Philadephia SE £/S Options
£31,250 (cents per £1)

Strike				Calls			Puts	
Price	Jun	Jul	Aug	Sep	Jun	Jul	Aug	Sep
1.725	10.65	10.70	10.65	10.65	–	0.06	0.50	1.04
1.750	8.15	8.20	8.15	8.17	–	0.23	0.89	1.64
1.775	5.75	5.79	5.95	6.12	–	0.58	1.60	2.46
1.800	3.28	3.72	4.14	4.45	0.04	1.15	2.53	3.48
1.825	1.27	2.18	2.76	3.12	0.59	2.22	3.76	4.84
1.850	0.26	1.16	1.79	2.19	2.11	3.72	5.31	6.46
1.875	0.03	0.54	1.08	1.43	4.28	5.62	7.14	10.18

Previous day's open Int: Calls 343,878 Puts 546,226 (All currencies)
Previous day's volume: Calls 56,656 Puts 27,881 (All currencies)

Source: *Financial Times,* June 9, 1992, p. 34. Reprinted with permission. Chicago portion: Reuters, Ltd., June 9, 1992. Reprinted with permission.

Exhibit 4 Excerpts from Global Financial Markets

In some respects a FRN is like a short-term money market instrument. The rate on the FRN is set at issue high enough that the note is worth 100. At each reset period, the rate is raised or lowered to match the prevailing market rate. So credit risk changes aside, its price should return to 100. That means you could buy it today (a reset date) and sell it six months later at par, collecting your six-month coupon, just like a Eurodollar CD. Even if you made some other assumption about the "rollover price" (the price at the next reset date) you could use this approach to calculate the money market return.

Call this somewhat naive approach the money market method. It is helpful to those who wish to compare the yield on an FRN held as a short-term investment in lieu of another money market instrument, and the fact that the rate is reset to market offers some comfort to such investors. But not much. FRNs are medium or long term bonds, and their prices at reset dates can and have deviated far from par, for reasons associated with general FRN market conditions as well as the creditworthiness of the specific issue. Thus we can identify three distinct influences on the price of an FRN:

1. *Credit condition of the issuer.* The price at the reset date will fall below par if the promised margin relative to LIBOR is perceived as insufficient reward for an issuer's deteriorated credit condition. The most direct measure is the issue's *credit rating.* A note issued as an AA may be downgraded to A or worse for reasons specific to the issuer.

2. *Market perceptions of FRNs in general.* Changes in investors' perceptions of the FRN market as a whole or of a particular segment of the market may cause a particular issuer's FRN to trade above or below par on reset dates. In the early days of the market many issues were seen as generously priced and traded above 100. Then in the late 1980s the opposite happened. Subordinated bank debt was priced in much the same way as unsubordinated debt until the Bank of England changed its rules concerning the investment by one bank in the debt of another bank. After the change, the market reassessed the relative risk of subordinated to unsubordinated FRNs. This resulted in a sharp widening of required margins and a fall in bid prices on subordinated debt relative to unsubordinated debt of the same issuers. The most visible and devastating effect was on the price of perpetual FRNs.

3. *Money market rates.* Changes in short term rates — specifically, the level of LIBOR between now and the next coupon reset date. A change in this rate will change the FRN's value as if it were a money market instrument maturing on the reset date.

The method used for pricing and comparing FRNs reflects the fact that they are in some respects bond and in some respects money market instruments. When comparing two straight bonds, the standard approach is to consider the yield to maturity of each bond and the liquidity and credit risk of the bonds. The yield is sometimes expressed as a spread over "benchmark" U.S. Treasury yields. But because the FRN's coupon rate fluctuates, the standard yield measures are useless. For this reason and because so many FRNs are held by those seeking a spread over their short term cost of funds, the market has developed a measure of an FRN's effective spread over LIBOR. To get the effective spread over the instrument's remaining life, we adjust the quoted margin by amortizing the premium or discount at which the FRN is trading. For example, on November 18, 1991 an Electricidad de Madrid FRN maturing on September 4, 1995 was offered in the London market at 99.64. The stated margin over six month LIBOR was 0.10 percent over six month LIBOR, but the effective or discounted margin was 0.21 basis points. This *discount margin* approach is the industry standard for comparing FRN spreads.

* * *

The discount margin is a measure of the effective spread, relative to LIBOR, that an investor would earn if he bought the FRN at some price today and held it to maturity. It is the margin relative to LIBOR that is necessary to discount the cash flows from an FRN so that the sum of the present value of the flows is equal to the gross price of the note. It is calculated in a manner similar to the yield to maturity of a fixed rate bond. Because the coupon stream is uncertain it is necessary to make some assumption about average LIBOR from the next coupon date until maturity, although fortunately the discount margin is not very sensitive to the assumption made. Naturally nobody can be sure what rates will prevail over the life of the FRN, but one acceptable method is to use the implied forward rate for the remaining life from the yield curve for equivalent fixed rate instruments. Better still, use the swap yield curve: this is preferable because, as will be seen in the chapter on swaps, an FRN can be converted into the equivalent of a fixed rate bond using an interest rate swap.

Source: From Ian H. Giddy, *Global Financial Markets,* © 1993. Reprinted with permission of D.C. Heath and Company.

Gunter Dufey

Case 6

Roach Hotel
International Investment Sales

It is late afternoon after a quiet trading day. You are sitting on the desk, watching the screen absentmindedly, and chatting on the phone with Joe Dominick, who handles the investments for Roach Hotel Corporation Intl. He is very pleased with the $3 million worth of Dow Chemical Euroyen bonds that you sold him in early December 1984, in spite of the fact that a slight rise in Japanese interest rates caused the bonds to be quoted now at 97–98. However, Roach Hotel International had bought the bonds, issued by DC Capital (Delaware) in bearer form, on behalf of its captive Bermuda insurance company, which carried the liability risks from operating two hotels in Japan. Because of earthquake and fire danger in that country, these risks were considerable.

Suddenly Joe says, "hey, look at the Reuters news page." And there you see it coming across the screen: "After earlier providing indications that the withholding tax on domestic yen and Euroyen bond issues by Japanese companies would be removed, Japanese officials served notice today that they would submit legislation to extend the withholding tax to all yen bonds in order to regain effective control over the use of their currency worldwide." Joe barks angrily on the phone, "What are we going to do now? How come you stuffed me with that paper? Didn't you see it coming?"

What would you reply? Would you advise to sell, buy, or to hedge? Which crucial pieces of information from the prospectus would you bring to Joe's attention?

Gunter Dufey

| **Case 7** |

Compañia Nacional de Tubos Ltda. (CNT)

THE FOUNDING OF THE COMPAÑIA NACIONAL DE TUBOS LTDA. (CNT) / ACQUISITION OF AN EQUITY PARTICIPATION IN COMPAÑIA MEXICANA DE ACERO S.A. (CMA).

In the early 1950s, German industry, for the first time since the war, was again faced with the question of investment abroad. Metall AG (Metal Corporation), whose operations primarily involved the manufacture of

The original case from which this translation was made was prepared by Messrs. Storck and Wussow under the direction of Professor Busse von Colbe of Universitätsseminar der Wirtschaft as the basis for discussion in seminars rather than to illustrate either effective or ineffective handling of an administrative situation.

steel pipe, had traditionally been oriented toward investment abroad and hence was one of the first German enterprises to resume foreign operations after World War II.

At this time Mexico was at the beginning of a period of intense industrial development. Characterized by a stable political climate and an ample labor supply, Mexico was especially receptive to German industrial investments.

Because of a shortage of domestic production facilities, the Mexican market for pipe was supplied primarily by imports from the United States. A rapidly growing market for pipe material was taken for granted, an expectation reinforced because of the country's size. Consequently Metall AG decided to establish a plant in Mexico for the production of seamless pipe. Tampico, which is located on the Gulf of Mexico about three hundred miles northeast of Mexico City and approximately the same distance from the U.S. border, was chosen as the location for the new plant. Here it was possible to work in cooperation with a Mexican foundry, Compañia Mexicana de Acero S.A. (CMA), which would supply the necessary preworked metal stock from which piping is formed. Availability of such metal stock is typically a decisive factor in the selection of a site for a seamless metal pipe plant. A preliminary long-term contract for the supply of pipe material was agreed upon by CMA and Compañia Nacional de Tubos Ltda. (CNT), the new wholly owned subsidiary of Metall AG. At the same time, CMA agreed to lease, for 99 years, 75 acres of real estate conveniently located to CNT for the construction of the new pipe plant. The ties between Metall AG and CMA strengthened over several years as Metall AG gradually acquired a 25 percent interest in CMA. In the long run, the acquisition of a majority holding was contemplated.

The new plant was equipped with automated pipe-forming machinery on which seamless pipes of diameters ranging between 4″ and 12¾″ could be produced. The plant was designed for an eventual maximum production of 300,000 tons per year. Initial production was to start at 90,000 tons per year and to eventually be increased to 180,000 tons per year within five years. The results of a market study showed these tonnages to be saleable. The capacity for finished output and other aggregates was estimated to be about 225,000 tons per year. Approximately six hundred laborers and office workers were to be initially employed.

From an analysis of the production costs and net revenues, it was expected that sales of 120,000 tons per year would be necessary to break even, and that anticipated future sales indicated that the operation would have earnings after about two years.

The market analysis was based on the feasibility of virtually displacing the U.S. imports by approximately 120,000 tons per year and the possibility of retaining 60 to 70 percent of the annual market size growth within

Mexico. The market analysis predicted an annual growth of the market by 10 to 15 percent. The pipes were to be distributed via two CNT sales corporations, in Mexico and in the United States respectively. Investment in plant and equipment for the new plant amounted to DM150 million ($32 mil) during 1956 and 1957. The equity portion of this investment amounted to DM100 million, which at the current exchange rate corresponded to $24 million.

CNT'S PROGRESS

1. The strategy which led to the founding of CNT failed for two reasons:
   a) The Mexican market in general, and the pipe market along with it, did not attain the growth rates anticipated in the preliminary market study.
   b) A much more serious problem was that the rolling process for pipe production advanced more rapidly than had originally been anticipated. Seamless pipe could now be manufactured at a lower cost and sold at a lower price, which led to cut-throat competition in the pipe market.
2. The corporation attempted to adapt to this new development by slowly retreating from the market for standard, average quality piping and by switching to the manufacture of high-grade, specialized pipes, in particular highly refined casings for oil drilling. This specialization made it necessary to extend the market area beyond the Mexican border. Consequently the U.S. market, with its heavy demand for such casings, presented itself.

The corporation was successful in adapting to this specialized pipe market, and by 1965 production and sales had increased to 210,000 tons per year. Of this amount, 50 percent was sold in Mexico, 40 to 45 percent in the United States, and 5 to 10 percent at lower prices in other countries. CNT's share of the Mexican seamless pipe market was about 80 percent.

Despite the sales level attained by 1965 through the adoption of the altered market strategy the earnings level of the corporation still remained unsatisfactory.

Results for the years 1965 to 1970 were as follows:

	1965	**1966**	**1967**	**1968**	**1969**	**1970**
Sales	50.3	47.6	34.2	48.0	50.1	52.3
				($000,000)		
Earnings Before Taxes	3.0	1.7	(1.7)	.6	.8	.4

The corporation cited the following reasons for its unsatisfactory earnings:

a) The constant development of higher grade specialized pipes necessitated considerable research and development expenditures and various additional investments.

b) The extensive specialization in highly refined pipes led to a strong dependence on the drilling activities of large oil companies, and a dependence on exports to the United States, which were less profitable due to tariffs and freight costs.

c) The production of highly refined pipes placed specific quality requirements on the preworked metal stock. CMA was not equipped to meet these quality standards, so high quality production could be achieved only with added expense and difficulty.

d) In deciding to service this specialized market, CNT had to conform to the industry practice of maintaining warehouses in all localities with major drilling operations in order to be prepared to deliver at any time. As a result, liquid assets were tied up and interest costs were incurred for funds invested in nonearning assets.

e) The poor earnings as a percent of sales in 1967 were attributed to lengthy periods of plant shutdown at CNT.

f) In selling 40 percent of its production of highly refined pipes in the United States, the firm competed with large U.S. manufacturers. In comparison to these competitors, who generally worked in affiliation with steel manufacturing and rolling mills, CNT controlled a very small plant and had an equally low sales volume. The company's costs for development, technical management and administration, purchasing, supply maintenance, and distribution as a percentage of sales were all very high. The supply of metal stock from CMA was also very expensive when compared to the in-house production of the competitors.

3. In addition to the unsatisfactory earnings yield of the firm, Metall AG was adversely affected by changes in the par values of various currencies that paralleled the revaluation of the Deutsche mark, because the DM equivalents of the transferred profits sank accordingly.

CMA'S POSITION WITH RESPECT TO CNT/METALL AG

1. Deliveries of metal stock to CNT for the planned production of 300,000 tons of piping in 1971 meant a possible contribution to overhead of about $6 million for CMA. If deliveries were discontinued,

CMA would have no way for the next five years of recovering this
amount through increased sales of existing and new products.

2. Upon completing commitments to expand the capacity for steel output, CMA was interested in expanding the breadth of its operations
and particularly in taking on the production of piping. Cooperation
with Metall AG would simplify this process through the transfer of
know-how, patents, licenses, and the like. However, the heavy financial burden of the commitments to expand output capacity left no
margin for further investments during the next five years.

METALL AG'S POSITION WITH RESPECT TO CMA

The originally planned purchase of a majority interest in CMA required
reconsideration as it became apparent that the Mexican government might
take measures to protect domestic industry from foreign takeovers.

Exhibit 1 Compañia Nacional de Tubos Ltda.

June 1970

Board of Directors
Metall AG

Dear Sirs:

In compliance with your request, we have drawn up a plan for sales,
production, and earnings of Compañia Nacional de Tubos Ltda. (CNT),
which is enclosed.

As you can see from our planning, we are forecasting an improvement
in our earnings on a long-term basis, which would result from increasing
sales and simultaneously decreasing costs due to economies of scale.

We point to the fact that the realization of these plans depends on
whether the additional sales intended particularly for the Mexican market
can be achieved without price concessions and without such extraordinary
factors as political unrest or worsening of export proceeds.

On this basis we will attain an average return on investment of only 8.4
percent or 9.6 percent, depending on alternative shipping projections for
the period 1971–1975, and therefore will not attain the target return that
you require. Even in consideration of an optimistic forecast regarding the
volume of shipments, we would realize a ROI of only 14 percent by 1975
and thus be below your expected goal of 15 percent.

TABLE 1 Sales and profit plan, CNT 1971–75

	1971	1972		1973		1974		1975	
		pessimistic	optimistic	pessimistic	optimistic	pessimistic	optimistic	pessimistic	optimistic
— in 1000 t —									
Shipments									
Mexico	120	128	128	135	135	141	143	147	150
United States	90	90	95	92	99	95	102	98	105
Offshore	23	27	29	30	35	30	39	30	45
Total	233	245	252	257	269	266	284	275	300
— in Million $ —									
Net sales	*54.83*	*57.6*	*59.0*	*60.5*	*63.2*	*62.6*	*66.5*	*64.8*	*70.4*
Material cost	31.40	33.0	33.8	34.7	36.3	35.9	38.3	37.1	40.5
Processing cost	21.86	22.5	23.0	23.3	24.0	23.9	24.9	24.5	26.0
Cost of goods sold	53.26	55.5	56.8	58.0	60.3	59.8	63.2	61.6	66.5
Gross margin*	1.57	2.1	2.2	2.5	2.9	2.8	3.3	3.2	3.9
Adjustments	./0.37	./0.5	./0.5	./0.5	./0.5	./0.5	./0.5	./0.6	./0.6
Earnings before taxes	1.20	1.6	1.7	2.0	2.4	2.3	2.8	2.6	3.3
Earnings after taxes in CNT (tax rate 42%)	0.70	0.9	1.0	1.2	1.4	1.3	1.6	1.5	1.9
Earnings after taxes in Germany**	0.56	0.7	0.8	1.0	1.1	1.0	1.3	1.2	1.5

* Differences between estimated and book values.

** The dividend paid to the German parent is subject to a 20 percent withholding tax in Mexico and is not taxable in Germany.

Basis: Price level of 1970, no significant shifts between market sectors.

Assumption: Increased cost can be offset through increases in productivity or, alternatively, they can be passed on to customers. Pessimistic and optimistic planning data are solely due to different estimates of shipments. Other risks (price discounts, cyclical fluctuations) should be compensated for by a special factor.

The continued realization of 1975 results cannot realistically be expected.

57

The well-known difficulties with the Compañia Mexicana de Acero S. A. (CMA) concerning the quality, quantity, and timely delivery of metal stock supply still exist. Owing to the long-term supply contract, we can see no way to improve this situation decisively.

In view of the difficult situation with CMA, we have also contemplated establishing our own production facilities for metal stock. The management of CNT, however, has reached a unanimous decision on the basis of its analyses that this alternative must be discarded. Considering the limited demand for metal stock, it is felt that the proposed facilities could not be operated economically.

We have also recently concluded a study which investigated the possible expansion of production of welded pipes and cold-rolled steel pipes. In addition to the difficulties which could arise from the construction of the facilities on land leased from CMA and the already mentioned metal stock supply acquisition problems with CMA, our investigation has also revealed that considerable funds would be required to bring the proposed facilities into operation. The investment necessary would amount to approximately $10 million for the welded pipe facility and $12 million for the cold-rolled steel pipe facility. The ROI for these investments would only be 9 percent or 10 percent.

In addition, the construction of a welded pipe facility would be of limited value since even our present production facilities are not operating at full capacity.

We suggest that the problems mentioned should be discussed at the next Board meeting.

Sincerely yours,

CNT Management

Enclosures

Exhibit 2 *Metall AG*

July 1970

Management
Compañia Nacional de Tubos Ltda.

Dear Sirs:

We thank you for your exposition of your economic situation along with the possible alternative courses of action for your company. As you know, we emphasized the difficulties in metal stock shipments during the last CMA Board meeting. It seems, however, that the solution to this problem cannot be reached in the present way of operating.

Based on experiences in our other plants, we view the present form of cooperation agreement as the primary cause for the difficulties. Directly coordinating metal stock material requirements with the appropriate departments in the rolling mills could result in an improvement.

We are convinced that the structural disadvantage of your operation, as well as the lack of your own metal stock supplies and the unfavorable ratio of overhead expenses to sales, can be eliminated only through close cooperation with CMA.

We therefore agree to discuss these points during the next Board meeting. Preliminary to this meeting we request that you consider possible benefits which would result from closer cooperation with CMA and then prepare the following material.

1. Quantify changes in earnings of CNT and CMA which would result from consolidating both stages of production.
2. Comment on the new Mexican legislation on foreign takeovers, which is presently being drafted.

In view of the legal question we ask that you invite your lawyer to the next Board meeting.

Sincerely yours,

Metall AG

Exhibit 3 *Excerpt from the minutes of CNT board meeting on September 30, 1970*
Third point on the agenda

GENERAL ECONOMIC CONDITION OF CNT AND POSSIBLE COURSES OF ACTION

In connection with CNT's unsatisfactory situation, its report explains in detail sales and profit plans from 1971 to 1975 and medium-term alternatives.

The material requested by Metall AG is presented and explained. After a detailed inquiry, a $2.2 million reduction in annual overhead expenses at CNT was considered feasible on a long-term basis (Table 2). Moreover, this reduction in expenses in the steel production and rolling stage and metal stock preworking stage has been determined to amount to approximately $1.8 million per year (Exhibit 4). CMA's expected economic benefits from the combined responsibility for production from raw material to the finished pipe are based on the data that have been attained in Metall AG's integrated foundry, rolling mill, and pipe works. As a consequence of integration, savings will also be made in the inventory of metal stock (Exhibit 5).

The detailed discussion on the potential to economize on overhead expenses shows that CNT's estimates are optimistic, but that at least 60 percent should be attainable.

The participants of the discussion all agree that cooperating with CMA is the best course of action. Therefore, CNT and CMA should be consolidated.

The expected profits for 1971–1975, according to the plan, make a takeover of CNT by CMA very interesting, especially in combination with the synergistic effects considered possible.

Mr. Fulano, the corporate legal counsel, presented the following views: The draft of the bill limiting foreign influence on domestic industries that is presently under consideration in Parliament provides for considerable limitations on foreign capital. In particular, foreign companies shall no longer be permitted to acquire a majority ownership share of Mexican companies. The date on which the bill is to be passed has not yet been set; however, an increase of Metall AG's share in CMA could accelerate this legislation and create considerable opposition. Already, any intended acquisition of additional shares by foreign companies must be registered.

Mr. Shultz, Senior Vice-President of Finance at Metall AG, states that this information, together with other intelligence reports available in Germany, confirms the change in attitude of Mexican officials toward foreign investment. For this reason, an increase in CNT's ownership share in CMA must be eliminated as an alternative as far as the Board of Metall AG is concerned, even though it would be the most rational solution economically.

In addition, Mr. Fulano refers to the following matters:

1. Consideration of the benefits of the consolidation under discussion in connection with this type of valuation study is new in Mexico.
2. During negotiations on cooperation with CMA, the impression should not be left that Metall AG, as major shareholder of CMA, could gain unfair advantage (reference to arm's-length clause).
3. Also, with regard to its own Board of Directors, CMA will request that a valuation study be made.
4. Because of its own plans for expansion and the restriction coven-

TABLE 2 Compañia Nacional de Tubos Ltda., Tampico, August 1970
(Summary of possible cost savings, especially in overhead expenses when steel and rolling operations are integrated)

Cost center ledgers	Actual 1.1–6.30.70 × 2 = expenses budget 1970	Compound effect (CNT)* Profit per year**	Loss per year**	Investment savings***	Remarks
4 Plant service I.	$ 10,532	—	—	—	
40 Roads and parking	607,170	—	—	—	
41 Tube mill buildings					
42 Utility systems					
4201 Water distribution system	$ 38,576	—	—	$100,000	Water settling basin and oil skimming facility
4202 Compressed air	14,914	—	—	—	
4203 Gas system	8,156	—	—	—	Natural gas (difference in contract price)
4204 Heating	63,302	$ 6,000	—	—	(difference in contract price)
4205 Electric power	469,402	150,000	—	—	
4206 Butane plant	13,914	—	—	—	
4207 Trolley wire system	750	—	—	—	
4208 Waste heat boiler	—	—	—	—	
43 Plant protection and safety	104,398	20,000	—	—	1 messenger, 2 guards
44 Plant cleaning	36,008	18,000	—	—	Reduction of office space
45 Stores	212,698	180,000	—	—	15 men
46 Hot mill offices	198,398	12,000	—	—	1 assistant superintendent
47 Hot mill tool processing	148,570	10,000	—	—	1 foreman
49 Grounds maintenance	59,996	20,000	—	—	Lower billet inventory
Subtotal	*$1,986,784*	*$416,000*	—	*$100,000*	

TABLE 2 (*Cont.*)

| | | Compound effect (CNT)* | | | |
| | Actual 1.1–6.30.70 × 2 = expenses budget 1970 | Compound effect (at CNT) | | | |
Cost center ledgers		Profit per year**	Loss per year**	Investment savings***	Remarks
5 Plant Service II.					
50 Inspection department	1,002,732	100,000	—	—	1 superintendent, 1 foreman, 8 men
51 Mechanical maintenance	1,431,036	36,000	—	—	4 operators
52 Machine shop	147,994	10,000	—	—	1 foreman
53 Labor pool	163,052	10,000	—	—	
54 Electrical maintenance	442,778	—	—	—	
55 Finishing mill tool grinding	74,526	—	—	—	
56 Cold straighteners	125,170	—	—	—	(Operating cost center)
57 Test preparation	85,684	20,000	—	—	Test department (2) for special investigations
58 Shipping department	465,788	30,000	—	50,000	1 foreman and 3 men, 1 diesel locomotive
59 Finishing mill offices (foreman)	211,268	—	—	—	
Subtotal	*4,150,028*	*206,000*	*—*	*50,000*	
6 Operating cost centers (*Hauptkostenstellen*)					
60 Billet department	385,914	40,000	—	45,000 / 20,000	Based on lower inventory: 1 straddle-carrier, 1 Michigan front loader,
61 Hot mill	2,681,184	36,000	—	10,000	1 Caterpillar, and 2 men Natural gas (difference in contract price)
62 Finishing department cut-off A	543,964	—	—	—	
63 Reclaim department A (Grinding)	461,608	—	—	—	

#	Department					Natural gas (difference in contract price)
64	Finishing Department Threading B	310,394	—	—		
65	Testing Department	574,166	—	—		
68	Heat Treat Department	766,274	22,000	—	—	
69	Nondestructive Testing	803	—	—		
70	Ultrasonic Testing	1,925	—	—		
71	Reclaim Department C (Adjustage)	63,660	—	—		
72	Finishing Dept. Cut-off C	69,016	—	—		
76	Coupling Department—Cut-off	40,882	—	—		
77	Coupling Department—Boring	162,890	—	—		
78	Coupling Department Tapping	166,270	—	—		
79	Coupling Department Electric Plant and Paint	62,954	—	—		
Subtotal		*6,291,904*	*98,000*	—	75,000	
8	Plant administration Cost Centers					
80	General operating	103,570	103,570	—		
81	Production planning department	87,030	25,000	—		1 superintendant and 1 man
82	Metallurgical department	216,932	60,000	—		1 superintendent and 2 phys. testers, and 1 metallurgist
83	Engineering department	102,472	30,000	—		1 superintendent and 1 man
84	Industrial engineering	168,146	75,000	—		1 superintendent and 5 men
89	Customer complaints	44,026	—	—		1 superintendent and 1 man
Subtotal		*722,176*	*293,570*	—		

TABLE 2 *(Cont.)*

		Compound effect (CNT)*			
	Actual 1.1–6.30.70 × 2	Compound effect (at CNT)			
Cost center ledgers	= expenses budget 1970	Profit per year**	Loss per year**	Investment savings***	Remarks
9 General Admin. and Sales Cost Center					
90 Corporate Management	262,912	262,912	—	300,000	Office building
91 Industrial relations department	66,212	50,000	—	—	except 1 man
92 Office service department	150,720	100,000	—	—	Communications, Depreciation on office equipment
93 Administration and finance expenses	447,712	165,000	—	—	Reduction of Interest due to lower Billet Inv. (7,000 t) and Compt. office.
94 Accounting department	214,680	170,000	—	—	except 4 people
95 Data processing department	214,976	170,000	—	—	
96 Purchasing department	40,616	40,616	—	—	except 4 people
97/98 Sales department	286,242	219,744	—	—	except "Traffic-Billing"
99 Outside pipe storage	285,720	—	—	—	
Subtotal	1,969,790	1,178,272	—	300,000	
Total	15,120,682	2,191,842	—	525,000	

The savings shown represent optimistic assumptions and can be realized to a certain extent only over an extended period of time.

*Synergistic effects

**Current cost savings with respect to increases p.a.

***Savings of investment funds when it is possible to rely on appropriate, sufficiently large-scale operations in another plant (which is the rule in an integrated steel and rolling mill).

ants[1] associated with long-term borrowing, CMA has no funds for such investments. CMA must not incur any additional debt that would show on its balance sheet.

5. A general increase of the equity capital for CMA is not considered feasible because of the presently low price of CMA common stock on the exchange.

6. CMA has no experience in the production and marketing of pipe.

7. Basically, CMA expects a before-tax return on equity of 18 percent, in which case the current balance proportions would be considered as adequate.

Talks with CMA concerning a consolidation of CMA and CNT have been decided upon. Upon convening a meeting, Mr. Shultz will speak to CMA's Board of Directors and will suggest that CMA appoint a committee for the negotiations. It shall be proposed that the committee consist of three members from each of the two parties.

For the time being, the committee members of CNT/Metall AG are to develop suggestions that might serve as a basis for the negotiations on CMA's takeover of CNT. Among other things, CMA's financial situation and its lack of know-how in the area of pipe production and sales must be specifically taken into account.

Enclosures

Exhibit 4 *Tampico, Mexico*

September 1970

Memorandum

TECHNOLOGICAL ADVANTAGES OF AN INTEGRATED FOUNDRY AND PIPE FACILITY (IMPROVEMENT OF OUTPUT, MANUFACTURING METHODS, AND PRODUCTION FACILITIES)

1. Improvement of output in the steel plant through increased use of exothermic hot tops. These are special covers for the molds into which the liquid steel is poured. They permit the slowest possible

[1] Regarding the structure of the balance sheet: the fixed assets, when increased by the amount of an additionally planned debt, must add up to at least two and one-half times the long-term debt (including the new loan). Regarding earning capacity: the earnings after tax must amount to at least three and one-half times the interest for long-term debt (including new loan) in the year prior to receipt of the additional debt. CMA was not in compliance with this restrictive condition.

hardening of the liquid steel on the surface so that impurities can rise, thus avoiding the formation of air pockets inside the steel block.

Normally, the application of exothermic hot tops improves the output. However, the reduction in the quality of the surface must be taken into account when the steel is rolled. Metall AG has considerable know-how in this area and can use these exothermic hot tops specifically for molding up to 90 percent of the different qualities of metal stock for pipe material. This exchange of know-how is consistently possible only if the production of both metal stock supply and pipe is under centralized control, since decisions on the most practical methods of the process demand thorough knowledge of pipe production and since specific decisions are necessary for each production run.

2. Matching of quality requirements of specific orders better throughout the individual stages in production particularly affects the finishing of the pipe output. In order to satisfy the *general* quality requirements of the customer CNT, the metal stock must be "soaked" or kept in a high temperature oven for a period of time. By taking the specific quality requirements into consideration, the extent of the soaking process can be calibrated much more precisely and the output can thus be improved. To that extent it would also be more practical to integrate the pipe material soaking process with the pipe manufacturing plant when combining foundry and pipe production. For reasons of pipe quality control, this is not possible without integrating all processes.

3. Leftover piping, which without consolidation has to be scrapped or at least depreciated in value, could be used partially for pipe manufacture when operations are integrated. Moreover, with integrated plants it is possible to deliver piping in roll-lengths and divide them up according to exact information on how they are to be employed, which would considerably reduce the amount of scrap lengths left over.

Furthermore, in integrated plants it is possible, within certain limits, to produce pipes from piping which does not fully meet the quality demanded.

To a considerable extent, good pipe can still be produced from this lower grade material.

With respect to the production of about 300,000 tons of piping the following quantifiable advantages would result from the above change.

Item 1	Approximately $0.6 million per year
Items 2 and 3	Average between pessimistic and optimistic estimate: approximately $1.2 million per year.

Exhibit 5 *Compãnia Nacional de Tubos Ltda., Tampico*

August 1970

INVENTORIES

The special situation of CNT, which was characterized by its dependence on a third party for the supply of metal stock and by correspondingly long lead times for scheduling the semifinished metal stock, demanded a considerably higher inventory compared to our other integrated pipe plants.

The volume of additional inventory required was estimated at about 15,000 tons and, according to a cautious assessment, was worth around $100 per ton. The expenses resulting from this (interest and warehouse costs) amounted to at least $0.15 million (10 percent).

Exhibit 6 **Compañia Nacional de Tubos Ltda., balance sheet, December 31, 1970**

Assets	$	$
CURRENT		
Cash		171,000
Accounts receivable		5,805,000
Due from subsidiary companies		1,665,000
Inventories, at lower of cost or market		
Finished goods*	7,563,000	
Work in process	2,121,000	
Raw materials	2,880,000	
Spare parts and supplies	1,353,000	
Total inventory		13,917,000
Production tools		426,000
Prepaid expenses		228,000
Total current assets		22,212,000
Investment in subsidiary companies, at cost		312,000
Fixed assets, at cost	43,509,000	
Accumulated depreciation	21,822,000	
Net book value		21,687,000
		44,211,000

Liabilities	$	$
CURRENT		
Bank loan		11,289,000
Accounts payable and accrued liabilities		7,479,000
Employees' withholding and other taxes payable		336,000
Due to subsidiary companies		357,000
Total current liabilities		19,461,000
Deferred income taxes		306,000
Shareholders' equity:		
Capital		24,000,000
Retained earnings		444,000
		44,211,000

* As to final product inventories in the U.S. they are on the books of the U.S. sales company ($7.2 mil on Dec. 31, 1970).

Exhibit 7 *Compañia Nacional de Tubos Ltda., statement of profit and loss and retained earnings, year ended December 31, 1970*

	1970 $
Sales, less discounts and allowance	52,254,000
Interest charged to subsidiary company	615,000
	52,869,000
Cost and expenses:	
Cost and expenses excluding the following	49,386,000
Depreciation	2,520,000
Interest	543,000
	52,449,000
Net profit before taxes and extraordinary items	420,000
Income taxes	240,000
Net profit before extraordinary items	180,000
Add extraordinary items:	
Income tax credit	87,000
Net profit for the year	267,000
Retained earnings, beginning of the year	177,000
Retained earnings, end of the year	444,000

Exhibit 8 **Compañia Mexicana de Acero S.A., consolidated balance sheet, December 31, 1970**

Assets		Liabilities	
	$		$
Current:		**Current:**	
Cash	3,957,000	Accounts payable and accrued	43,026,000
Short-term investments, at cost	28,595,000	Provision for income and other taxes	14,381,000
Accounts receivable	53,911,000	Dividend payable	3,650,000
Inventories	79,389,000	Current portion of long-term debt	1,172,000
Prepaid expenses	881,000		
Total current assets	166,733,000	Total current liabilities	62,229,000
Investments in associated companies, at cost	11,117,000	Long-term debt	55,113,000
Unamortized debenture issue expense	482,000	Provision for deferred income tax	76,000,000
		Shareholders' equity	
Fixed assets		Capital	65,700,000
Raw material properties, at cost	77,010,000	Retained earnings	201,565,000
Manufacturing plants and properties, at cost	461,722,000		
	538,732,000		267,265,000
	256,457,000		
Accumulated depreciation	282,275,000		
	460,607,000		460,607,000

Exhibit 9 *Appraisal, RCN value and RCLD value, summary classified by accounts, October 1970*

Accounts	Reproduction cost new (RCN)	Reproduction cost less depreciation (RCLD)
Buildings and structures	$16,945,484	$12,985,725
Residences	230,220	163,692
Misc. construction (paving, etc.)	550,607	442,950
Machinery and equipment	36,544,046	26,714,186
Misc. equipment	2,841,873	1,231,405
Power feed wiring*	240,225	215,549
Office furniture and equipment	442,463	309,725
Transportation equipment	960,218	641,863
Hot mill rolls	1,685,005	405,585
Subtotal	*$60,440,141*	*$43,110,680*
add:		
General overheads (Organization, administrative, and legal expenses, engineering and supervision, interest, taxes, and insurances during period of construction and installation)	10,758,150	7,674,750
Subtotal	*$71,198,291*	*$50,785,430*
Property in construction	1,947,972	1,947,972
Total	*$73,146,263*	*$52,733,402*

* These accounts include miscellaneous items of wiring and piping, as the major portion of this material is included with buildings and structures.

The revenue from the sale of individual pieces of equipment has been estimated at $10.2 mil.

Study Questions

1. What are the problems facing MAG's management?
2. Does MAG still have a foreign direct investment strategy?
3. What are MAG's alternatives?
4. How would you go about quantifying these alternatives?
5. What are the key issues of each alternative?
6. Which is your suggestion? Summarize the arguments you will use to sell it to your top management.
7. Would you lend to CMA for the purpose of acquiring CNT?

Ian H. Giddy

Case 8

Imperial Power — Spain

Late in 1978 Imperial Power Company (IPC) management was considering expansion of the firm's involvement in international business. IPC was a Chicago manufacturer of a variety of electric motors for use in automobiles, household goods, and industrial equipment. All of the company's sales were to other manufacturers, primarily in the automobile industry. IPC's worldwide market was supplied from subsidiaries in France, Germany, Brazil and the Philippines as well as the United States. The company's success in Europe was based primarily on its technical expertise and prompt delivery of equipment meeting a variety of industrial needs. This success led top management to believe an expansion of IPC's European capacity was needed.

The French and German subsidiaries of IPC distributed and assembled electric motors. They also performed a limited amount of manufacturing when special adaptations were required. With the maturing of European markets, particularly that for automobiles, an expansion of capacity to produce standard five-horsepower motors was required. The French subsidiary's management had urged IPC (U.S.) to expand facilities in France. However, Spain had much lower labor costs and certain government incentives that were not available in France, so IPC's president had asked the treasurer's staff to prepare a financial evaluation of a possible investment in Barcelona, Spain.

The proposed Spanish subsidiary of IPC would be a wholly owned venture producing electric motors for the Spanish domestic market as well as for export to other European countries. The initial parent-supplied equity investment would be $1.5 million, equivalent to Pts. 105 million at the current exchange rate of Pts. 70 to the U.S. dollar. An additional $600,000 would be raised by borrowing from Banque de la Société Financière Européenne, Paris-based consortium bank. Interest of 10 percent would be payable annually, and the entire principal would be due in ten years. However IPC-Spain did not anticipate any difficulty in renewing the loan indefinitely. The combined capital of $2.1 million would be sufficient to purchase equipment of $1 million and finance working capital requirements. No new working capital would be needed in the foreseeable future, and ten-year straight-line depreciation would be applied to the original cost of the equipment.

The project was regarded as an ongoing operation and therefore should, in principle, be evaluated for an indefinite time horizon. However, because of the difficulty of forecasting demand beyond a few years, the procedure used by IPC was to make cash flow forecasts only four years into the future and to treat the value of the subsidiary at the end of the fourth year as the present value of a constant annual cash inflow equal to that forecast for the fourth year.

(If, for example, the cash inflow forecast for year 4 were $150,000, then that amount was assumed to be the inflow for years 5, 6, and so forth. The net present value of this annual inflow can be found from the formula for the present value of a constant annuity:

$$\text{NPV} = \frac{\text{annual cash inflow}}{\text{discount rate}}$$

Assuming a 10 percent discount rate, the net present value at the end of the 4th year in this instance would be $150,000/0.10 = $1,500,000.)

The firm's overall marginal after-tax weighted-average cost of capital was about 12 percent. However, because of the higher risks associated with a Spanish venture IPC decided that a 16 percent discount rate would be applied to the project.

The initial sales price of an electric motor was to be Pts. 1,300 in Spain. Because of Spain's high tariffs on competing imports, this price would enable the Spanish operation to sell 50,000 units domestically and 150,000 in the export market. Spanish inflation would probably force the company to raise its sales price by 15 percent per annum, which would not affect domestic demand but might reduce forecast export sales unless the inflation were offset by a depreciation of the peseta. Discussions with the manager of the French subsidiary suggested that the price elasticity of demand in Europe was about 1.5; that is, for each 1 percent increase in the relative price of IPC's electric motors over the immediately prior year, demand would fall by 1.5 percent. Inflation in all Europe (except Spain) and in the United States was expected to run at a 5 percent annual rate.

For convenience, start-of-year prices and exchange rates would be used to calculate demand, sales prices, and operating costs for each year. However, interest (to the consortium bank) and royalty fees (to the parent) would be paid on December 31st at the year-end exchange rate.

In the absence of any price change or exchange rate change, sales for the first four years were forecasted as follows:

Year	Price (pesetas)	Price (French francs) (16.67 ptas/FF)	Domestic sales (units)	Export sales (units)
1979	1,300	77.98	50,000	150,000
1980	1,300	77.98	60,000	165,000
1981	1,300	77.98	65,000	181,500
1982	1,300	77.98	70,000	199,650

The capacity of the Spanish plant would be 350,000 units per year.

Variable cost per unit was estimated to be Pts. 840. Of this, 20 percent was for materials imported from the United States, 40 percent for domestic materials and the remainder for labor. Domestic costs could be expected to rise at the forecast inflation rate of 15 percent per annum. Annual fixed costs consisted of manufacturing overhead of Pts. 75 million, depreciation of the equipment over ten years with no salvage value, and royalty fees to the parent of $30,000 per year.

Spanish taxes consist of a 30 percent corporate income tax and a 10 percent witholding tax on dividends. No carry forward of losses is allowed. The U.S. income tax rate is 50 percent, with a credit allowed for foreign income and withholding taxes paid. Although the company expected that some of the subsidiary's earnings might be reinvested, for the purpose of evaluation, all profits were to be treated as if repatriated at the end of the year.

The project evaluation team at IPC was asked to evaluate the project on the basis of the above information, together with the following exchange rate forecasts received from the company's bank:

Currency Forecasts, 1978–1982 (Units of Foreign Currency Per U.S. Dollar)

December 31	Spanish pesetas/$	French francs/$
1978	70.0	4.20
1979	70.0	4.00
1980	85.0	3.50
1981	95.0	3.50
1982	110.0	3.50

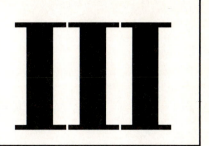

Funding and Capital Structure

Gunter Dufey

Case 9

Kent Consolidated Overseas

Kent Consolidated Overseas Manufacturing Company (KCO) was a highly integrated manufacturer of trucks for both commercial and industrial applications. More than 90 percent of its business was in the manufacture of industrial trucks, axles, transmissions, and related components. Rental of its products and sale of replacement parts were also important phases of the company's operations. KCO had some eleven manufacturing plants in the United States and manufacturing and sales subsidiaries in England, France, and Germany as well as Canada and several South American countries. Sales in 1974 were $987 million, with net income of $36.1 million. Of this, overseas sales (excluding $95 million in exports from the United States) were $209 million, of which $151.7 million (72.6 percent) were accounted for by subsidiaries in England, France, and Germany.

KCO operations worldwide had experienced substantial growth in recent years and overall company volume had doubled since 1970. Management felt that the addition of much-needed plant and equipment was necessary for the continued success of the company; thus, production capacity was scheduled to increase by 22 percent during 1975. KCO's projected capital expenditures companywide for 1975 were $64.8 million (as compared to $51.8 million in 1974). Partially because of the scale of the expansion program, KCO had recently secured additional financing: $72 million were raised through an offering of debentures and notes, and revolving credit agreements with seven major banks were increased to $109 million (up from $35 million in 1973).

Kent Consolidated also controlled Kent Credit Corporation (KCC), a wholly owned, nonconsolidated domestic finance subsidiary of the company, which financed retail time sales of Kent products through Kent's independent dealers and retail branches. Kent subsidiaries in England, France, and Germany also had wholly owned subsidiaries which assisted in financing their sales. These non-U.S. finance subsidiaries were combined with Kent Credit for administrative and reporting purposes, and the combined financial statements of Kent Credit were reported separately from KCO's operations (but the income of Kent Credit was included in the consolidated income of the company). In 1974, Kent Credit raised an additional $36 million in capital with an offer of five-year debentures, and another $18 million in the form of a five-year subordinated bank note.

COMPANY DEBT POSITION

At year-end 1973, Kent Consolidated's total debt was $130.2 million; by year-end 1974 it had risen to $196.4 million, an increase of $67.7 million. The company's treasury department was kept busy during the year financing this growth and estimates were that by year-end 1975, total company debt would reach approximately $303 million. Although the company had received an "A" rating by both Moody's and Standard & Poor's, both investment services indicated that this was despite Kent's coverage of its fixed charges (earnings coverage of interest expenses), which had been declining.[1] By the end of the year, Kent's net tangible assets were expected to be only 1.21 times long-term debt compared with Standard & Poor's mini-

---

[1] Standard & Poor's minimum coverage guideline for an "A" bond rating was five times before taxes and two to three times after taxes.

Exhibit 1 *Kent consolidated overseas balance sheet ($000)*

	1973	1974
Assets		
Current Assets:		
Cash	$ 19,983	$ 28,820
Accounts & Notes		
Receivable	54,769	96,324
Inventories	268,952	334,145
Prepaid Expenses	6,242	9,623
Total Current Assets	349,946	468,912
Rental Equipment:	41,312	39,373
Investments & Advances		
Finance Subsidiaries	57,319	53,691
Minority-owned Companies	13,244	15,109
Property, Plant, & Equipment	110,998	147,069
	$572,819	$724,154
Liabilities		
Current Liabilities:		
Notes Payable	$ 24,484	$ 54,534
Accounts Payable	70,696	88,060
Accrued Payrolls	16,215	19,102
Accrued Other	12,452	16,848
Installment Obligations	10,954	12,827
Taxes on Income	12,166	1,889
Current Installment on Debt	3,269	11,518
Total Current Liabilities	150,236	204,778
Long-Term Debt:		
Borrowings	100,160	170,771
Installment Obligations	29,995	25,613
Accrued/Deferred Items:		
Accrued Items	6,403	7,305
Rentals	16,556	20,491
Income Taxes	14,240	19,755
Shareholders' Equity:		
Common Stock	106,554	106,901
Retained Earnings	148,675	168,540
Total Equity	255,229	275,441
	$572,819	$724,154

mum guideline of 2.25 times. Working capital would be equal to 76 percent of long-term debt compared with Standard & Poor's minimum guideline of 80 percent. (See Exhibit 1 for Kent Consolidated's 1973–1974 assets and liabilities.)

Kent's average borrowings, interest expense and average cost of funds from 1972 through 1974 for the parent and the subsidiaries as a group were as follows:

	Average borrowings ($000)	**Interest expenses ($000)**	**Average cost of funds (%)**
Parent:			
1972	$30,096	$1,440	4.90
1973	$41,472	$3,024	6.62
1974	$83,016	$7,992	9.36
Subsidiaries:			
1972	$54,792	$5,040	9.20
1973	$63,576	$6,984	11.04
1974	$94,464	$14,040	14.83

Kent Credit and its subsidiaries had a long-term debt position at year-end 1974 of $169.5 million in senior and senior-subordinated securities. United States lines of short-term credit were $150 million, with $41.5 million outstanding. Canadian lines of short-term credit were $26.6 million, with $21.5 million outstanding, while Eurodollar Revolving Credit agreements amounted to $23.8 million, with no outstanding balance. Overseas finance subsidiaries had additional short-term bank lines of credit in the amount of $62.1 million, of which $19.7 million was unused. At year end, the average interest rate on outstanding short-term bank borrowings was 11.21 percent, and 10.36 percent on commercial paper.

BORROWING LIMITATIONS

In February 1972, the Board of Directors of Kent Consolidated adopted a policy of borrowing limitations for the parent company and for its subsidiaries. This policy placed certain ratio limitations on the borrowing of Kent, the parent, and other ratio limitations on the consolidated subsidiaries as a group. For the parent these were: (1) working capital not less than $57 million, (2) working capital must exceed funded indebtedness, and (3) a current ratio of not less than 2.00. For the subsidiaries as a group the limitations were: (1) a minimum working capital of $18 million,

(2) working capital not less than funded indebtedness, and (3) a current ratio not less than 1.5.

A large portion of the debt of Kent's subsidiaries was guaranteed by the parent. By year-end 1975, Kent's (the parent) funded indebtedness was expected to exceed working capital by $23 to $69 million, with the difference accounted for by whether the debt of Kent's subsidiaries as a group was borrowed long-term and guaranteed, or borrowed short-term — where the guarantee would not be considered as a debt of Kent, the parent. If the debt was guaranteed, the total guarantees to subsidiaries by year-end would be an estimated $78 million. Kent's financial executives believed, after lengthy discussions with Kent lenders around the world, that if the company established most of its consolidated subsidiaries on a viable financial basis, guarantees of the indebtedness of these subsidiaries could be eliminated. If this were done, by year end the company's violation in its working capital guidelines would be considerably less than $69 million, which was the estimated shortfall should the continued guarantee route be followed.

Under terms of loan agreements with private lenders (insurance companies), any loans with a maturity of more than one year and guaranteed by Kent were considered indebtedness of the parent. For Kent's financial managers this meant that the ability of the parent to leverage its own balance sheet was dependent upon the maximum amount of funds that could be obtained for the subsidiaries based upon their own financial statements. Lenders in nearly all countries had indicated that they would be willing to lend to the company's subsidiaries in their respective country without a Kent guarantee, provided the subsidiary committed itself to maintain senior liabilities not greater than two times the equity of the subsidiary plus subordinated debt.[2] Subsidiaries would also be required to maintain a current ratio of at least 1.5.

Kent would also be required to agree to do one of the following should nonperformance arise: (1) cause the subsidiary to repay its loans, (2) guarantee the subsidiary's loans, or (3) cause the subsidiary to reestablish the ratios. This requirement was imposed by the banks because it was their view that Kent, since it was the sole shareholder, could take action that could cause a default, leaving the banks with a debtor that was insolvent. From Kent's standpoint, this arrangement did not constitute a guarantee, because Kent had the option of taking action prior to any default that

---

[2] Lenders generally wished to include as senior liability for this ratio 10% of the indebtedness of any finance subsidiary, 10% of any discounted obligations for which the subsidiary might be liable, and 100% of any guarantees made by the subsidiaries of the indebtedness of third parties.

would prevent the subsidiary from going into default. In Kent's view, this action could take many forms besides having Kent increase its investment in the subsidiary and, as one example, management cited the option of liquidating some of the assets of the company. Management felt that the overall "debt transfer" approach might be beneficial, as this would permit the parent to leverage the balance sheets of each of its subsidiaries with a minimum effect on the borrowing capacity of the parent.

Kent's foreign subsidiaries were subject to numerous laws and regulations of foreign governments relating to investments, operations, currency restrictions, and revaluations and fluctuations of currencies.[3] On the question of how to finance projected capital increases in foreign subsidiaries, management was concerned with three issues: (1) Where to source the required capital and in what form, (2) the optimum manner in which to transfer the funds through the firm, and (3) in what form the monies should be put into the affiliates where they would be ultimately used. Additionally, worldwide economic factors led management to expect a high degree of uncertainty in financial markets, which made contingency planning for the company's funding activities all the more important. With these issues in mind, Kent financial management turned to financing the projected requirements of its three biggest subsidiaries: Kent Limited (England), Kent–France, and Kent–Germany. (See Appendix 1 for an abstract of the 1974–1975 international financial environment and Appendix 2 for a description of Kent's business strategy.)

KENT LIMITED (UNITED KINGDOM)

For the period 1970 through 1974, Kent Limited lost $15.3 million on a legal basis, and although capital was increased by $7.7 million in 1972, by year-end 1974 the subsidiary had a deficit net worth position of $7.2 million. Kent Limited had been financed primarily by intercompany loans, first from Kent Consolidated and then from Kent Credit. Kent and its operating subsidiaries had advances to Kent Limited totaling $3.6 million, and Kent Limited had bank lines totaling £3.0 million (US$7.0 million), with £1.44 million (US$3.38 million) outstanding. In 1969, Kent Limited had borrowed £4.3 million (US$10.4 million) from three mutual funds in the United Kingdom on a "back-to-back" basis, while another Kent subsidiary had lent these same mutual funds the $10.4 million. Kent Limited loans from private lenders were guaranteed by the parent at an interest

---

[3] Foreign currency losses which resulted in deductions from KCO's income were $2.3 million in 1973 and $1.9 million in 1974.

rate of 6 percent to 8 percent per annum. Kent Limited's other loans had an interest rate of 5 percent to 7 percent, about 1 percent below the interest rate on pound sterling loans.

The Bank of England required that foreign-owned British companies have equity plus funds borrowed outside the United Kingdom equal to at least 7 percent of their fixed assets. Because of Kent Limited's losses, Kent was required to finance 70 percent of these losses from funds outside the United Kingdom. For a British company to borrow outside the country it was required to obtain permission from the Bank of England, which was usually given, provided the loan was for a term of not less than two years. In order for Kent Limited to get back into compliance with the fixed asset ratio imposed by the Bank of England, the subsidiary would have to borrow, outside the United Kingdom, $3.2 million at the beginning of the year and $11.0 million by year-end 1975, based on company projections (see Exhibit 2 for the three subsidiaries' 1974 and estimated 1975 assets and liabilities).

In August 1974, Kent Consolidated's Board of Directors authorized an increase in its capital in Kent Limited by £3.6 million (US$8.3 million) in order to eliminate the subsidiary's deficit net worth position and reduce interest expenses.[4] The effect of this capital increase would be to transfer the debt that Kent Limited had under its lines of credit to the debt of the parent, which would put the interest expense for these borrowings in KCO, where they would be tax deductible. Because of Kent Limited's past losses there was no possibility of having the subsidiary borrow on its own financial structure, and KCO management felt the subsidiary's balance sheet ratios were meaningless. With respect to operational needs, if assumptions based on historic inventory turnover were considered, the subsidiary's projected requirement was $2.88 million. If both historic inventory and earnings performance ratios were applied, cash requirements for the year would be $8.7 million. On this basis, the total need for direct KCO loans and guarantees for the year would be $17.0 million.

United Kingdom tax law permitted 100 percent depreciation on new capital assets in the year of acquisition. The tax deferral aspects of this provision had substantial cash flow value to a profitable company, but were without value to a subsidiary such as Kent Limited, which paid no U.K. taxes. Consequently, long-term leasing of fixed assets had grown substantially in recent years since it shifted the depreciation advantage to a leasing company, which then passed most of this advantage on to the lessee in the form of a lower effective interest rate. Fixed asset leasing had an ad-

---

[4] In the Spring of 1975, KCO was still awaiting approval from the Bank of England for this investment.

Exhibit 2 **Kent consolidated overseas subsidiary balance sheets: 1974, 1975 (est.)**
England, France, Germany (U.S. dollars, amounts in thousands)[1]

	England		France		Germany	
	1974	1975 (est.)	1974	1975 (est.)	1974	1975 (est.)
Assumptions						
Sales	$33,500	$57,537	$48,989	$82,110	$69,254	$94,398
Net income	$(4,600)	$(6,330)	$(2,066)	$(2,053)	$ 2,079	$ 1,889
Return on sales	(13.7)%	(11.0)%	(4.2)%	(2.5)%	3.0%	2.0%
Capital appropriations	$ 785	$ 1,148	$ 1,018	$ 2,277	$ 1,785	$ 5,806
Capital expenditures	$ 462	$ 1,346	$ 706	$ 1,161	$ 1,856	$ 3,564
Inventory turnover to sales	2.4X	3.0X	3.0X	3.9X	2.8X	3.3X
Comparative Balance Sheets						
Inventories	$17,003	$21,501	$19,567	$24,790	$29,040	$34,014
Other current assets	3,852	2,897	20,607	26,726	4,812	4,963
Total current assets	20,855	24,398	40,174	51,516	33,852	38,977
Rental Equipment	1,838	4,680	1,728	2,616	4,110	5,421
Investments and advances	1,720	2,472	1,124	4,149	3,135	4,724
Net properties	1,237	2,220	3,259	3,665	8,660	11,315
Total assets	$25,650	$33,770	$46,285	$61,946	$49,757	$60,437

Exhibit 2 *(Cont.)*

	England		France		Germany	
	1974	1975 (est.)	1974	1975 (est.)	1974	1975 (est.)
Short-term debt (*)	$ 8,163	$ 3,765	$26,153	$24,378	$ 128	$ 2,252
Other current liabilities	8,685	8,130	13,031	12,230	11,440	14,067
Total current liabilities	16,848	11,895	39,184	36,608	11,568	16,319
Long-term borrowings (*)	13,603	13,971	4,564	1,464	24,983	18,549
Rental equipment obligations	2,452	5,015	—	2,617	5,014	6,546
Accrued items and deferred credits	—	—	—	—	—	—
Capital stock	8,094	16,446	6,178	6,178	7,723	7,723
Retained earnings	(15,347)	(22,239)	(3,641)	(4,144)	469	1,313
Total shareholders' equity	(7,253)	(5,793)	2,537	2,034	8,192	9,036
Additional funds required (*)	—	8,682	—	19,223	—	9,987
Total liabilities	$25,650	$33,770	$46,285	$61,946	$49,757	$60,437
Total debt (*)	$21,766	$26,418	$30,720	$45,065	$25,111	$30,788

1. Financial statements of subsidiaries operating outside the United States were translated into U.S. dollar equivalents at (1) current exchange rates for net current assets, except inventories and long term debt, (2) exchange rates applicable at the time of acquisition of inventories and properties, and (3) average exchange rates for the year for income and expense amounts, except depreciation. Translation gains and losses were included in current income. Inventories of foreign subsidiaries were valued at the lower of cost or market on the first-in, first-out method.

ditional advantage for foreign-owned companies in the United Kingdom, since leased assets were excluded from the Bank of England's requirement that foreign-owned companies finance a minimum percentage of their fixed assets through either equity or foreign borrowings. In the case of Kent Limited, the leasing of new fixed asset acquisitions under a Kent guarantee would mean significant interest savings and a reduction in the extent to which Kent Limited would have to be supported by direct intercompany loans or equity investments.

The British prime rate was 8.5 percent at the end of 1972, 14 percent at the end of 1973, and 13 percent by the end of 1974. The rate was expected to average 11.25 percent during 1975. Kent Limited's average borrowings, interest expense, and average cost of funds for the last three years were as follows:

	Avg. borrowings	Interest exp.	Avg. cost[5] of funds
1972	$10.6 million	$0.86 million	8.30%
1973	$10.7 million	$0.65 million	5.91%
1974	$13.1 million	$1.37 million	10.69%

The subsidiary's total debt was projected to increase to $26.4 million by year-end, assuming the £3.6 million capital increase would be effected during the year, in which case changes in total debt would be the net of the capital increase. For KCO financial planners, the question was to what extent the funds requirements should be financed through a combination of local borrowing and leasing of facilities, and to what extent they should be met through (foreign currency) intercompany borrowings. If the new funds, in addition to the capital increase, could be obtained in the U.K. they would probably have to be guaranteed by the parent. Funds obtained in other currencies would be at a lower interest cost but with consequent foreign exchange risk.

KENT FRANCE

Kent France was financed primarily with local borrowings within France on a short-term basis from French banks and the French branches of some of Kent's U.S. banks. Of $26.2 million short-term debt on its balance sheet (not including discounted receivables), $7.3 million were loans denomi-

[5] Because the subsidiary paid no U.K. income taxes, after tax cost of borrowings was the same as before tax cost.

nated in U.S. dollars, of which $1.44 million had been borrowed from Kent's U.S. finance subsidiary. The French Central Bank annually reviewed the credit files of large borrowers for the purpose of authorizing access to its relatively low-cost trade note discounting program. Comments by the bank on financial conditions of borrowers carried great weight in French domestic financial markets, as most of the major banks were nationalized. Although French financial authorities were generally not permitting banks to accept new guarantees from outside of the country in support of domestic credit facilities, to date, French leaders had been willing to extend credit to Kent France based on outside guarantees. Kent management felt this arrangement was not acceptable on a long-term basis, particularly since in its most recent review of Kent France, the French Central Bank indicated the subsidiary was in need of an immediate increase in its capital position.

Borrowing requirements of Kent France had grown substantially as a result of the expansion of French retail distribution activities for truck products, French government restrictions on the ability of Kent France's finance subsidiary to factor receivables, and unprofitable operations on a legal entity basis. As a result, the company's year-end borrowings of FF81.8 million (US$18.4 million) were extremely high in relation to the subsidiary's capital base. Management felt this debt-ratio problem could be solved by the increase in Kent France's capital position to FF36 million (US$8.1 million).

Depending on whether the restrictions on the growth of the finance company were lifted during the year, the subordination of intercompany loans (including those already outstanding) of an additional FF36 million might be necessary. If restrictions were eased, the need for subordinated borrowings at year end could drop to an estimated FF14.4 million (US$3.2 million). In order for Kent France to borrow without a Kent guarantee, it was felt that KCO or one of its subsidiaries should subordinate existing intercompany debt and extend subordinated intercompany loans to Kent France up to a total of FF43.2 million (US$9.6 million).

Kent France's total debt was $30.7 million at year-end 1974 and was expected to total $45.1 million at year-end 1975, based on sales projections. Bank lines totaled FF113.8 million (US$25.6 million) and borrowings outstanding under these bank lines were FF109.4 million. Long-term borrowings totaled $4.6 million (FF20.7 million), virtually all of which matured in 1976. These funds had been borrowed under a term loan guaranteed by KCO with Bank of America and a French bank.

The French prime rate was 9.15 percent at the end of 1972, rose to 12.45 percent by the end of 1973, and was approximately 14.45 percent during 1974. In 1975 the rate was expected to average 13.75 percent. Kent

France's average borrowings, interest expense, and average cost of funds was as follows:

	Avg. borrowings	Interest exp.	Avg. cost of funds
1972	$5.9 million	$0.43 million	7.32%
1973	$6.2 million	$0.86 million	14.45%
1974	$18.4 million	$2.88 million	15.87%

Kent France's total liabilities were 12.07 times Kent's investment and were expected to increase by year-end 1975 to 29.44 times investment, based upon company projections and the assumption that Kent would not increase its investment in the subsidiary, and including intercompany loans as liabilities. Kent France's current ratio was 1.06 and at year-end 1975 was expected to be 1.4, assuming additional funds were borrowed on a long-term basis.

For Kent France's capital structure to be put on a sound footing from a credit standpoint, Kent would have to increase its investment in Kent France by $13 to $15 million, provided Kent subordinated its $1.44 million of intercompany loans to Kent France. The alternative to this would be for Kent to guarantee the debt of Kent France, which would mean that $39.9 to $45.0 million of Kent parent's domestic borrowing capacity would be used up on these guarantees. If the guarantee route was followed, Kent would still be forced to increase its investment in Kent France, but by a much smaller amount, and the guarantee approach would not solve the potential problems of Kent France being required to borrow more funds outside of France (although these foreign loans could be guaranteed just as well as borrowings inside of France).

KENT GERMANY

Until 1970 Kent Germany was financed primarily with intercompany loans from Kent Credit and secondarily with short-term bank borrowings within Germany. In 1970 the Germans established regulations requiring noninterest-bearing deposits (bardepot) to be placed with their central bank by any German entity that borrowed from lenders outside of Germany. Originally this deposit was 25 percent of the foreign loans, but was eventually raised to 100 percent.[6] To avoid these deposits, Kent financed

---

[6] The bardepot was still in effect by the end of 1974.

Kent Germany with borrowings from German banks and the German branches of the company's U.S. banks. In order that these borrowings would be classified as long-term debt on the balance sheet and to assure availability of the money, the company set up revolving credit agreements.

Kent Germany had revolving credit agreements guaranteed by KCO with nine banks, totalling DM114.0 million (US$47.3 million), of which about DM56 million (US$23.3 million) had been borrowed. The interest rate on these borrowings fluctuated with the German prime bank rate. At the end of 1972 the prime rate was 8.50 percent, in 1973 it rose to 14 percent and subsequently dropped to 11 percent by the end of 1974, where it was expected to remain during most of 1975. Kent Germany's average borrowings, interest expense, and average cost of funds were as follows:

	Avg. borrowings	Interest exp.	Avg. cost of funds
1972	$8.2 million	$0.50 million	6.01%
1973	$12.9 million	$1.22 million	9.59%
1974	$20.7 million	$2.74 million	13.24%

Kent Germany's liabilities (including intercompany loans) were projected to grow from 3.2 times KCO's investment to 4.6 to 5.7 times by year's end, depending on operating results. If Kent Germany's balance sheet was to be put on a sound credit basis so that its total liabilities did not exceed twice KCO's investment, Kent would have to increase its investment in its subsidiary by $9.4 to $13.0 million. This would, in the opinion of management, allow Kent to eliminate its guarantee of Kent Germany's debt. Kent was considering authorizing the parent or one of its subsidiaries to increase the investment in Kent Germany to DM21.6 million (US$9.0 million) through either (1) an increase in capital stock, (2) subordinated company loans, (3) guaranteed third party loans, or some combination of these. Additionally, authorization might be required for new subordinated intercompany loans of up to DM8.6 million (US$3.5 million) that might be needed to support the subsidiary's projected 1975 growth. The subsidiary's current ratio was projected at 1.73 by year-end, which was above the "rule of thumb" minimum because Kent Germany's borrowings were classified as long-term. Management felt, however, that any lender to the subsidiary would be satisfied as far as the company's liquidity was concerned even without a guarantee of the loans by the parent.

Appendix One

Kent Consolidated Overseas

FINANCIAL ENVIRONMENT

In late 1974, government policies became expansive in the United States, the United Kingdom, Germany, and elsewhere, and were expected to become even more so in 1975. A major element introducing uncertainty was the trend in wages, the most important element in the cost of doing business. If wages were to continue to rise in line with the rise in demand for output brought about by stimulative government policy, the result would be higher rates of inflation. As far as the general financial outlook was concerned, Kent management felt developments pointed to lower interest rates and continued availability of short-term funds, particularly as governments were inclined to pursue expansive policies. Continued high rates of inflation, however, were expected to make markets for long-term funds for corporations difficult and expensive worldwide. These difficulties were expected to be reinforced by the investment behavior of the oil exporting countries and the high demands of increased deficit financing by public borrowers.

THE UNITED KINGDOM

Retail prices increased by 19 percent during 1974 and real output amounted to 1 percent less than in the year earlier. Governmental attempts at restraint through fiscal and monetary policies resulted in higher interest rates, while controls were in effect over price increases allowed by business firms. At the same time, wage levels rose 26 percent. This led to severe liquidity problems in the business sector and to a general decrease in investment. The country's balance of payments deteriorated during the year to a $10 billion deficit on current account. The British pound weakened in foreign exchange markets against other European currencies, and the weakness would have been more pronounced were it not for capital inflows. High nominal interest rates, aggressive borrowing by the British government, and large investments by some oil exporting countries in combination with the prospects for North Sea oil kept Sterling stronger on foreign exchanges than underlying conditions would otherwise warrant. In November, British economic policy became mildly expansionary, but what the resulting effects would be was uncertain.

FRANCE

The French economy had experienced relatively good growth beginning in 1974, supported by expansive economic policies and favorable underlying long-term growth conditions. Subsequently, consumer prices rose by 15 percent and the balance of payments current account deteriorated. As a consequence, the government switched to restrictive policies in terms of monetary aggregates, credit ceilings, and special tax measures, resulting in reduced corporate profits, construction slowdowns, and rising unemployment (2.3 percent). The French franc appreciated slightly relative to other currencies on a trade-weighted basis, due primarily to capital inflows. Projections were that credit conditions would remain tight with little change into 1975, after which a forecasted shift in monetary policy might ease conditions somewhat.

GERMANY

Although the German economy was relatively weak in 1974 (real output up only 1 percent, and unemployment at 3.7 percent, an eighteen-year high), management felt it represented one of the few bright areas worldwide. German authorities were the first to switch to a policy of fiscal and monetary restraint in early 1973. These policies were followed rather thoroughly and sustained. The result was a rate of inflation that went from 7.9 percent to 6.5 percent during the year. With domestic demand curtailed, especially in the automotive, construction, and textile industries, the combination of domestic slack and strong foreign demand for capital goods resulted in a German export boom. Together with reduced rates of inflation and high interest rates, the Deutsche mark strengthened in 1974. In the latter part of the year, monetary policy became more expansive and interest rates declined. This was coupled with a fiscal policy that provided an effective tax cut for lower income groups and an investment tax credit for business.

Appendix Two

Business Strategy and Market Characteristics of Worldwide Operations

KCO had essentially two product lines: Industrial trucks (lift trucks) and heavy-duty axles, transmissions for off-highway vehicles, and similar engineering products. Accordingly, the company's activities were divided into two product groups, "Materials Handling" and "General Products," each directed by a Group Vice-President who reported directly to the CEO.

Worldwide sales of the Materials Handling Group in 1974 were $647 million. General Products accounted for $545 million in worldwide sales; however, $205 million of this amount was accounted for by sales to the Materials Handling Group. The remaining $340 million in sales went to unrelated manufacturers of construction machinery. In this industry segment KCO had a strong market position because of the quality and high technological standards of its power-trains.

While KCO's operations in Latin America were quasi-self-sufficient because of local content regulations, KCO's activities in North America and Europe were highly integrated. Large trucks were manufactured in the U.S. plants and then shipped to Europe (and elsewhere) as needed. In this line, KCO's trucks were the leaders in the field, because of product quality and excellent after-sales service. All of these trucks were powered by gasoline engines that the company purchased under long-term contract from a U.S. supplier.

Only about 15 percent of KCO's output of large trucks was shipped to Europe, because customers in that market preferred smaller sizes, with either diesel or electric engines. Thus, the European plants specialized in small lift trucks, whereby diesel-powered units were produced in Germany and electric trucks were built in the United Kingdom. Sixty percent of all the power-trains needed came from the United States; the remainder were built in the German plant by the General Products Group. Approximately 70 percent of the output of the United Kingdom plant was sold in the domestic market, where occupational safety rules mandated the use of electric trucks in warehouses. The problem with the United Kingdom market was not only its small volume, but KCO had to fight for the market with two domestic competitors, who had 50 percent and 20 percent of the market respectively. The lack of economies of scale and continuing labor problems caused nothing but grief for the Vice-President of the Materials Handling Group.

Germany was a somewhat different story: it was KCO's largest operation in Europe. Fifty percent of its output of trucks was sold domestically, 35 percent went to France and the remainder was sold in the smaller European countries and elsewhere. Only 5 percent was shipped to the United States.

In Germany the company had a strong market position; it faced three medium-sized domestic competitors and was only occasionally bothered by Japanese imports. The big problem was the French market, which was wide open to imports and where a domestic competitor was dominant. KCO's marketing operation in France was a big headache, but management felt it could not abandon the market since its German plants would lose so much production volume that it too would become unprofitable.

KCO's production facilities in France were under the General Products Group. They were the results of a somewhat misguided acquisition in the late 1960s. The plant produced construction machinery, transmissions, and axles, but not the type used in trucks. Most of the output (60 percent) was sold in France, but 40 percent was exported to the Middle East and French-speaking Africa, where the company had carved out a respectable and rapidly growing market share in direct competition with United States and Japanese competitors.

Ian H. Giddy

Case 10

New Hampshire Tea Kettle

In late 1990 the New Hampshire Electric Tea Kettle Company, an independently managed subsidiary of Raytheon, was considering several alternative financing sources to obtain $35 million (or equivalent). The money would be used both to expand production in New Hampshire, and to develop marketing and distribution in Canada.

The company manufactured plug-in kettles and other small household appliances. While the focus had originally been the New England market, the plug-in kettle had never really caught on in the United States. Now the major market for electric kettles was in English-speaking Canada. By keeping costs down, New Hampshire Electric had gained a major share in the Canadian market. Its only serious competitor was a Canadian company located in Ontario.

Until now, the company had always financed itself with U.S. dollars. One of its bankers was now advising the company to consider financing the expansion with Canadian dollars. The bank pointed out that the inverted yield curve in Canada made this an excellent time to lock in long-term funding.

The following options were possible methods of funding:

1. Finance by discounting its three-month receivables from exports to Canada, which were invoiced in U.S. dollars. The cost would be US$ LIBOR+40 basis points. US$ LIBOR was 7.35 percent.
2. Switch invoicing to Canadian dollars, and finance through the Canadian Bankers Acceptance Market, at approximately C$ LIBOR+30bp. C$ LIBOR was currently 10.97 percent.
3. Obtain a six year US$ revolving facility, under which the company could borrow at LIBOR+25bp with an annual commitment fee of .25 percent.
4. Issue a six year Eurodollar bond. The firm had been advised that it could raise funds at the prevailing AA swap rate, which was U.S. Treasuries plus 75bp. The six year benchmark Treasury Yield was currently 8.2 percent.
5. Issue a six year EuroCanadian dollar bond at the AA rate of 9.5 percent.
6. A final alternative was to apply for a regional development loan at 7 percent from the New Hampshire Development Authority. This would require conforming to the employment requirements of the authority, but the company felt that this would not be a problem given the expanded production that was anticipated.

Which choice of funding should New Hampshire Electric use? Be sure to consider interest rate, maturity, currency and availability of funds.

Arthur I. Stonehill

Case 11

Tektronix, Inc.

In June 1974 Ken Knox, Assistant Treasurer, Tektronix, Inc., was trying to arrive at a rational policy for determining the most desirable financial structure for Tektronix UK, a British manufacturing subsidiary of Tektronix, Inc., U.S. In particular he wanted to determine how much debt, if any, Tektronix UK should carry, and in what currency the debt ought to be denominated. He realized that the policy decision on Tektronix UK might serve as a new guideline for the desired financial structures of the other foreign subsidiaries of Tektronix, Inc. The policy also needed to be consistent with recent corporate decisions to refund existing corporate short-term debt either in the United States or abroad, and to reduce exposure to foreign exchange losses.

BACKGROUND

Tektronix is the world's leading producer of oscilloscopes. It was founded in January 1946 by Howard Vollum and Jack Murdock. Howard Vollum had worked with radar in the military during World War II and recognized the need for a better oscilloscope. Jack Murdock was also a veteran with a similar belief and good skills in business administration. During the first year the founders developed an oscilloscope for use in the electronics industry that was technically superior in reliability and performance to any on the market at the time. The firm occupied an 11,000 square foot building in Portland, Oregon, in March 1947. In May 1947 the first oscilloscope was delivered. Its technical superiority and low price soon created an outstanding reputation for Tektronix and the problem soon became producing enough oscilloscopes to meet demand. The product line was also broadened to include additional types of oscilloscopes and related instruments.

Sales grew dramatically from $257,000 in 1948 to $4,022,000 in 1951. Production facilities were moved to the new 20,000 square foot Sunset plant west of Portland in 1951. Sales and profits continued to expand. Production facilities were expanded greatly by the purchase of a 300-acre farm near Beaverton, Oregon, and its conversion to a model industrial park. The product line continued to be broadened in oscilloscopes, and in the late 1960s into related technologies such as information display equipment (graphic computer terminals). Sales and profits continued to grow unabated as shown in Exhibit 1. During the fiscal year ending May 25, 1974, net sales reached $271 million. The main customers continued to be the manufacturers of electronic equipment, electrical equipment, and computers. Other customers were government agencies, research laboratories, educational institutions, and the broadcast and TV industry.

INTERNATIONAL ACTIVITIES

In the early years Tektronix marketed oscilloscopes through existing distributors and commission agents in the United States and abroad. It soon became apparent, however, that the technical nature of the product required a closer relationship with the customer and greater attention to quality control and servicing. Therefore Tektronix developed its own direct selling organization in the United States starting in 1950. Its first non-U.S. direct selling sales office was started in Canada in 1957. Wholly owned marketing subsidiaries were established in Switzerland in 1961, United Kingdom and Australia in 1963, France in 1966, Denmark in 1969, The Netherlands and Sweden in 1970, and Belgium in 1971.

Exhibit 1 *Tektronix consolidated financial statistics (Dollars, shares and square feet in thousands)*

Fiscal year ending in May	1974	1973	1972	1971	1970	1969	1968	1967	1966	1965
NET SALES	271,428	202,855	167,482	149,442	168,939	151,011	135,021	129,961	102,162	81,364
EARNINGS	21,353	16,739	11,764	9,904	15,005	14,572	13,810	13,620	11,111	7,347
Per Share	$2.47	$1.94	$1.37	$1.16	$1.75	$1.72	$1.64	$1.64	$1.33	$0.88
% of Sales	7.9%	8.3%	7.0%	6.6%	8.9%	9.7%	10.2%	10.5%	10.9%	9.0%
% of Beginning-of-Year Shareowners' Equity	13.7%	12.1%	9.3%	8.6%	15.0%	17.4%	20.3%	24.8%	25.1%	19.1%
INCOME BEFORE INCOME TAXES	38,497	30,479	21,008	16,806	26,398	26,379	25,825	25,611	19,703	13,608
% of Sales	14.2%	15.0%	12.5%	11.2%	15.6%	17.5%	19.5%	19.7%	19.3%	16.7%
Income Tax Rate	44.5%	45.1%	44.0%	41.1%	43.2%	44.6%	46.0%	46.6%	43.6%	46.0%
PAYROLL BEFORE PROFIT SHARE	94,258	70,949	58,609	56,338	60,281	49,214	41,625	38,413	32,605	26,111
EMPLOYEE PROFIT SHARE	18,706	14,875	10,462	8,275	13,144	13,360	13,542	13,744	10,810	7,553
Facilities in Use at Year End (in Square Feet)	2,940	2,612	2,429	2,329	2,111	1,813	1,711	1,596	1,441	1,203
COST OF FACILITIES	111,302	89,681	84,947	81,381	76,146	59,256	47,638	41,447	35,986	30,893
INVESTED IN FACILITIES (during year)	23,530	7,075	4,915	6,047	17,289	12,269	6,644	5,889	5,728	3,915
FACILITIES DEPRECIATION (mostly accelerated)	7,525	6,834	6,394	5,898	4,904	3,870	3,470	3,008	2,470	2,358

ACCUMULATED DEPRECIATION	49,947	43,514	37,726	32,140	26,789	22,348	18,955	15,929	13,197	11,323
TOTAL ASSETS	251,061	206,599	173,743	157,808	155,619	127,813	107,552	93,348	76,459	59,402
ACCOUNTS RECEIVABLE NET	55,230	44,417	32,833	27,113	29,165	27,428	22,873	21,675	17,111	12,701
INVENTORY (including supplies)	97,230	72,904	56,066	63,085	59,252	41,599	35,289	34,305	28,537	19,727
CURRENT ASSETS	176,405	151,033	120,539	101,991	101,506	86,728	74,840	63,375	52,975	39,180
CURRENT LIABILITIES	68,484	46,644	31,802	28,963	38,674	27,042	22,183	23,480	20,935	14,513
WORKING CAPITAL	107,921	104,389	88,737	73,028	62,832	54,686	52,657	39,895	32,040	24,667
LONG-TERM INDEBTEDNESS (including current portion)	973	1,100	1,288	1,930	429	501	988	2,134	610	583
Common Shares Outstanding at Year End	8,651	8,651	8,602	8,588	8,572	8,555	8,456	8,323	8,336	8,360
SHAREOWNERS' EQUITY	175,488	155,630	138,488	126,338	115,841	100,297	83,824	67,897	54,938	44,335
COMMON-SHARE CAPITAL	12,213	12,158	9,357	8,889	8,325	7,774	7,507	6,009	6,009	6,009
REINVESTED EARNINGS	163,966	144,140	129,186	117,467	107,532	92,546	78,320	64,511	50,892	39,781
Number of Employees at Year End	12,693	10,580	8,334	9,091	9,957	8,813	7,892	7,302	6,500	4,992

Foreign manufacturing facilities were established in 1958 on the Isle of Guernsey in order to serve customers in the European Free Trade Association without having to surmount restrictive trade barriers and tariffs. This operation also received British Commonwealth preference treatment. The Isle of Guernsey uses the pound sterling as its normal currency and for all practical purposes is treated as if it is part of the British Isles for monetary purposes. Guernsey residents must abide by the same regulations set by the Bank of England as other British residents.

A secondary manufacturing operation was started at Heerenveen, The Netherlands, in 1961. This served the Common Market countries from within the common external tariff barrier. In 1965 Tektronix established a fifty-fifty joint venture with Sony Corporation to serve the Japanese market. In 1970 the marketing subsidiary in the United Kingdom was merged with an independent oscilloscope manufacturer (acquired in 1967) to form Tektronix UK.

In addition to avoiding tariff barriers, Tektronix preferred to compete on the home markets of potential competitors to insure that the competitors did not have an easy base from which to compete in the United States and other markets.

International operations played an important role in the spectacular growth of sales and earnings. In 1974 non-U.S. sales were $116 million or approximately 40 percent of consolidated sales. The corresponding figure for foreign net earnings was $9 million, or about 50 percent of total net earnings.

International activities received all the attention they deserved since many of the key corporate officers had come up through the "international group." This included Tektronix's President and several of the Vice-Presidents. Les Stevens, Group Vice-President — Finance, had been International Finance Manager before becoming the chief financial officer. Ken Knox had assisted him on the international headquarters staff prior to being appointed Assistant Treasurer.

FINANCIAL STRUCTURE

Tektronix followed a policy of trying to finance its growth almost entirely from its own cash flow without resort to external long-term borrowing. As a result, with the exception of the period 1961–64, there were insignificant amounts of long-term debt in the financial structure. Current liabilities were also modest compared to current assets and the overall debt ratio (total debt/total assets) was usually under 30 percent from 1965 until 1974.

The rate of growth of Tektronix was not constrained significantly by its reliance on internal cash flow. Instead, growth was directly related to its market opportunities in the test and measurement field and later in the information display field as well. It had been corporate policy not to stray outside of their area of technological expertise. No attempt was made to diversify as a means of reducing business risk. The steady growth of the oscilloscope field, and Tektronix's very strong market position as leader in the field, combined to establish a relatively stable return on assets and equity. The general feeling was that potential risk reduction from diversification outside of the industry would have been less than the added risk from a managerial and expertise viewpoint.

The low debt–low diversification policies also reduced the perceived need for Tektronix to calculate what an upper limit might be on its debt ratio. The financial executives did not worry about finding an optimal debt ratio which might theoretically minimize its cost of capital although they were quite familiar with the theory. In fact management had not been overly concerned about the level of fluctuations in market price of Tektronix's common stock. It was publicly traded starting in 1963 and soon listed on the New York Stock Exchange. They were very concerned, however, about return on sales, and growth in earnings.

One factor that favored the above goals was that almost from the start Tektronix had a very generous profit-sharing plan. Typically the employees received 35 percent of consolidated profit before income taxes and charitable deductions. Profit sharing was an important part of each employee's total compensation package. In the early years, prior to going public, an employee common stock ownership plan was in effect. As much as 12 percent of the common stock became employee-owned. Stock options continued to be granted in later years but employee ownership as a proportion of the total did not grow substantially.

In June 1974 Tektronix decided to modify its traditional no-debt finance structure policy. It was motivated by a belief that the tight credit conditions of the previous years might continue for several more years. A brief easing of credit conditions and interest rates, because of the Federal Reserve Board's desire to stimulate the lagging U.S. economy, convinced management that the time was ripe to borrow long term as insurance against the day when they might need the funds and not be able to borrow them easily. This had not occurred in the past but the frightening degree of inflation worldwide had increased the need for working capital just to maintain the same pace. Furthermore, both domestic and foreign sales continued to climb dramatically. With the prospect of further high rates of real and inflation-induced growth, management felt that it was now opportune to consider $20–40 million in long-term debt which would refund existing short term borrowings of $23 million. Long-term debt was less than $1 million at the May 1974 year end.

FINANCIAL STRUCTURE OF FOREIGN SUBSIDIARIES

Tektronix followed a policy of starting new foreign subsidiaries with inter-company credit from sister subsidiaries or the parent firm. Typically, equity would be extremely small but the debt would be entirely accounts payable to related companies. This arose from importing the initial inventory on extended payment terms or direct loans from affiliates. As a result the apparent debt ratio of the new subsidiary appeared quite high relative to local norms but was almost riskless since the debt was internal to Tektronix. Thus, the entire original capital could be considered equivalent to equity from the viewpoint of an outside creditor or supplier. Because of the rapid rate of growth in earnings, each of the Tektronix subsidiaries soon were able to repay the original debt out of cash flow, thus acquiring more normal balance sheet ratios.

The decision to borrow locally for working capital needs was made by corporate headquarters rather than local managers. Tektronix believed that leads and lags in the intercompany trade accounts was the optimal method of local financing considering its flexibility, high local interest rate costs, and effective local income tax rates. In addition, control by head-quarters permitted better coordination of exposure to foreign exchange losses.

The cost of local debt varied widely among countries of concern to Tektronix. Exhibit 2 shows key interest rate indicators. Generally Tektronix could borrow locally on a short-term basis at rates close to money market rates. Medium- and long-term borrowing for Tektronix, however, would probably cost approximately 2–4 percent over the host country government bond rate to reflect the normal risk differential between public and comparable risk private borrowing.

The after-tax cost of debt also varied widely due to differing effective corporate income tax rates and qualifications for deductibility of interest. Effective corporate income tax rates for Tektronix in the United States were 50 percent, in the United Kingdom 48 percent, in the Netherlands 48 percent, and the Isle of Guernsey 20 percent. In the United Kingdom, how-ever, interest paid to related companies could not be deducted for tax purposes. Thus, interest paid by Tektronix UK to Tektronix, Inc. or other affiliates could not be deducted for tax purposes. On the other hand inter-

Exhibit 2 Interest rates

Central Bank Discount Rates
(End of period quotations in percent per annum)[1]

	1962	1963	1964	1965	1966	1967	1968	1969	1970	1971	1972	1973			1974				
												II	III	IV	Jan	Feb	Mar	Apr	May
United States	3.00	3.50	4.00	4.50	4.50	4.50	5.50	6.00	5.50	4.50	4.50	6.50	7.50				7.50	8.00	8.00
United Kingdom	4.50	4.00	7.00	6.00	7.00	8.00	7.00	8.00	7.00	5.00	9.00	7.50	11.50	13.00	12.75	12.50	12.50	12.00	12.00
Industrial Europe																			
Austria	5.00	4.50				3.75		4.75	5.00	5.00	5.50	5.50							6.50
Belgium	3.50	4.25	4.75		5.25	4.00	4.50	7.50	6.50	5.50	5.00	5.50	6.50	7.75		8.75			8.75
Denmark	6.50	5.50		6.50	7.50	6.00	6.00	9.00	9.00	7.50	7.00	7.50	8.00	9.00	10.00				10.00
France	3.50	4.00		3.50		3.00	6.00	8.00	7.00	6.50	7.50	7.50	11.00						11.00
Germany	3.00		3.50	4.00	5.00	3.00		6.00	6.00	4.00	4.50	7.00							7.00
Italy	3.50							3.75	5.50	4.50	4.00		6.50						6.50
Netherlands	4.00	3.50	4.50	5.00		4.50	5.00	6.00	5.50	5.00	4.00	5.00	6.50	8.00					8.00
Norway	3.50			5.50	6.00		5.00	7.00	7.00	4.50	5.00						5.50		5.50
Sweden	4.00		5.00	5.50	6.00		5.00	7.00	7.00	5.00									6.00
Switzerland	2.00		2.50		3.50	3.00		3.75	3.75	3.75					5.50				5.50
Canada	3.24	4.00	4.25	4.75	4.75	6.00	6.50	8.00	6.00	4.75	4.75	6.25	7.25	7.25				8.25	8.75
Japan	7.30	5.84	5.84	6.57	5.48	5.48	5.84	6.25	6.00	4.75	4.75	5.50	7.00	9.00	9.00				9.00

[1] See country pages for changes within each year or quarter.

Exhibit 2 *(Cont.)*

Money market and Euro dollar rates
(In percent per annum)

	1962	1963	1964	1965	1966	1967	1968	1969	1970	1971	1972	1973 II	1973 III	1973 IV	Jan	Feb	1974 Mar	Apr	May
United States[1]	2.78	3.16	3.55	3.95	4.88	4.33	5.35	6.69	6.44	4.34	4.07	6.61	8.39	7.46	7.76	7.06	7.96	8.33	—
United Kingdom[1]	4.18	3.66	4.61	5.91	6.10	5.82	7.09	7.64	7.01	5.57	5.54	7.36	10.24	11.62	12.09	11.92	11.96	11.51	11.35
Industrial Europe																			
Belgium[2]	2.13	2.29	3.35	3.17	3.88	3.19	2.84	5.40	6.25	3.70	2.46	3.19	5.77	7.10	8.52	7.94	8.96	9.21	9.52
France[2]	3.61	3.98	4.70	4.17	4.79	4.80	6.15	8.95	8.68	5.84	4.95	7.61	9.26	11.27	13.53	12.48	12.15	11.83	12.91
Germany[2]	2.66	2.99	3.29	4.11	5.34	3.35	2.58	4.81	8.67	6.05	4.30	11.05	12.06	11.25	10.40	9.13	11.63	5.33	8.36
Netherlands[2]	2.51	2.82	3.75	3.73	6.42	5.67	5.19	7.76	7.96	5.20	1.93	2.93	9.04	12.29	11.82	10.86	9.07	9.86	9.10
Canada[1]	4.00	3.56	3.75	3.99	4.99	4.64	6.27	7.19	5.99	3.56	3.56	5.19	6.14	6.44	6.22	6.07	—		
Japan[2]	10.31	7.54	10.03	6.97	5.84	6.39	7.88	7.70	8.29	6.42	4.72	6.13	7.88	9.44	11.65	12.10	12.48	12.04	12.00
Euro Dollar London[3]		3.95	4.32	4.81	6.12	5.46	6.36	9.76	8.52	6.58	5.46	8.47	10.99	10.13	9.37	8.50	9.23	10.53	11.67

[1]Average tender rate for three-month Treasury Bills.
[2]Average of daily or weekly Call Money rates.
[3]Average of daily quotations for three month deposits.

Central Government Bond Yields

(Average yields to maturity on issues with at least 12 years' life in percent per annum.)

	1962	1963	1964	1965	1966	1967	1968	1969	1970	1971	1972	1973 II	1973 III	1973 IV	1974 Jan	1974 Feb	1974 Mar	1974 Apr	1974 May
United States	3.95	4.00	4.15	4.21	4.66	4.85	5.26	6.12	6.58	5.74	5.63	6.22	6.59	6.31	6.56	6.54	6.81	7.04	—
United Kingdom	5.90	5.43	5.98	6.56	6.94	6.80	7.55	9.04	9.22	8.90	8.91	10.03	11.16	11.93	12.89	13.50	13.68	14.21	13.80
Industrial Europe																			
Belgium	5.24	4.98	6.41	6.44	6.62	6.70	6.54	7.20	7.81	7.35	7.04	7.32	7.46	7.69	7.92	8.14	8.22	8.36	8.71
France	5.02	4.97	5.08	5.27	5.40	5.66	5.86	7.64	8.06	7.74	7.35	7.99	8.47	8.80	9.32	9.73	9.98	—	10.31
Germany[1]	5.9	6.1	6.2	7.1	8.1	7.0	6.5	6.8	8.83	8.0	7.9	9.3	9.8	9.6	9.6	9.9	10.4	10.4	10.6
Italy	5.78	6.10	7.41	6.94	6.54	6.61	6.70	6.85	9.01	8.34	7.47	7.41	7.41	7.46	7.43	7.49	7.80	8.27	—
Netherlands	4.21	4.22	4.92	5.50	6.59	6.18	6.49	7.51	8.22	7.35	6.88	7.33	8.33	8.33	9.17	9.19	9.74	10.08	—
Sweden	4.89	4.93	5.64	6.18	6.57	6.06	6.31	6.98	7.39	7.23	7.29	7.39	7.41	7.39	7.30	7.27	7.15	7.73	7.83
Switzerland	3.13	3.25	3.97	3.95	4.16	4.61	4.37	4.90	5.82	5.27	4.97	5.38	5.60	6.07	6.41	6.72	7.09	7.27	7.30
Canada	5.09	5.09	5.19	5.21	5.69	5.94	6.75	7.58	7.91	6.95	7.23	7.62	7.76	7.65	7.75	7.74	—	—	—
Other Countries																			
Australia	4.92	4.58	4.72	5.21	5.25	5.25	5.21	5.81	6.75	6.92	6.03	6.63	7.50	8.50	8.50	8.50	8.50	8.50	8.50
India	4.36	4.68	4.73	5.32	5.54	5.52	5.07	5.00	5.00	5.00	5.00	5.00	5.00	5.00	5.00	5.00	5.00	5.00	5.00
New Zealand	5.25	5.15	5.06	5.10	5.28	5.51	5.53	5.54	5.51	5.52	5.52	5.59	6.01	6.05	6.06	6.04	6.04	6.05	—

[1] Bonds of local authorities.

Exhibit 2 *(Cont.)*

End of Month Forward Rates

Three-months rates of the currencies shown against the US dollar

Expressed as a premium or discount (−) on the spot rate, in percent per annum

| | 1973 | | | | | | | | | | 1974 | | | | |
	Mar	Apr	May	June	July	Aug	Sept	Oct	Nov	Dec	Jan	Feb	Mar	Apr	May
Pound sterling	−2.78	−2.41	−1.54	−1.91	−3.10	−4.39	−4.51	−4.35	−5.50	−6.54	−10.54	−9.20	−9.36	−5.10	−3.06
Belgian franc	5.99	3.17	2.33	2.44	3.57	3.77	7.37	1.74	1.72	2.61	− 2.83	−6.54	−6.88	−3.41	−7.66
French franc	.70	.17	.63	.29	1.94	1.85	−1.60	−2.63	−1.25	−2.04	− 5.02	−4.90	−3.36	−2.36	−2.36
Deutsche mark	8.17	4.65	5.86	2.80	2.04	1.62	1.65	.65	−2.14	−1.04	− 2.01	−2.25	− .48	2.12	−2.06
Netherlands guilder	8.15	4.86	3.95	1.07	2.15	.89	.16	.31	− .43	−3.40	− 3.16	−1.29	—	.92	1.21
Swiss franc	4.82	5.06	6.20	11.62	10.47	5.94	4.50	3.75	−1.75	1.11	− 4.13	−1.54	−1.07	.82	2.69
Canadian dollar	2.48	1.63	1.05	1.60	2.52	2.55	1.43	− .08	.36	.32	− .12	− .37	.74	—	—

Source: International Monetary Fund, *International Financial Statistics*, July 1974, page 26.

est income from affiliates was taxable in all countries of concern to Tektronix.

DIVIDEND POLICY FOR FOREIGN SUBSIDIARIES

The European subsidiaries of Tektronix were owned by a Swiss subsidiary which was in turn wholly owned by Tektronix, Inc. Dividends passed through the Swiss subsidiary and were subject to various national dividend withholding taxes depending on the particular bilateral tax treaties. The average withholding tax was 15 percent, but the net cost to Tektronix, Inc. was negligible because these dividend withholding taxes could be used as tax credits against U.S. income taxes on foreign earnings repatriated by Tektronix, Inc. There were no significant dividend restrictions except for the normal limitation of not paying dividends greater than historical retained earnings. Dividend decisions were made by corporate headquarters in Beaverton, Oregon.

FOREIGN EXCHANGE MANAGEMENT

Starting with the currency crisis of August–December 1971, and the official devaluation of the dollar by 8.6 percent in December 1971, the problem of foreign exchange management became more acute. Under the subsequent "managed float" system, exchange rate movements were much more volatile than under the fixed rate system established in 1944 at Bretton Woods. Exhibit 3 shows movements in major currencies since 1971. Exchange rate movements of the British pound sterling and the Dutch guilder were particularly important to Tektronix because of the locations of its manufacturing plants. Between 1971 and June 1974 the pound had declined from $2.4442 to $2.3902 and looked to be heading further downward. On the other hand, the Dutch guilder had appreciated from $.28650 to $.37747 in the same time span.

As a result of floating exchange rates, Tektronix's income was actually increased by $56,644 in 1971; $1,151,315 in 1972; and $606,008 in 1973. However, it was decreased by $1,015,161 in fiscal 1974. Typically a foreign exchange gain or loss was made by foreign subsidiaries changing their local currencies into dollars to pay the Tektronix manufacturing subsidiaries for products the importing subsidiaries had previously purchased. Foreign exchange gains or losses also resulted from translation of the foreign subsidiaries' local currency accounts into dollars in order to present a consolidated worldwide Tektronix financial statement. Tektronix used the

Exhibit 3 *Foreign exchange rates (In cents per unit of foreign currency)*

Period	France (franc)	Germany (Deutsche mark)	Japan (yen)	Netherlands (guilder)	Switzerland (franc)	United Kingdom (pound)
1971	18.148	28.768	.28779	28.650	24.325	244.42
1972	19.825	31.364	.32995	31.153	26.193	250.08
1973	22.536	37.758	.36915	35.977	31.700	245.10
1974–June	20.805	39.603	.35340	37.757	33.449	239.02

Source: Board of Governors of the Federal Reserve System, *Federal Reserve Bulletin,* July 1975, page 75.

monetary-nonmonetary method for translating its subsidiary statements. In particular, the strength of the Dutch guilder resulted in translation gains when the Dutch manufacturing operation was consolidated on the parent's dollar books.

As a result of the fiscal 1974 foreign exchange loss, Les Stevens, Group Vice-President — Finance, initiated a review of Tektronix's international financial policies. He recognized that methods proven to be successful in the 1960s may not be the best approach in the future. This review would include start-up capitalization, working capital financing, long-term debt, dividends, and the currency and inflation problems now impacting those policies. Based on long experience in the international finance function, Les Stevens knew of the poor results most companies and banks, as well as advisory services, had achieved in forecasting the timing and magnitude of currency movements. He was aware of the increased attention Wall Street analysts were giving publicly held international companies and the impact on earnings caused by their currency exposure. This belief caused a strong bias for a policy of neutral currency exposure. This would mean balancing exposed assets and liabilities wherever feasible so that Tektronix would be basically indifferent to shifting currency values. This fit well with overall corporate philosophy, which favored conservative accounting methods and frowned on speculative financial practices. Les Stevens assigned Ken Knox, Assistant Treasurer, to review the financial structure of each subsidiary in light of these policy issues.

TEKTRONIX UK

Ken Knox's first priority was to examine the financing of Tektronix UK because he believed the United Kingdom economy, and its currency, were fundamentally weak. He felt that an analysis and solution of the Tektronix

UK situation would provide him a chance to determine reasonable financial policy guidelines for the other foreign subsidiaries as well.

Tektronix originally entered the United Kingdom market through an independent distributor. However, in accordance with corporate policy of selling direct, Tektronix bought out the distributor's interest in June 1963 and formed Tektronix UK as a 100 percent owned marketing subsidiary. As was its custom, Tektronix provided a minute amount of equity capital but financed the import of inventory on extended terms from its manufacturing plants in the United States and on the Isle of Guernsey. An additional reason for the low equity base was a capital tax which was levied on equity in the United Kingdom. In any case, the small size and lack of outside stockholders in Tektronix UK made its financial structure invisible to the outside world, and no local credit was being requested.

In 1969 one of the United Kingdom's many currency crises caused the Bank of England to impose a 50 percent import deposit requirement for six months on goods bought from outside the United Kingdom. In order to avoid the import deposit it was necessary to manufacture within the United Kingdom. In 1970 a merger was consummated between Tektronix UK and Telequipment Ltd., a previously acquired U.K. manufacturer of oscilloscopes. It was agreed that the surviving name would be Tektronix UK.

As a result of the floating exchange rates after 1971, and the corresponding weakness of the pound, Tektronix UK generated a considerable foreign exchange loss during the next few years, as did the sterling subsidiaries on the Isle of Guernsey. In early 1974 a "minimum distribution" dividend was paid by Tektronix UK to the parent firm in order to establish the foreign exchange losses for tax purposes. A mere translation loss would not result in any tax savings although it appears in statements prepared for financial reporting purposes.

The imposition of the import deposit scheme and the growth in the U.K. manufacturing operations had caused severe strain on Tektronix UK's working capital. The intercompany accounts and loans from Tektronix Guernsey had been used extensively to finance the U.K. operations. Exhibit 4 shows the balance sheets of the European manufacturing subsidiaries of Tektronix as of May 31, 1974. Exhibit 5 shows the income statements for the fiscal year ending May 31, 1974, for the same subsidiaries.

In determining financial policy for Tektronix UK, and ultimately the other foreign subsidiaries, Ken Knox knew that he must justify his recommendation to the Corporate Finance Committee in Tektronix, Inc., the outside directors of the subsidiaries, and perhaps the host country monetary authorities. In so doing he needed logical answers to several problems. One problem was how to coordinate foreign borrowing, if any, with the probable need for Tektronix as a whole to raise external debt of some sort,

Exhibit 4 Balance sheets as of March 31, 1974, for the European manufacturing subsidiaries of Tektronix, Inc. (in thousands)[1]

	TEK United Kingdom		TEK Guernsey		TEK Netherlands	
	pounds sterling	dollars included	pounds sterling	dollars included	guilders	dollars included
Cash and short-term investments	£ 100		£ 100		FL12,500	$4,000
Accts. receivable: non-affiliates	4,000		200	$ 480	8,000	3,016
Accts. receivable: affiliates	100		1,200	2,880	8,000	3,016
Inventory	3,300		3,000		12,500	
Total current assets	£ 7,500		£ 4,500		FL41,000	
Net plant and equipment	1,300		800		6,900	
Long-term notes of affiliates	—		3,800[2]		1,300[3]	
Total assets	£ 8,800		£ 9,100		F 49,200	
Accts. payable: non-affiliates	£ 900		£ 200		FL 800	
Accts. payable: affiliates	1,000	$1,000	300	$ 720	4,800	$1,810
Notes payable	—		—		300	
Other current	700		100		2,400	
Total current liabilities	£ 2,600		£ 600		FL 8,300	
Long-term notes to non-affiliates	—		—		800	
Long-term notes to affiliates	3,200[2]		—		—	
Capital stock	500		1,500		7,000	
Retained earnings	2,500		7,000		33,100	
Total liabilities and net worth	£ 8,800		£ 9,100		F 49,200	

[1] TEK UK and TEK Guernsey are shown in pounds sterling. TEK Netherlands is shown in guilders. Figures in the "dollars included" column show portions of the total balance which are actually denominated in U.S. dollars. For example, TEK UK owes other affiliates the equivalent of £1,000,000. This amount includes $1,000,000 denominated in dollars; the remainder is denominated in sterling. The pound sterling is translated at $2.40 and the guilder at $0.377. Actual numbers are disguised.

[2] TEK UK owes TEK Guernsey £ 3,200,000, mostly for inventory. The debt has an indefinite maturity and no interest charge.

[3] Scandinavian affiliates owe TEK Netherlands 1,300,000 guilders.

Exhibit 5 *Income statements for fiscal year ending May 31, 1974, for the European manufacturing subsidiaries of Tektronix, Inc. (in thousands)**

	TEK UK	TEK Guernsey	TEK Netherlands
	(pound)	(pound)	(guilder)
Sales	£ 15,000	£ 10,000	FL 53,000
less cost of sales	−12,000	−7,000	−40,000
Gross Profit	3,000	3,000	13,000
less operating expenses	− 2,000	− 600	− 5,300
Income Before Profit Share	1,000	2,400	7,700
less profit share	− 300	− 700	− 2,700
Income After Profit Share	700	1,700	5,000
less non-operating expense (income)			
Interest Income	—	(300)	(1,300)
Interest Expense	—	—	—
Foreign Exchange Loss (Gain)	200	100	(2,700)
Other	100	100	5,300
Income Before Taxes	400	1,800	3,700
less income taxes	− 200	− 400	− 1,800
Income After Taxes	200	1,400	1,900

*Not actual numbers.

whether in the U.S. capital market, host country capital markets, or the Eurodollar market. He knew the Board of Directors were considering adding corporate debt in the $20–40 million range.

A second problem was to coordinate any foreign borrowing with the recently adopted program to reduce exposure to foreign exchange rate fluctuations. In this respect local borrowing was only one alternative to reduce exposure. For example, another alternative would be to purchase hedging contracts (see Exhibit 2 for forward exchange rates). Considering the costs of local borrowing or hedging, however, it was unclear to Ken Knox if the benefits of reducing foreign exchange losses alone were worth the costs to accomplish it. Furthermore, any program that was only designed to reduce translation or transaction exposure could have an impact on underlying economic exposure. He was unsure how to measure economic exposure but felt it should not be neglected.

In the event that he recommended some borrowing by Tektronix UK, it would be necessary to specify where the funds would be raised and in what currency. Tektronix UK could borrow dollars internally from Tektronix, Inc., or other currencies from sister subsidiaries, either as a direct loan or through changing the payment terms of accounts receivable and/or payable. It could also borrow pounds or Eurodollars in the U.K. from the London branch of one of the major U.S. banks or from Tektronix's British banks. However, at this time resident sterling was under extreme credit restrictions imposed on both U.S. and British banks by the Bank of England. The Bank of England would have to approve any nonsterling loan to Tektronix UK whether from a Tektronix affiliate or from the Euro-markets.

All U.K. residents, including Tektronix UK and Tektronix Guernsey, could not purchase nonsterling securities with resident sterling. A separate kind of pound sterling held in the so-called investment pool could be used to purchase nonsterling securities, but this "investment sterling" sold at a premium of 10–40 percent above resident sterling, depending on supply and demand conditions, and was currently at a 25 percent premium. For example, Tektronix UK could borrow resident sterling and convert it into dollar-denominated time certificates of deposit by first purchasing investment sterling at a premium. If Tektronix UK then wished to convert back from these dollar CD's to sterling, it would be allowed to sell 75 percent of the dollars for investment sterling, thereby recapturing a premium, but the remaining 25 percent of the dollars would need to be sold for resident sterling without any premium. Thus the cost to Tektronix UK of raising dollars would be increased by the need to use more sterling (investment sterling at a premium) for a given number of dollars than would be needed for a normal trade transaction (resident sterling). Furthermore, 25 percent of this premium paid for investment sterling would be lost on conversion from dollars back to sterling. The remaining 75 percent of the premium might or might not be recaptured on conversion of dollars to sterling, depending on whether the premium had changed in the meantime due to supply and demand conditions in the investment sterling market.

Extensive external borrowing by Tektronix UK might raise some eyebrows in London. Although the firm had been virtually invisible to the British financial community this borrowing might increase its visibility slightly. A very high debt ratio for Tektronix UK would cause its debt ratio to stand apart from British firms in the same industry. On the other hand, Ken Knox was not overly familiar with British finance structure norms and was of the opinion that the British might be indifferent to what finance structure Tektronix UK carried as long as it promptly paid its obligations. This attitude might or might not prevail elsewhere, but just in case country norms were important, he had Exhibit 6 prepared. It shows what typical debt ratios might be in the countries where Tektronix and its manufactur-

Exhibit 6 *Average corporate debt ratios in selected countries and years*[*]

Country	1966	Year 1970	1972
U.K.			
Electronics Industry	47%	33%	27%
All Manufacturing	45	35	35
The Netherlands			
Electronics Industry	45	53	55
All Manufacturing	49	56	59
The U.S.			
Electronics Industry	43	46	48
All Manufacturing	42	46	47
Japan			
Electronics Industry	63	63	61
All Manufacturing	69%	69%	69%

* Total debt as a percent of total assets at book value. Each company is weighted equally.

ing subsidiaries are located. It excludes Guernsey because of its size and the fact that it would probably be using U.K. norms.

Ken Knox would like to have had time to analyze and forecast the future exchange rate prospects for various currencies, but he needed to make a recommendation within two weeks in order to contribute to the overall corporate decision on borrowing externally. For what it was worth, the financial press was full of speculation that the dollar was really undervalued in June 1974, but this did not seem to show up in the spot or forward exchange markets. In any case, his recommendation had to include policy for all foreign subsidiaries, whether or not they normally dealt in dollars.

Gunter Dufey and Ian H. Giddy

Case 12

Metall AG's Eurobond Issue

Dr. jur. Gerhart Wendt ("call me Gary" to his Anglo-Saxon friends who did not take well to German formalities), a member of Metall AG's management board, recently took on responsibility for the group's finances. Previously he had served many years as head of the Legal Department and subsequently the Administration Department, which included Personnel, Accounting, and a number of other staff functions.

A NEED FOR FINANCING

A few weeks ago, in early March, the head of his Financial Planning Group had presented a report that strongly suggested that Metall AG would soon reach what management historically considered to be the upper limits of short-term sources of funds, from banks and the commercial paper (CP) facilities in both the Euromarket and the newly created DM CP market. "Sooner or later, we will need more term funding. And in view of our international expansion plans, this should preferably be dollar debt, although major European currencies and even an ECU issue could be justified under our new exposure guidelines," said Wendt. He explained that the company had some leeway under those guidelines because any deviation from the desired currency composition could be adjusted by changing draw-downs of bank lines and, if absolutely necessary, via the judicious use of currency swaps. Wendt, however, was not fond of "derivatives." He had learned long ago that they consumed bank lines, and caused problems with counter-party risks, which he had always found difficult to explain to his colleagues on the management board.

METALL AG

As one of Germany's premier engineering companies, Metall AG had a long history. It had survived two world wars, the punitive period of dismantling of production facilities after World War II, and a number of recessions since. Carefully nurturing its core competency of engineering skills, it had adapted to changing markets, reinforcing its reputation for designing and building state-of-the-art factory equipment, first in Germany, then in Western Europe, and increasingly in the rest of the world. Its reputation for first-class products gave it a visibility beyond the small circle of engineering experts who were involved with purchasing factory equipment. While its products were always in the upper price range, its core of traveling, well-trained technicians gave it a name for quality installation, operator training, and superb after-sales service. Thus, while not exactly a household word, Metall AG had a worldwide reputation as a German blue chip. Within this spirit, its shareholders had done well, but not spectacularly.

U.S. MARKET VERSUS EUROMARKET

When the possibility of a substantial dollar denominated bond issue came up, Wendt's first thought turned to the U.S. market. The company had made several acquisitions of engineering service companies in the United States and one in Canada, and the board had discussed the possibility of establishing production facilities in the United States, as wages and other costs in Germany went up relentlessly. "Why not a public issue in the U.S. market," he mused. This would be popular with his colleagues in management who found the U.S. market a difficult operating environment and would love to have Metall AG be better known in the U.S. financial community and beyond. Wendt quickly dismissed the idea. He remembered an incident from his days as head of the Legal Department a few years ago. At that time, Metall AG was approached by the Bank of New York which wished to sponsor an ADR issue to increase the distribution of Metall's equity in the United States. Obviously, this would be attractive for the company because it would provide access to the liquid U.S. equity markets, but also it would make it much easier to retain and reward key U.S. management employees through stock option plans, a necessity in the United States to retain key management personnel.

Wendt had felt obliged to kill the plan, against the wishes of his colleagues. He did this after studying a legal brief by Cuthbert and Cuthbert, the firm's U.S. lawyers, that indicated the legal risks of such an action would be considerable since the German company was not willing to provide consolidated financial information that conformed to (U.S.) generally accepted accounting principles.

More recently the issue had flared up again, prompted by an initiative of the New York Stock Exchange. Seeing that its business was being eroded by competition from electronic markets, such as NASDAQ, as well as by foreign exchanges, such as London (that had persuaded many large companies to list their shares on its exchange, the ISE), the NYSE proposed to make it easier for foreign multinationals to be listed. The New York Stock Exchange initiative was supported by the EC Commission which suggested its adopted principle of the "EC passport," that implied home country recognition of regulatory supervision, might also be good enough to govern U.S.-EC listing arrangements. Unfortunately, the SEC wanted to hear nothing of it. Foremost, U.S. firms had no difficulty obtaining a listing on foreign exchanges, so there was no push from a strong constituency; all the European exchanges that mattered accepted U.S. financial disclosure practices. Further, the SEC argued that to admit foreign companies using lower disclosure standards would give foreigners an unfair advantage in competition for the capital of U.S. widows and orphans, since U.S. companies would still be forced to follow the more extensive U.S. disclosure rules.

Last, but not least, the SEC, Chairman Breeden particularly, was concerned that any exception given to foreign firms would be a Trojan horse to introduce "softer" U.S. disclosure standards to the United States. Such standards had always been attacked by U.S. managers as costly and onerous in a global competitive environment.

Yet even the U.S. authorities recognized that sophisticated institutional investors did not require molly-coddling, so in April 1990 the SEC adopted Rule 144A that allowed, for the first time, immediate resale of certain privately placed securities to *qualified* institutional buyers. Under this rule, non-U.S. issuers can offer securities in the U.S. without incurring the costs associated with SEC registration or with the historic illiquidity of private placements, since the SEC also approved the first trading system in the U.S. for privately placed securities through a system called "private offering, resale, and trading through automated linkages" — or for short, PORTAL.

DISCUSSIONS WITH BANKS

Wendt instructed his staff to begin more intensive negotiations with a number of international banks and securities houses to see what was available to the company, both in the 144A market as well as the Eurobond market. If possible, he thought it would be nice to have something positive to report at the company's annual shareholder meeting besides increased costs, depressed margins, and mediocre earnings.

During March, Metall's financial staff signalled its interest in raising approximately US$250 million in long-term bonds to four international houses, and of course its house bank. A long tenor was important as the company preferred a fixed rate as well as covenants that would not restrict management's prerogatives in running the company. The issuing vehicle would probably be Metall Capital B.V., Amsterdam; however, other alternatives would be considered as long as the funds could be freely deployed worldwide, without causing withholding tax problems for either the company or bond investors.

During the first two weeks of March it was concluded that there was likely to be some advantage to the Company in issuing Eurobonds as compared to issuing bonds in the domestic U.S. market. The underwriting firms agreed to monitor market conditions for issues of similar quality to that of the Company and to keep the Company's treasurer informed.

During the second half of March, two of the Eurobond underwriters made specific proposals to the Company, providing indicative quotes based on various maturities and types of issue. These ranged from the simple "plain vanilla" U.S. dollar-denominated Eurobond to dollar/yen dual currency bonds to Australian dollar bonds swapped entirely for U.S. dollars by an affiliate of the lead manager. In the U.S.- dollar sector, the use of a medium-term Euronote issuing facility, as well as the issuance of Eurocommercial paper, were considered as alternatives.

Wendt and his associates came to the conclusion near the end of March that Hercules Bank PLC, a British investment banking subsidiary of a Swiss bank, provided the more imaginative financing alternatives and intensified their discussions with Hercules while remaining receptive to the proposals put forward by Credit Helvetique, a major Swiss investment bank. Both firms had analyzed the latest financial data on the Company in order to be ready for an offering of securities. By the end of March, however, Hercules had gained a psychological advantage.

At 5 P.M. on March 30, Wendt called an Executive Director of Hercules at home in London and asked him to send three proposals by telex the following morning, Eastern Time. The treasurer indicated he would not be interested in the dollar/yen dual currency market or any other financing that would leave an open foreign currency position.

By noon the following day, March 31, the Company's treasurer had received a telex containing three proposals from Hercules, as well as a telephone call from Credit Helvetique urging a dollar/yen dual currency issue.

The treasurer called Hercules for clarification of certain terms of the proposed issues, discussed the proposals briefly with the chief financial officer, and obtained approval for his own recommendation. By late afternoon he called Hercules and entered into an agreement to issue $250 million U.S. dollar-denominated bonds with a maturity of 15 years, retractable every five years, meaning that a new interest rate would be set every five years, with the holder having the option to put the notes to the issuer at that time.

PROPOSALS AND FEES

During the second half of March the underwriters submitted proposals, trying to differentiate themselves in various ways. Apart from a number of innovative features, one American bank suggested that its fixed price re-offer method of distribution would work particularly well in the issuing company's favor. The practice of selling a large proportion to select institutions below the "official" issue price would be detrimental on future trips to the market. Indeed, competition among underwriters to move up in the league tables and the concomitant underpricing of bonds turned out to be so pervasive that some brokers began to show lower prices on a "when issued" basis on the screens in the so-called "grey market."

This practice was much resented by the established underwriters because it made clear that they were willing to give up all or part of their underwriting fees which were set at the standard 2 percent level, consisting of a selling concession of 100-125 basis points, a management fee of roughly 36 basis points, and an underwriting fee of similar magnitude. In addition, there were out-of-pocket expenses for legal work and other administrative services of US$75-100,000, which the issuer was supposed to bear. In contrast, in the United States, underwriting fees were less than one-half of that amount, but the structure of the market was different. Fixed income securities were invariably sold to institutional investors in large lots. By contrast, the Eurobond market used to be primarily a retail dominated market of "Belgian dentists" and other people with investment accounts in offshore centers such as Switzerland, Luxembourg, and London. As institutions began to play a more important role as Eurobond market investors, underwriting and distribution practices developed for a retail market began to change and things became a bit schizophrenic as there were definitely two different classes of investors.

After years of losses in the late 1980s, attempts to reimpose discipline in the market by creating an underwriters' cartel, similar to that existing in the U.S. market, proved to be more difficult since the financial institutions active in London and elsewhere hailed from many countries and new entrants into the market disturbed any incipient oligopolistic structure.

WENDT CALLS A MEETING

On March 17 Wendt called a meeting with his Treasury colleagues. He passed around a fax he had received from one of the underwriters who laid out a detailed schedule about a hypothetical time schedule and documentary requirement for the Eurobond issues (Exhibits 1 and 2). Those at the meeting agreed on the need to elicit information from the underwriters about a number of technical points so that Wendt would be able to answer questions at the next board meeting. What Wendt was particularly interested in was how quickly a 144A deal could be done compared to a Eurobond issue. What he was not sure about was when the cost would be known and when the company would receive the funds. He also needed to know how to insure the pricing risk if there was an "event" in international markets. Of course, he wanted to know what would be cheaper and, primarily in this respect, which factors would influence the total cost. He told his colleagues about an article that he had just read that seemed to show that Eurobond issues were priced more aggressively whenever the dollar was strong. However it was not obvious why dollar strength would affect two market segments differently where paper was denominated in the same currency because of something extraneous such as currency gyrations.

Now, all we need is a good organized answer to these questions, Wendt thought. "Why don't we fax our friends in New York to see what they come up with," he suggested.

Exhibit 1 *The Underwriting Sequence*
Wednesday, April 1
(i) Financing offer formally accepted by telex from the Company to Hercules. Composition of Management group discussed between the Company and Hercules.

(ii)   Hercules extends invitations to proposed members of management group by telephone, confirmed by telex.

(iii)   Management group formed, based on verbal acceptances of invitations.

(iv)   Composition of selling group discussed among management group and the Company. Management group makes final decision. Invitation telexes sent to proposed selling group members.

(v)   Press Release issued in London and New York.

(vi)   Drafting by Hercules staff of selling documents, overnight printing, and facsimile transmission to New York of first proofs of:

(a)   Subscription Agreement

(b)   Selling Group Agreement

(c)   Letter to the Selling Group

(d)   Delivery Instruction Form

Thursday, April 2–Monday, April 6

Meetings at the Company's office and formation of a Working Group representing Hercules and the Company, including attorneys for both parties, to discuss and agree upon the:

(a)   Subscription Agreement

(b)   Selling Group Agreement

(c)   Offering Circular

Tuesday, April 7

(i)   Preliminary Offering Circular submitted to printer in New York and simultaneously printed in New York and London.

(ii)   Selling documents dispatched to selling group members from Hercules in London.

(iii)   Subscription Agreement and Agreement Among Managers sent to Managers by Hercules in London.

Tuesday, April 7–Friday, April 10

Comments on Offering Circular provided to Working Group by Hercules, management of Company, outside auditors and counsel for the Company and Hercules. Redrafting of Offering Circular and reprinting once a day.

Friday, April 10

(i)   Powers of Attorney received by Hercules from the Managers.

(ii)   Final Offering Circular printed.

Monday, April 13

THE SIGNING in London

(i)   Final indications of interest from Managers and Selling Group members notified to Hercules by telex.

(ii)   Selling group Agreement with completed Forms of Acceptance received by Hercules.
(iii) Subscription Agreement signed.
(iv)   Agreement among Managers signed.
(v)   The Company approves final Offering Circular and signs for identification.
(vi)   The Company signs the Listing Agreement with The Stock Exchange, London.
(vii) Hercules sends telexes to Selling Group members, allotting amount of Notes.

Tuesday, April 14–Wednesday, April 22
Working Group drafts documentation required for the Closing, in consultation with management of the Company and Hercules, outside counsel, and auditors.

Tuesday, April 14
Selling Group members are deemed to have accepted allotments unless they advise Hercules to the contrary.

Wednesday, April 22
Payment in U.S. dollars to Hercules in New York by Selling Group members.

Thursday, April 23
The CLOSING 15:00 hours London Time
(i)   Signing and delivery of:
       (a) No adverse change certificate — the Company
       (b) Auditors' Comfort Letter
       (c) Legal Opinions
       (d) Temporary Global Note
       (e) Agency Agreement
       (f) Trust Deed or Fiscal Agency Agreement
(ii)   Temporary Global Note delivered to Morgan Guaranty Trust Company of New York, London Office, as operator of Euro-clear Clearance System.
(iii) Payment of the net proceeds of the issue to a temporary account of the Company, established with a bank in London, and as a post-closing event, transfer of the funds to the Company's account in New York.

June 25
Tombstone advertisement published.

July 25
Definitive notes made available to Euroclear in exchange for the Temporary Global Note then returned to the Company marked cancelled.

Exhibit 2 **Principal Documentation**

SUBSCRIPTION AGREEMENT

An agreement between the Issuer and the Managers, establishing the terms and conditions of the offering of securities, including those presented in the Offering Circular which is incorporated by reference.

Typical agreements on the part of the issuer are:

1. That it has authorized the Managers to offer the securities for sale and that this action has been duly authorized under corporate authority.
2. That it will take the necessary action to have the securities listed (either on the London or Luxembourg stock exchange).
3. To pay the specified underwriting fees from the proceeds of the offering.
4. To make available the Temporary Global Note (or Bond) and the definitive Notes (or Bonds).
5. That the Offering Circular is not misleading in any material respect, and to indemnify the Managers for any losses caused by reliance on the information in the Offering Circular concerning the issuer.

Typical agreements on the part of the Managers are:

1. To sell the securities or buy the securities for their own account and to pay for the securities at the issue price. Typically, this is a joint and several obligation.
2. To indemnify the issuer in the event of any claims arising from the conduct of the underwriting and selling activity.
3. To comply with all applicable laws, particularly securities laws. While this seems obvious, it is very important in the case of Eurobonds, in order to ensure that the issue does not become subject to the issuer's domestic securities laws.

This agreement will also specify governing law. U.S. issuers sometimes choose English law and sometimes New York law. Other choices are also possible. The form of some of the documentation will depend on the choice of governing law. There is now a tendency to use English law and the trustee format. There was previously a tendency to use Fiscal Agency format under English law, and in the early days of the Eurobond market there was a preference for New York law which made the agreements seem more familiar to U.S. issuers.

Agency Agreement

The Agency Agreement is entered into between the issuer and the Paying Agent(s). Normally, the Lead Manager becomes Principal Paying Agent and its affiliates or other firms with which it has close relationships in other European cities and in New York are appointed Paying Agents.

For a fee, the Paying Agents effect payment of interest and principal when due, provided payment has been received from the issuer. In addition, the Paying Agents and the Principal Paying Agent have record keeping duties with respect to payment of interest and principal, cancellation and/or destruction of paid notes and coupons.

If the securities are convertible, callable or puttable, or if there are warrants or options involved, the Paying Agents are also appointed Conversion Agents or other appropriate Agents to enable the issuer and the holders to exercise their rights.

For Eurosecurities which may be issued in either the traditional bearer form or in registered form for U.S. holders, the Paying Agent in New York is also appointed Registrar, to enable conversion of bearer notes into registered notes and to maintain records of registered notes.

Trust Deed

The trust deed is entered into between the issuer and a trustee. The trustee is a firm qualified under English law (or other governing law) to act as trustee and receives remuneration for its services from the issuer, normally as a flat annual fee unless asked to perform extraordinary functions.

Fiscal Agency Agreement

A Fiscal Agency Agreement might be used instead of a Trust Deed, in which case there would normally be a Fiscal and Paying Agency Agreement replacing both the Trust Deed and the Agency Agreement. Under this structure, the Lead Manager would normally be appointed Principal Fiscal and Paying Agent.

In the case of fiscal agency rather than trust, there is no specific representative for the holders of the securities. The Fiscal Agent is an agent of the issuer, with prescribed duties. While this may place the holders at some disadvantage if problems arise, it also means that there is no holder representative with whom the issuer could negotiate in case of a problem. For this reason, the trust arrangement has gained ground after years during which the fiscal agency form predominated.

The case for the fiscal agency structure is that it reduces the number of parties involved in the issuance and administration of the securities issue.

Agreement Among Managers (Underwriters)

This agreement specifies the amount of securities underwritten by each Manager and defines the relationship among the Managers. Normally, there is a joint and several commitment, under which all other managers would be required to take up the commitment of a defaulting manager.

The Agreement Among Managers also defines the rights and responsibilities of the Lead Manager, such as the allotment of securities to Selling Group Members, accounting and record keeping for the issue, receipts and payments of cash, etc.

Selling Group Agreement

The Selling Group Agreement is a simple agreement between each Selling Agent and the Managers, setting forth the terms on which the selling agents may sell the securities, including their remuneration and their undertaking not to sell the securities in the United States, to U.K. persons other than dealers, or (in the traditional issues before 1984) to a Netherlands Antilles person.

Exhibit 3 *Other Major Documents*

OFFERING CIRCULAR

The Offering Circular (or Offering Memorandum) is the type of prospectus used in the Eurodollar bond market. It is a description of the securities and of the issuer. The offering document is not prescribed by law, since the Eurobond market is not regulated. However, the stock exchanges (London and Luxembourg) have certain requirements.

In the case of The Stock Exchange (London), the most important document is the Extel card, provided to The Stock Exchange via Extel Statistical Services, which incorporates most of the Offering Circular and which must be approved by The Stock Exchange.

In the case of Luxembourg, requirements are more informal, but the familiar format of offering circular is used. Since the offering circular is the selling document which is made available to all potential investors, it is considered very important regardless of legal requirements and is carefully drafted. Some major U.S. corporations also follow the theory that the offering document should meet SEC criteria for full disclosure.

Temporary Global Note

The requirement for a Temporary Global Note arose from the U.S. legal requirement that in order for securities to qualify for exemption from SEC registration, the securities must be issued under arrangements reasonably designed to prevent their sale to U.S. persons except for certain qualified sophisticated investors.

This requirement gave rise to the theory of a 90-day lock-up period during which ownership of the securities is evidenced by notation on the schedule attached to the temporary global note. Notifications of sale by the selling group members must be accompanied by certifications that the purchasers have declared that they are not U.S. persons. Once the 90 days have elapsed and the securities have been fully sold, the temporary global note is exchanged for definitive notes in bearer form (or in registered form for any non-exempt U.S. purchasers). This procedure is also relied upon to prevent distribution of Euroyen bonds in Japan.

Ian H. Giddy

Case 13

Arabian Nights

A U.S. manufacturer of medical diagnostic equipment was thinking of setting up a subsidiary in Saudi Arabia. The market looked good. But how should it be financed? What currency should be used to finance the venture, and what would be the appropriate capital structure for the subsidiary?

Foreign investors generally seek to finance a substantial proportion of foreign operations in the local market, in order to hedge currency and other risks. In Saudi Arabia, many investors used foreign finance (U.S. dollars) instead, because the Saudi riyal was fixed against the U.S. dollar and there were no exchange controls limiting funds going into or out of the country.

From the company's point of view, the special considerations for funding in Saudi Arabia include (a) the availablity of subsidized financing from the Saudi Industrial Development Fund (SIDF) (b) that to take advantage of tax and other benefits the investments should be joint ventures with a majority Saudi ownership, and thus must forego the full parent company backing that many investments in other countries enjoy, (c) the special nature of debt servicing in a country where the legal system is founded in Islamic law (i.e. the ordinary payment of interest may be contrary to the Koran), and (d) that Saudi Arabia, like many countries at a similar stage of development, possesses a bank-dominated financial system with only a very limited market for direct financing (equity and bonds) by companies. There are no insurance companies or pension funds, apart from the government social insurance agency.

The company's financing goals could be divided into three parts:

- A major consideration is how the investment will be *financed initially*.
- To conduct ongoing business, the firm will want *short term working capital* financing. The local money market should be capable of providing short-term bank loans, supplemented perhaps by other money market instruments such as bills of exchange, discounted receivables and commercial paper.
- The availability of supplementary sources of medium term funds is important for companies engaging in *subsequent expansion* of existing investments.

A typical initial financing mix for foreign companies in Saudi Arabia was:

SIDF	up to 50 percent
Medium term bank loans	25 percent
Saudi equity	12.5 percent
Foreign equity	12.5 percent

The U.S. company was willing to go along with this structure. Looking at each of the four potential sources in turn, however, it found that each had its disadvantages as well as its advantages:

- The **Saudi Industrial Development Fund (SIDF)** supposedly contributes up to half of the total initial financing of an industrial investment, at no explicit interest rate apart from up-front costs and an annual servicing fee of 1–2 percent. Because it is constrained to lend at below-market rates, those fees in no way reflect the riskiness of the project. Since SIDF cannot be compensated for taking risk, it must avoid it. This means it must undertake an abnormally stringent and time consuming evaluation and screening process before committing funds. Smaller, riskier ventures, especially if they are not backed by a prominent foreign partner, stand a good chance of being turned down. In addition the SIDF insists on taking a mortgage on the borrower's Saudi property and normally expects the parent company to guarantee its share of the firm's debt.

- Given the absence of long-term institutional investors, the gap between total financing needs and that satisfied by subsidized finance must be filled by medium- or long-term lending by the **commercial banks.** There was no shortage of bank funds in Saudi Arabia — indeed most of the banks' deposits were invested abroad in the international interbank market. Yet the banks are constrained by a lack of medium-term lending experience and the subordinated status that their loans must take relative to SIDF loans, considering that the latter typically appropriate the borrower's best assets as collateral.

- **Domestic equity investors** are expected to put up 50 percent or more of the equity capital in order to qualify for incentives and government contract eligibility. Yet local investors in a new venture in Saudi Arabia recognize that they may not have effective control, and where the poor state of development of the market for equity, as well as the difficulty of taking such companies public, mean that they have no assurance of liquidity for their stock. The supply of equity investment that is long term, i.e. unconcerned with liquidity, is limited by the absence of institutional investors such as pension funds and insurance companies.

- Finally, from the U.S. company's point of view, it would be willing to put up equity capital in a venture where the potential return may be high. But this was a part of the world known for conflict. And how much should one invest in a venture in which one cannot have a majority of the equity (without sacrificing many advantages important to the profitability of the venture)?

Foreign Exchange Risk Analysis and Management

Gunter Dufey and W.S. Carlisle, Jr.

Case 14

AC Tractors
Part A

The 1980s had not been kind to the people who were in the agricultural tractor business in North America. The problems started with the excess capacity build-up during the previous decade. Recession, changes in Federal support programs, and bad weather, including a series of droughts led to depressed markets for agricultural implements and tractors. A number of manufacturers were forced to scale down operations and some had to consolidate. Allied Chambers was the result of one of these mergers that originated from two formerly independent manufacturers, namely, Allied and Chambers. When the industry went through a crunch, the two companies consolidated their operations by combining dealer networks and

Copyright © 1991 by Gunter Dufey and W.S. Carlisle, Jr., for class discussion only. It is not intended to illustrate either effective or ineffective managerial practices. Pheng-Lui Chng assisted the authors. Support from the Business Fund for Canadian Studies in the United States is gratefully acknowledged.

keeping only their most efficient plants. Furthermore, they abandoned making their own engines and tied up with a German company, MAN, that built a high-quality air-cooled, medium sized diesel engine. This engine was very popular in Europe and promised to be popular with U.S. farmers because of its low maintenance cost. As a matter of fact, 60 percent of a diesel engine's maintenance costs are associated with its water cooling system.

The joint venture, AC-MAN, was not very successful either. During the first half of the 1980s, the farm industry in the United States had been over-leveraged and it took several years and substantial federal subsidies to pull agriculture out of its doldrums. AC-MAN failed and in late 1989 the joint venture partners decided to call it quits. It was sold in a leveraged buyout (LBO) to a new team of managers who hailed from various parts of the industry to form AC Tractors (AC). The deal was put together by a leverage buyout firm based in Dallas, Rainwater and Associates, who found the management team who in turn contributed a considerable part of the (small) equity capital out of their own funds. While management and the LBO firm had put up the equity, the vast proportion of the assets was financed with borrowed money, the source of which was ingeniously raised from one of the large captive finance companies, General Electric Credit Corporation (GECC). GECC in turn received a lien on all the assets, which consisted of 90 percent of dealer receivables to finance equipment on dealers' lots. The rest was spare parts. There was also an old manufacturing operation, but the book value of that plant was close to zero; its economic value not much more. The new management team decided to minimize manufacturing operations by necessity (there was no money) and because of the excess capacity in the industry. The company relied on engines imported from Germany which were installed in the tractors and combines. These, in turn, were assembled from parts purchased from a variety of outside venders, including competitors, who were only too happy to keep their plants working at higher capacity rates. The new management team knew something about selling tractors; most of them had come from senior positions with various competitors in the industry.

For a variety of reasons, the new company was very strongly represented in Canada; almost 50 percent of sales went to that market. Over time the U.S. and Canadian markets for tractors and farm equipment do not follow the same drummer. While weather related factors are similar, the crops in Canada are mainly wheat and corn, the major market segment for AC's equipment; agriculture in the United States has a much greater variety of products. More important than the weather and the crops were differences between the two government's support programs. While Canada frequently focused on overseas markets, the United States, for political and other reasons, did not like to sell there. Thus, the 50 percent sales distribution between the United States and Canada was not a stable magnitude.

The dominant competitors in the markets were John Deere and Case IH, the latter a combination of the old operations of J.I. Case and International Harvester. Together, those two companies had in excess of 75 percent of the tractor and farm implement market and were clearly market leaders. Thus, their smaller competitors, of which there were about a dozen, had to look for specific market segments. AC Tractors focused on the market for medium sized machines with air-cooled engines, large tractors, and combines. The German air-cooled engines were an important competitive factor, because they allowed the company to offer farmers a product that was significantly different. The engine was advertised as the "Mercedes" of farm tractor and combine engines. North American competitors were not able to supply air-cooled engines for these applications.

The LBO left the company with very limited operating cash. In turn, the distribution of tractors and combines in this industry required credit. With the economic life of an agricultural tractor in excess of 10 years, farmers demanded and received from competitors credit terms of approximately five years. Dealers were undercapitalized and expected to receive financing from the manufacturer as long as the equipment was on their lots, which averaged one to two years. Volume was driven by farmers' cashflows after the harvest: 50 percent of sales were in the second part of the year; half again were in the fourth quarter, and half of those sales occurred in December. Thus, it was not surprising that dealers' inventories were high with equipment usually on the lots at least a year. And if the dealer missed the selling season, financing was required for another year. The business actually was quite risky for the manufacturers because sales to the dealers were not final. When the dealer was unable to sell a tractor, he came back to the manufacturer and required — and under the competitive conditions usually received — a discount on the price in order to finally move the equipment.

Since this dealer financing business was quite risky, the cost of the floor plans ran at 2–6 percent over the prime rate, on a floating basis. In contrast, installment sales to farmers were often done on the basis of fixed interest, calculated on the prime rate that prevailed when the contracts were signed, plus a spread of 4–5 percent. The installment sales were amortized, at the farmer's choice, monthly, quarterly, or semi-annually; but the bulk was amortized annually to match the farmers' cashflows.

Obviously this business was not only risky but also ate up funds. Thus, selling receivables was the going practice in the industry. The large competitors, essentially Deere and Case, had their own captive finance companies. The remainder of the competitors sold their receivables to other finance companies. Some of those were the large captive ones, such as GECC, GMAC, or Whirlpool; some were leasing companies affiliated with large financial institutions; and some were independent finance companies. Uniformly, the receivables were interest bearing, both those to dealers and those to individual farmers. The manufacturer sold the receivables, both dealer paper as well as receivables from farmers, at a discount to the finance companies, whereby the size of the discount essentially equated a 3 percent "holdback." The holdback served as a reserve to compensate the finance company for default risk, warranty costs, and legal and administrative costs in collecting payments. If payments were delinquent, i.e., late or defaulted, arrangements varied, but losses were frequently split between the finance company and the manufacturer.

One interesting feature linked to AC Tractors' financing activities pertained to the sale of the Canadian dollar receivables to GECC. The finance company bought the paper at the U.S.$-CAN$ spot rate. When the Canadian dollar cashflows were received from dealers and farmers, they were in turn sold at the spot market for U.S. currency and the difference between the two spot rates became an obligation of the manufacturer. Thus, the manufacturer took the U.S.$-CAN$ exchange risk fair and square. The way this worked in practice was that the finance company ran a clearing account and if the spot rate for the Canadian dollar had fallen below the original spot rate, the clearing account accumulated a loss which AC Tractors had to make up. If, on the other hand, the Canadian dollar strengthened, the clearing account accumulated a surplus which was rolled forward to be available for future losses.

While these arrangements looked extremely profitable for the finance company, it was exposed to substantial risks. If the equity position of AC Tractors or one of its competitors were to be wiped out, which in that industry was easily possible, the finance company would be stuck with equipment outstanding, which may have little economic value. Thus, there were almost equity-type risks in this kind of paper and this method of financing. (It was not clear whether the shareholders of the finance company, or even senior management, recognized the full dimensions of the risks they were assuming.)

Total annual sales of new equipment (measured at the point in time when the equipment is placed with the dealers), amounted to approximately $200 million. Given the financing practices in the industry, these sales had to be supported with at least $300–$400 million in terms of receivables to make it work.

In addition, the company had approximately another $100 million of spare parts business. This was the truly profitable part of the whole operation. Indeed, many manufacturers in this business hope, with some luck, to break even on new equipment. All the profit, if there is any, is made through spare parts. While the margins are very high, many of the spare parts stay in inventory for lengthy periods of time, in some cases for years, during which time the purchase costs had to be financed.

Default rates of end users of the new equipment hovered around 5 percent in normal years; however, when agriculture was under stress — either by the weather, change in government programs, or some other calamity — that number increased to 10–15 percent. Dealer defaults manifested themselves in terms of repossessions of new equipment, but then, if it occurred at a bad time, the company had to slash prices substantially on that new equipment in order to move it. A further problem in implementing a cashflow and funding policy was that farmers tended to prepay their equipment when the farm economy did well. A five year annual pay note was paid off in two or three years if that occurred. This made the hedging of interest rate risks and the assurance of funding availability very important in developing sound financial policies.

In addition to the agricultural cycle, prepayment rates were, of course, also influenced by interest rates. As a matter of fact, interest rates interacted in very peculiar ways with agricultural cycles. When interest rates fell and the farmers had lots of cash, they prepaid in spades. When the agricultural economy went bad, no matter what interest rates did, farmers kept their notes outstanding to the very end, indeed, sometimes stretching time periods involuntarily.

Questions:

1. What should AC Tractors do?
2. How could AC Tractors establish a foreign exchange hedging system to take care of its Canadian dollar problems that would be a durable solution?
3. What other financial problems do you see?

TABLE 1(a) Farm Income and Expenses—United States (1979–88)
($ billions)

	Gross Income	Expenses	Net Income
1979	150.7	123.3	27.4
1980	149.3	133.1	16.1
1981	166.3	139.4	26.9
1982	163.5	140.0	23.5
1983	153.1	140.4	12.7
1984	174.9	142.7	32.2
1985	166.4	134.0	32.4
1986	160.4	122.4	38.0
1987	171.6	124.5	47.1
1988	177.6	132.0	45.7

Source: U.S. Bureau of the Census Statistical Abstract of the U.S. (1990 edition)

TABLE 1(b) Canada — Net Income of Farm Operators from Farming Operations, 1983–87 (C$ million)

	Realized Gross	Total Net Income
1983	18,976.7	2,700.2
1984	20,596.9	3,382.5
1985	20,173.3	4,332.6
1986	20,739.9	5,558.4
1987	21,128.3	5,425.4

Source: *Canada Year Book* — 1990, Minister of Supply and Services, Ottawa: Statistics Canada, Nov. 1989, p. 9.24.

TABLE 2(a) United States — Average Wheat Price ($/per ton)

1984	124.55
1985	113.16
1986	88.91
1987	94.42
1988	135.94

Source: *Statistical Abstract of the U.S.,* U.S. Bureau of the Census, 1990, p. 660.

TABLE 2(b) Canada — Average Wheat Prices (C$/per ton)

1982–83	204.64
1983–84	215.21
1984–85	235.33
1985–86	249.12
1986–87	180.72

Source: *Canada Year Book — 1990,* Minister of Supply and Services, Ottawa: Statistics Canada, Nov. 1989, p. 9.37.

Exhibit 1 *Key Exchange Rate. Canadian Dollar/U.S. Dollar*

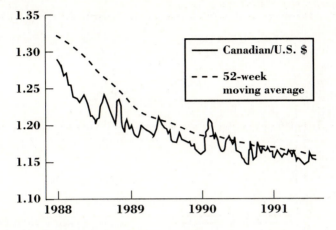

Source: *Currency & Bond Market Trends,* International Fixed Income Research, Merrill Lynch, August 29, 1991.

Exhibit 2(a) *Call Money Rates (Weekly Series)*

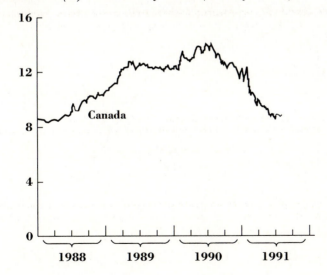

Source: Division of International Finance, Board of Governors of the Federal Reserve System. "Selected Interest and Exchange Rates: Weekly Series of Charts," August 19, 1991.

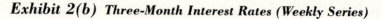

Exhibit 2(b) **Three-Month Interest Rates (Weekly Series)**

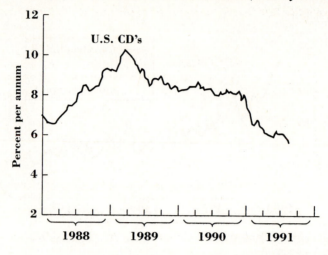

Source: Division of International Finance, Board of Governors of the Federal Reserve
System. "Selected Interest and Exchange Rates: Weekly Series of Charts," August 19, 1991.

Exhibit 2(c) **Three-Month Interest Rates (Weekly Series)**

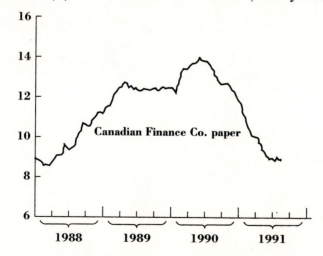

Source: Division of International Finance, Board of Governors of the Federal Reserve
System. "Selected Interest and Exchange Rates: Weekly Series of Charts," August 19, 1991.

Exhibit 2(d) **Three-Month Forward Exchange Rates.**
Premium (+) or (−). (Averages for week ending Wednesday)

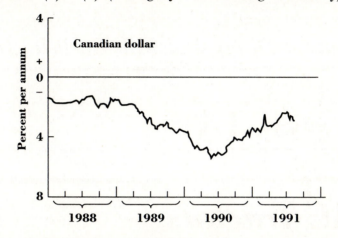

Source: Division of International Finance, Board of Governors of the Federal Reserve System. "Selected Interest and Exchange Rates: Weekly Series of Charts," August 19, 1991.

Gunter Dufey and W.S. Carlisle, Jr.

Case 14

AC Tractors
Part B

A short time after taking control in the beginning of 1990, the management of AC Tractors discovered they had purchased a major problem. While the company had bought the assets from MAN and Allied Chambers very cheaply, it did not obtain any commitments on the price of either original equipment or the engines. Those engines were priced in Deutsche marks, and during 1989 the Deutsche mark was on a constant up-tide vis-a-vis the U.S. dollar (see Exhibit 1). This, of course, raised the dollar cost of the equipment in the United States. In addition, MAN increased the DM price of the engines by 25 percent, having no real stake in AC Tractors and the U.S. market anymore.

Copyright © 1991 by Gunter Dufey and W.S. Carlisle, Jr., for class discussion only. It is not intended to illustrate either effective or ineffective managerial practices. Pheng-Lui Chng assisted the authors. Support from the Business Fund for Canadian Studies in the United States is gratefully acknowledged.

Unfortunately, the company had very little leeway in terms of obtaining price increases in the North American market. While the farm economy was not bad and farmers, after a few good years in both the United States and Canada, had money again, somehow Deere and Case IH, the dominant competitors in the agricultural equipment market, kept prices for medium size tractors stable **in dollar terms** (although they too sourced the equipment for this segment of the market out of their German subsidiaries). Industry observers speculated that these companies were "operationally hedged," since they sourced many components for their European and German operations, including a lot of their spare parts, out of the United States. In addition, some of the agricultural specialty implements were brought in from the United States. (Note, the European markets and the U.S. markets require quite different farm equipment since European farming is small scale for the most part, while North America is large scale and requires not only larger equipment but a wider range of equipment.)

Therefore, management desperately looked for a different supplier who was competitive not only in terms of prices but also in product features. After a considerable search, AC Tractors management thought they had found an alternative. One of the Italian manufacturers, Ital Tractor S.p.A., was most eager to expand in the North American market. They offered a full line of medium sized tractors at prices considerably below the Germans (the cost was similar to what MAN used to charge) and they were willing to allow AC Tractors to put its brand name on the equipment. In other words, they were willing to pursue private label manufacturing for North America.

The negotiations with Ital Tractor focused primarily on volume. The Italians, interested in keeping their plants running at full capacity, insisted on firm commitments. They agreed to a rough estimate of annual sales, but then insisted on four months of firm orders prior to shipment of the tractors. The equipment was to be shipped monthly. Table 1 shows the intended shipment volume. The total estimated annual "bring-in" amounted to roughly $25 million, comprising roughly 2,500 units. The economic shipping quantity was about 300 tractors.

There was considerable confusion during negotiations about invoicing and pricing. The original proposal by the Italians was to invoice the U.S. company at the agreed price in dollars, but they wanted to maintain the right to adjust the dollar price whenever the lira moved up against the dollar by more than 5 percent on orders. The adjustment presumably was then to reflect fully the new lira-dollar relationship. This, of course, would put the exchange risk squarely on the U.S. company and it was felt, especially by the senior financial officer of AC Tractors, that this was not acceptable because it would jeopardize the company's survival.

He persuaded his colleagues to present a counter-proposal to the Italians. He argued he would rather accept straight lira invoicing, get a better price, and manage the exchange risk out of the United States corporate office. This, of course, raised the question of how *lira prices* were to be established. The Italians left that point deliberately vague. The U.S. negotiators insisted on a more rational approach to this issue. One possibility that was to be included in the proposal for the negotiations was to start with the "general" wholesale list price of the Italian manufacturer, which it used to offer its products to its own dealers in Italy and/or in Western Europe in general, and take a discount to reflect AC Tractors' large volume purchases.

There was also some discussion on limiting the price increases in terms of Italian lira by the increase in the wholesale price index in the United States. If, for example, wholesale prices in Italy went up by 10 percent and in the United States by 4 percent, the Italians could raise lira prices only 4 percent. This feature, of course, was designed to deal with the problem of "deviations from Purchasing Power Parity" — whether this intent would be realized was another question. And whether Ital Tractor was willing to accept this clause was a different matter altogether. In any case, financial management argued, "we can take care of the exchange risk but we cannot take care of purchasing power risks."

In establishing a hedging program, the financial staff quickly ran into a few nasty problems. First, the shipping date was not relevant for the price commitment; volumes and lira prices had to be set four months prior to shipping date. In addition, it was not known how long the company would be exposed to the economic risk of the tractors which lasted at least until dealers had made final sales if not longer.

The arrangement provided for payment for the tractors under a letter of credit (L/C) arrangement. Accordingly, the L/C had to be opened on order date and be negotiated (drawn) on shipping date. Since the company had pledged all its assets to GECC as part of the receivables financing (indeed financing of the whole company!) the banks were willing to open L/Cs on behalf of the company favoring the Italian manufacturer **only** if the company "prefunded" the L/C through a deposit. Fortunately, the company was currently in a (modest) cash position. The shipment of the tractors took at least 30 days before they could be placed with the dealers and the dealer paper could then be factored with GECC.

Even if the company could find a way to hedge the four month period, which was relatively straightforward, it was still left with the economic exchange risk: whenever the lira appreciated, the company's dollar price (hedged for four months) went up and given that European currencies did not influence tractor prices in North America, AC Tractors saw its margins evaporate. In waiting to manage that risk they ran into a number of problems. First of all, the commitment of the company, and therefore its risk, did not stop until the final sales of dealers. Thus, the potential margin squeeze, or economic exchange risk, had no precise time horizon. It lasted until (a) either the lira reversed itself and depreciated so the company's (dollar) margins were reestablished, or (b) if the lira stayed up, the only way the company could react to its predicament was to find another supplier. There were indeed some candidates, such as a Finnish company in Brazil which was eager, for a price, to sell their products in the United States. However, this switching of suppliers was not easy and in any case would take at least two years to fully implement.

Given the uncertainties of time and volume, the financial staff at AC Tractors started to consider using options. These instruments also had, in the eyes of the senior financial officer, the advantage of minimizing accounting problems: option premia would be expensed over the life of the contract; forwards and futures, however, would affect the P & L adversely without the company having offsetting income to show in the same period.

Question:
How would you establish a hedging system for AC Tractors whose equipment is sourced out of Italy and sold in the North American market?

TABLE 1 Scenario 1: LOC Repayment Cash Flow Projections—Same(S+L+H) Tractor Imports

($ in 000s US)	1991 Jan	Feb	Mar	Apr	May	Jun	Jul	Aug	Sep	Oct	Nov	Dec	Total
Amount Ordered	0	11,888	6,022	0	5,456	3,845	1,805	0	2,732	3,296	3,485	3,118	41,646
Open Orders	0	11,888	17,910	17,910	19,029	15,323	11,106	11,106	8,382	7,832	9,513	12,630	12,630
Future Plan Orders	41,646	29,758	23,737	23,737	18,280	14,435	12,630	12,630	9,899	6,603	3,118	0	0
Begin D-A Inventory	0	0	0	0	0	4,337	11,888	14,134	10,374	12,086	12,202	10,293	0
P.O. Shipment/Recpt	0	0	0	0	4,337	7,551	6,022	0	5,456	3,845	1,805	10,293	29,016
Billed Inventory	0	0	0	0	0	0	(3,776)	(3,760)	(3,745)	(3,729)	(3,714)	(3,699)	(22,422)
End D-A Inventory	0	0	0	0	4,337	11,888	14,134	10,374	12,086	12,202	10,293	6,594	6,594
Payments	0	0	0	0	(4,337)	(7,551)	(6,022)	0	(5,456)	(3,845)	(1,805)	0	(29,016)
Payable Balance	0	0	0	0	0	0	0	0	0	0	0	0	0
Plan Purch–Lira (000)	0	0	0	0	4,985,982	8,716,576	6,980,277	0	6,377,367	4,512,539	2,126,988	0	33,699,728
Plan Purch–$US	0	0	0	0	4,298	7,514	6,017	0	5,498	3,890	1,834	0	29,051
Purch–$US Forward	0	0	0	0	4,337	7,551	6,022	0	5,456	3,845	1,805	0	29,016
Variance	0	0	0	0	(39)	(36)	(4)	0	41	45	29	0	36
Planning Rate		1160.0	1160.0	1160.0	1160.0	1160.0	1160.0	1160.0	1160.0	1160.0	1160.0	1160.0	
Forward Rate Lira/$US		1135.0	1139.8	1144.6	1149.6	1154.4	1159.2	1164.0	1168.8	1173.6	1178.4	1183.2	
Future: 1992													
Plan Purch–Lira (000)			6,670,000			6,670,000			6,670,000			6,670,000	26,680,000
Plan Purch–$US			5,750			5,750			5,750			5,750	23,000
Purch–$US Forward			5,615			5,509			5,447			5,386	21,957
Variance			135			241			303			364	1,043
Planning Rate			1,160.0			1,160.0			1,160.0			1,160.0	
Forward Rate Lira/$US			1,187.8			1,210.8			1,224.6			1,238.4	

**TABLE 2 United States—Producer Price Index (1985 = 100)
and Consumer Price Index (1985 = 100)**

		Producer Prices	Consumer Prices
1988	Q-I	143.2	107.9
	Q-II	146.9	109.2
	Q-III	147.8	110.7
	Q-IV	152.4	111.8
1989	Q-I	161.6	113.1
	Q-II	173.2	114.9
	Q-III	188.2	115.9
	Q-IV	189.8	117.0
1990	Q-I	186.6	119.0
	Q-II	196.2	120.2
	Q-III	190.8	122.3
	Q-IV	178.9	124.3
1991	Jan.	184.2	125.1
	Feb.	205.9	125.3
	Mar.	212.7	125.5
	Apr.	216.6	125.7
	May	216.6	126.0

Source: *International Financial Statistics*, various issues, prepared by the Statistics Department of the International Monetary Fund.

Exhibit 1 *Key Exchange Rate. Deutsche mark/U.S. dollar*

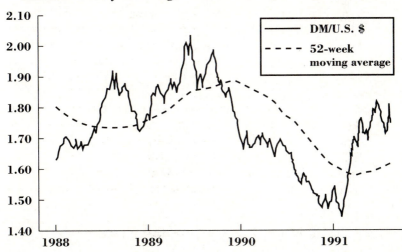

Source: *Currency & Bond Market Trends*, International Fixed Income Research, Merrill Lynch, August 29, 1991.

Exhibit 2 *Lira Exchange Rates and Relative Prices*

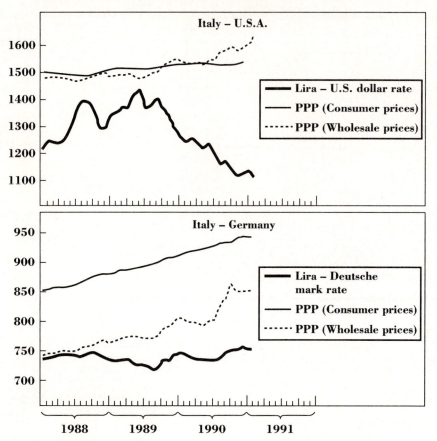

Source: *The Italian Economy,* Economic Research Department, Banca Commerciale Italiana. N. 138 – June 1991, p. 22.

Exhibit 3 **Prices and Wages — Italy**

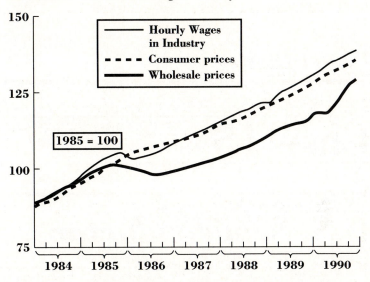

Source: *The Economist Intelligence Unit Country Report* (Italy), No. 2, 1991

Gunter Dufey

Case 15

U.S. Semiconductor

In early 1980, U.S. Semiconductor, a large specialized semiconductor manufacturer headquartered in Santa Clara, California, decided to make a strategic move into the United Kingdom market. Until this time the company had a small sales office in London that serviced clients in that country. The product, semiconductors, were shipped by air freight from warehouses in Silicon Valley to London's Heathrow Airport, and distributed to various customers.

Due to increased competition from other American firms, the company decided to establish a distribution center and technical support facility in the U.K. A location was found approximately 50 miles west of Heathrow Airport near the small town of Swindon. A business plan was established that provided for the construction of a special, climate-controlled warehouse to protect the chips, the acquisition of a number of small yellow trucks to move them around, and some storage and inventory control equipment.

The legal/tax department advised that all these assets should be "housed" under a corporate umbrella called U.S. Semiconductor Ltd, a wholly-owned subsidiary of the parent company incorporated in Delaware. By the same token, the entity should be capitalized with minimal equity investment. The remainder of the assets, including the high-value inventories, should be funded with debt.

It was at this point that U.S. Semiconductor's Finance Department got involved. This group had responsibility not only for the funding operations at home and abroad but was also in charge of risk management, particularly exchange risk management. Assistant Treasurer Marcel Godfrey began to work with a number of commercial banks headquartered both in the United States and in the United Kingdom with whom U.S. Semiconductor had previously established relationships. He solicited them for financing proposals. The company decided to go for "plain vanilla" debt financing rather than a legally complex leasing arrangement.

When everything was said and done and analysts at U.S. Semiconductor had sorted out the numbers, it came down to two financing alternatives; both incorporated the usual, standard documentation with a strong comfort letter from the parent. When all front- and side- and back-end fees were included, the choice was between two five-year fixed rate term facilities in either U.S. dollars at 8 percent per annum or pound sterling at 12 percent per annum. The spot rate for STG was quoted at approximately USD 2.40; long dated forward cover for five years was available at roughly USD 1.97.

This was where the difficulties began. Local management supported by the Group Vice President for European Operations insisted on pound sterling funding because they did not want to have any exchange risk. They argued that there was no other choice anyway, because Chief Executive Officer Andrew Godfornough, an immigrant Soviet physicist, had long ago laid down the policy that financial risks should be minimized in view of the big gambles that the company took since its business was extremely cyclical and characterized by dynamic changes in technology. Thus, the guiding principle was "hedge everything."

Some staffers at headquarters, however, argued differently on the same principle: since the semiconductor business worldwide was a "dollar driven" business, it would be prudent to use dollar denominated debt. In addition, they argued, it was obviously cheaper!

The Director of Foreign Exchange, who had recently been hired away from the foreign exchange trading operations of a major U.S. West Coast bank, insisted that the company should borrow in sterling since that currency would be weak as oil prices would drop over the coming years. "This is a chance for Treasury finally to make some money and become a profit center rather than a constant drain on the company resources by paying out interest and fees to the bankers," he wrote in a memo to Marcel Godfrey.

Others on the finance staff argued that a compromise was appropriate: the subsidiary should simply fund its debt half in dollars and half in sterling since nobody could really tell which way exchange rates would go. However, all shipments from the warehouse in Santa Clara to the facility in Swindon should be hedged by selling U.S. dollars forward against pounds by way of three-month contracts.

At this point, the controller's group put its advice in a special memorandum. They argued that maybe they could persuade the outside accountants to treat all these assets of U.S. Semiconductor Ltd. as *de facto* dollar assets on the basis that the dollar would be the "functional" currency of that business in the United Kingdom. The new accounting standard 52 provided for just such a contingency.

By now, the new V.P. of Finance decided that what was needed was a weekend meeting at a small hotel in Monterey to bring all the issues to the table and reach an agreement that could be sold to the Board's Finance Committee at the next meeting. He invited some of the company's bankers and a consultant to advise the company on its international funding and risk management strategy.

Gunter Dufey and Thomas Hofstedt

Case 16

The Uncovered Transaction: Rolls Royce Australia

Assume that an Australian importer contracts to buy five Rolls Royce automobiles from a British company for £100,000. The contract is signed on February 1, the cars are shipped on May 1, and the account is settled on October 15 of that same year. The cars are sold on October 30 for A$250,000. Exchange rate movements over that time period are shown at the top of the next page. Show the accounting and cash flow implications for the Australian importer by completing the work sheet on the bottom of the next page.

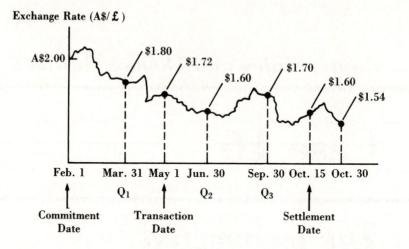

Exchange Rate (A$/£)

Worksheet for the uncovered transaction

Date	Balance sheet		Income statement
	Assets	Liabilities	Profit/Loss
Feb. 1			
Mar. 31			
May 1			
June 30			
Sept. 30			
Oct. 15			
Oct. 30			

Breakdown of revenues, costs and foreign exchange gains or losses

	A. Anticipated (economic) as of Feb. 1	B. Ex post (accounting) as of Oct. 30
Revenues		
COGS (Expenses)		
Operating Profit		
FX Gains/Losses		
Net Cash Inflows		

Gunter Dufey

Case 17

Kemp Corporation
(Funding Multinational Operations)

In 1975, Kemp Corp. USA decided to expand the production facilities of its French subsidiary, Kemp France SA, located near Muhlheim, in order to serve the expanding markets for heavy construction machinery in the Middle East from this plant. While these markets were expanding very rapidly, they were dominated by Caterpillar, Komatsu, and Terex (an affiliate of General Motors in Ohio). Kemp, being in a very cyclical business, was well capitalized and currently enjoyed an A bond rating, and S&P had given its credit subsidiary a commercial paper rating of A2-P2. Kemp, the parent, was never stingy with guarantees, but its treasury department demanded the same fine rates worldwide that it obtained at home.

As a banker to Kemp, you can offer the company the following funding choices:

1. Commercial paper issued in the U.S. market, supported by the usual short-term backstop line costing ¼ p.a., at 8.5 percent for 180 days.
2. A U.S.$ term loan, priced at 10 percent, subject to renewal at market rates after 24 months.
3. A six year revolving Eurodollar facility, currently priced at 9 percent for six months, or 10 percent for 24 months.
4. A six year revolving Euro French franc facility at 13 percent for six months, or 14 percent for 24 months.
5. A domestic franc overdraft facility; 10 percent current cost.
6. A two year term facility in domestic French francs at 11 percent, renewable at market rates.
7. A multicurrency facility consisting of UAE dinars, KDs and SRs, currently available at an all-in cost of 10 percent for 90 days, sourced out of a Bahrain OBU.

Issues:

A. What is the best French franc option Kemp can obtain, given the nature of its needs?
B. What is the least cost $ option that you can provide to Kemp?
C. In which currency(s) should Kemp France be funded? Why?
D. Summarize your advice to Kemp.

Gunter Dufey

Case 18

General Electric's Yen Payables
or which exchange risk do you want to cover?

In January 1982 Bill Straub, the finance manager of General Electric's Videotape Recorder division, was confronted with a nasty dilemma: What should he do with a big chunk of yen payables that his unit accumulated in the course of marketing a line of videotape recorders under the G.E. label in the United States?

Like all videotape recorders sold in the U.S. market, G.E.'s were made in Japan by one of the four manufacturers that dominated the business and its associated technology. Steady advances in that technology and production processes had put VCR prices on a long-term downward trend of approximately 12 percent p.a., a trend that was expected to continue (see

©1989 Gunter Dufey. The facts of the case have been sufficiently disguised to protect the innocent. Any similarity with real persons, institutions, and situations is purely accidental. The case serves as a basis for discussion only; it is not designed to present an illustration of effective or ineffective decision making. Developed from publicly available information by G. Dufey, The University of Michigan.

figure). The four Japanese manufacturers sold machines under their own labels, but they also supplied U.S. marketers who sold them under their own names, and G.E. was one of them. Because the Japanese manufacturers had the field all to themselves, they invoiced their customers in yen, giving the customary ninety-day terms.

Bill Straub's dilemma was in part accentuated by the conditions on the distribution side of the videotape recorder business: There were about ten competitors active in the U.S. market, including the four captive marketing companies of the Japanese manufacturers. During the recession, demand for videotape recorders had slowed considerably as consumers' buying intentions had weakened. As a result of soft demand and intense competition, margins were razor thin. In this environment, hedging costs began to matter. To make things worse, they were at a record high: The yen had weakened a bit over the past months from Y242 per U.S. dollar to Y250. Ninety-day forwards at this time ran at Yen 246, reflecting approximately a 6.5 percent U.S. dollar premium to Yen when converted to an annual basis. The cost of U.S. dollar debt at the time was 15.5 percent, while rates for "Euroyen" (yen credits available from banks outside of Japan) were about 9 percent per annum.

In 1981, Bill's strategy of leaving the payables uncovered had turned out to be a brilliant tactical move. Not only had the dollar value of the yen decreased, but Bill's action had saved the division 6.5 percent hedging costs per annum — as he was careful to point out in his annual report. But now for 1982, what was he going to do as an encore? He recognized that the same superiors who patted him on the back for his success, would sacrifice him without mercy if the yen turned the wrong way. As long as that currency would appreciate by no more than four yen for every ninety days, Bill could always argue that the hedging cost savings roughly equalled the translation losses. However, a glance at the historical evidence told him that the Japanese currency was given to abrupt swings and Bill wondered whether this was not the time when caution was the better part of valor.

Since any hedging strategy would represent a major change in financial policy for the division, Bill recognized that he had some persuading to do. In particular, senior management had to be told about the accounting and cash flow implications as well as the various hedging alternatives.

Could you help Bill prepare his presentation?

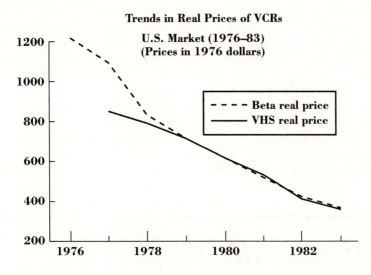

Trends in Real Prices of VCRs
U.S. Market (1976–83)
(Prices in 1976 dollars)

Ian H. Giddy

Case 19

Morris de Minas

It was August 1984 in New Jersey and the management of Morris Mini Mainframe Computer Company was looking for the most desirable alternative to finance the working capital needs of its Brazilian affiliate, Morris de Minas Ltda. The total need was for 82,650 million cruzeiros, or US$39,320,000 at the then-prevailing exchange rate of 2,102 cruzeiros per United States dollar.[1] The funds were required to meet competition by

Copyright © 1985 by Ian H. Giddy. Prepared by Geraldo Valente and Ian Giddy.

[1] The cruzeiro (Cr$) is the Brazilian currency. Its exchange value was set in relation to the US dollar, and exchange rates against other currencies were determined from their rate relative to the US dollar. For instance, while the Cruzeiro/US dollar exchange rate remained fixed until it was adjusted, the Cruzeiro/Deutsche mark exchange rate varied daily, according to the free-market fluctuations of the Deutsche mark/US dollar exchange rate. Under the minidevaluation system that had been prevailing in Brazil since 1968, the cruzeiro was continually devalued by small amounts at frequent intervals in order to take account of the chronically higher inflation rate

providing installment credit for increased sales forecast for the first half of Morris de Minas' fiscal year (Exhibit 1); this was a level of sales that the company felt it could sustain in the future.

BACKGROUND

Morris was a manufacturer of "supermini" computers based in Hacketts-town, New Jersey. It had gone international a long time ago and by 1983 about two-thirds of its revenues were earned outside the United States. Morris (USA) entered the Brazilian market in 1971 by assembling and distributing computers in Belo Horizonte, in the state of Minas Gerais. Late in the 1970s, after it became known for the high quality of its products, Morris (USA) expanded its operations in Brazil to manufacture and distribute a line of superminis, which included a full line of disk drives, printers, and other peripherals. Sales in Brazil focused on medium-sized enterprises, foreign and domestic, and were made on a revolving and installment credit basis. Such sales had amounted (excluding financial charges) to 36,246 million cruzeiros (Cr$) in fiscal year 1982, 86,593 million cruzeiros in 1983, and 158,916 million cruzeiros in 1984 (Exhibit 1). Morris was beginning to feel the pinch of competition from the North American minicomputer manufacturers, who, having been excluded from the Brazilian market in their principal products by severe import controls, had moved aggressively into the one segment, halfway between minis and mainframes, that remained the principal domain of foreign producers.

Past experience in several countries, including the United States, had shown that the availability of credit was fundamental to maintaining a market position. This aspect was even more important in Brazil, where

---

in Brazil than in most of its trading partners. Prior to the introduction of the minidevaluation policy, the cruzeiro came to be overvalued as a consequence of prolonged high inflation periods without adjustments in the exchange rate. Expectations of large devaluations were built up, encouraging the delay of exports, anticipation of imports, and, more important, eroding the competitive position of Brazilian goods in international markets. On the other hand, to the extent that the magnitude of the smaller and periodical devaluations reasonably matched inflation, this policy of minidevaluations avoided the occurrence of destabilizing speculation, especially in the form of capital outflows. Furthermore, it guaranteed the competitive advantage of the Brazilian exports. At least on two occasions, however, the Brazilian government had failed to adjust the cruzeiro exchange rate adequately by minidevaluations. Thus in December 1979 and in February 1983 two minidevaluations of 30 percent (each) had broken the continuity of the minidevaluation policy, raising, as a consequence, some doubts about the credibility of this exchange rate system. *Sources:* Financing Foreign Operations (FFO), "Domestic Financing: Brazil," June 1984. Peat, Marwick, Mitchell & Co., "Banking in Brazil," 1982.

Exhibit 1 *Morris de Minas selected financial data (Cr$ Million)*

	Fiscal (August 31)		Forecast for first 6 months of fiscal	
	1982	1983	1984	1985
Total Sales	36,246	86,593	158,916	166,194
Time Sales	30,954	75,865	142,548	152,063
Ending Balance Time Sales Receivables	18,525	49,236	92,484	175,134
Net Earnings Before Foreign Exchange Loss	4,952	6,321	14,927	15,964
Return on Net Worth Before Foreign Exchange Loss	13%	8%	11%	
Return on Investment After Foreign Exchange Loss	3%	1%	5%	

Working Capital Needs: Cr$ 82,650 Million
US$ 39,320 Thousand (Cr$2,102/US$1)

Equity: Cr$16,530 million   *Debt:* Cr$66,120 million
US$ 7,864 thousand   US$31,456 thousand

companies frequently incurred indebtedness in the hope of benefiting from the chronically high inflation rate. Therefore, to assure sales, Morris de Minas would need to extend its investment in receivables from time sales for the foreseeable future.

Until recently, Morris (USA) had followed a policy of financing its growth almost entirely from its own cash flow without resort to external borrowing. For subsidiaries operating in countries with high inflation rates and soft currencies, that policy had sometimes led to heavy foreign exchange losses, as reflected in Morris de Minas' profitability in years 1982 and 1983, when equity was by far the most significant source of the affiliate's funds (Exhibits 1 and 2). However, during the fall of 1983, in a move aimed at limiting exposure to exchange losses, Morris (USA) management had set new equity participation limits for all subsidiaries potentially subject to high foreign exchange risk. According to the new policy the parent company would commit equity capital to its Brazilian affiliate only to the extent of 20 percent of its present working capital needs. The implication was that Morris de Minas would have to obtain Cr$66,120 million from outside sources in this instance.

David Albuquerque, the vice-president of finance for the Latin Ameri-

Exhibit 2 *Morris de Minas balance sheets (CR$ Million)*

	Fiscal (August 31)		
	1982	1983	1984
Assets			
Cash and Marketable Securities	2,658	3,597	7,086
Accounts Receivable	4,282	6,046	14,513
Time Sales Receivable	18,525	49,236	92,484
Inventory	7,947	16,319	29,486
Total Current Assets	33,412	75,198	143,569
Net Fixed Assets	16,452	43,341	121,485
Total Assets	49,864	118,539	265,054
Liabilities			
Accounts Payable	4,795	16,286	59,239
Accrued Taxes	1,846	5,211	13,180
Other Liabilities	3,652	9,142	45,236
Total Current Liabilities	10,293	30,639	117,655
Notes Payable	2,311	5,341	16,462
Capital Stock	29,325	70,986	111,469
Retained Earnings	3,149	5,135	9,152
Reserves	4,786	6,456	10,316
Total Liabilities	49,864	118,539	265,054

can Division, was in charge of exploring possible financing arrangements and preparing a financing plan. Albuquerque realized that both the Brazilian expected inflation rate and tax legislation, as well as the future behavior of the exchange rate, would play major roles in his analysis. These were difficult to predict; nevertheless he regarded this as a good opportunity to stack up the company's financing choices against one another in a systematic fashion and perhaps also to give some thought to the total financial structure of the Brazilian subsidiary.

BRAZIL'S ECONOMIC ENVIRONMENT[2]

Brazil's rate of economic growth had been impressive for most of the past twenty years, up to 1980, except in the beginning of the 1960s when the

[2] Most of this synthesis is based on material from: Financing Foreign Operations (FFO), "Domestic Financing: Brazil," June 1984. The Economist Intelligence Unit

Exhibit 3 *Morris de Minas, Brazil's gross domestic product*

	1979	1980	1981	1982	1983
Total (CR$ billions)					
At Current Prices	6,239	13,104	26,833	53,150	130,805
Real Increase (%)	6.8	7.9	−1.9	1.4	−3.3
Per Capita (CR$ thousands)					
At Current Prices	54	110	220	425	1,021
Real Increase (%)	4.2	5.4	−4.1	−0.8	−5.4

Source: *International Monetary Fund*

GDP (Gross Domestic Product) growth rate fell to 1.6 percent, mainly due to a marked slowdown in the manufacturing sector. However the recovery occurred rapidly, and from 1968 through 1973 the economy expanded at impressive rates averaging over 10 percent per annum. Following this period of "economic miracle" GDP increased at a rate above 5 percent per annum between 1974 and 1980, except for 1978.

However, in order to support its massive program of development, Brazil had incurred an extremely high level of indebtedness. Brazil's foreign debt had reached US$100 billion in 1984. High interest rates on dollar funds and the unwillingness of foreign lenders to advance additional loans provoked a deep economic recession. The initial effect of the severe reduction in the pace of economic growth was felt through a fall in GDP of 1.9 percent and a decline in per capita income of 4.1 percent in 1981 (Exhibit 3). In 1982 there was a recovery in the rate of growth of the GDP that registered 1.4 percent. Nevertheless, this improvement was short-lived; in 1983 Brazil returned to a negative rate of economic expansion, with the GDP falling by 3.3 percent. 1983 showed an even more pronounced decrease in per capita income of 5.4 percent, in contrast with 0.8 percent in 1982. Adding to this, an unfavorable export performance had affected Brazil's capacity to meet the financial obligations pertinent to its huge foreign debt, since Brazil had lost a critical amount of foreign reserves. As a consequence the Brazilian government, whose basic goal was the stabilization of the balance of payments, had to ask the International Monetary Fund (IMF) for funds, which involved submitting to a rigid program of economic austerity developed by the Fund and the country's main private creditor banks.

While in 1984 there was an expectation of small but positive GDP

(EIU), "Quarterly Economic Review of Brazil: Annual Supplement," 1983. The Economist Intelligence Unit (EIU), "Quarterly Economic Review of Brazil," No. 3 1984. Peat, Marwick, Mitchell & Co., "Banking in Brazil," 1982.

growth, due mainly to an impressive export performance, the outlook for 1985 was more uncertain because it was believed that the inflation rate would remain high, at least for the first half of the year.

Public expenditure had been among the most prominent causes of Brazil's lack of financial stability for a long time. Brazil had three separate, unconsolidated budgets: the fiscal budget, the monetary budget, and the budget for state-owned firms. In recent years it had proved to be politically impossible to finance the public deficits by noninflationary means. While fiscal budget surpluses had been achieved every single year since 1976, it was not until 1983 that the monetary budget introduced a liquidity squeeze, reduced credit subsidies, cut the public enterprise budget, and effected a transfer of funds from the fiscal to the monetary budget. 1983 also marked the beginning of an attempt to control the spending and borrowing activities of the nearly six hundred public sector companies in foreign markets. This was part of a greater effort directed towards the reduction of the public sector financing needs from 17 percent of GDP in 1983 to 5 percent in 1984 and 4 percent in 1985. The state companies were still expected to register deficits in 1984, but limits had been set in order to keep the deficit under control.

The rate of growth of the money supply (M1) had increased from 36.8 percent in 1974 to 87.6 percent in 1983 (Exhibit 4); current policy for 1984 was to keep monetary growth under 50 percent. In the early months of the year, however, the money supply growth rate was far beyond the desired

Exhibit 4 *Morris de Minas, money supply and inflation in Brazil*

	Percentage Change Over Previous Year	
	Money Supply (M1)*	General Price Index**
1974	36.8	34.6
1975	35.6	29.4
1976	42.3	46.2
1977	37.0	38.8
1978	40.9	40.8
1979	53.2	77.2
1980	76.4	110.3
1981	65.1	95.1
1982	75.4	99.7
1983	87.6	211.0

*Source: International Monetary Fund
**Source: Getulio Vargas Foundation, Rio de Janeiro, Brazil

level, which made more strict measures seem inevitable. Monetary expansion in the first seven months of 1984 alone had risen to over 139 percent.

The pace of inflation had similarly accelerated over the last decade. In every year but three since 1974, the inflation rate had increased, reaching 211 percent in 1983. Frequently cited causes for this included strong internal demand, unchecked monetary expansion, acute increases in prices in world markets (especially for petroleum), and some food supply related problems. In addition, recent salary increases above the amount permitted by the wage legislation, price adjustments allowed to industry and commerce who in turn passed them on to consumers, and the reduction of subsidies for oil, sugar and wheat had made it certain that the inflationary wave would continue. By the end of August 1984 the annual rate of inflation stood at 219.3 percent, and higher industrial costs were expected to cause a further rise in the overall price level of the economy. Moreover, the funding crisis facing the government was having an impact on industry's costs by means of very high interest rates. Therefore it was very unlikely that Brazil would come into 1985 with less than 230 percent inflation. Both inflation and monetary expansion were expected to stay high, up to the time when a combination of growth and structural changes could relieve the pressure caused by the financing of the nearly US$25 billion internal debt from domestic financial markets.

The exchange rate of the cruzeiro had weakened from 7.44 cruzeiros to the U.S. dollar in the end of 1974 to 252.67 at the end of 1982 (Exhibit 5). On February 18, 1983 the government devalued the cruzeiro by 30 percent, partly influenced by the negotiations with the IMF concerning the debt

Exhibit 5 *Morris de Minas, exchange rate and monetary correction in Brazil*

End of period	CR$/US$	O.R.T.N. (CR$)
1974	7.44	105.41
1975	9.07	130.93
1976	12.35	179.63
1977	16.05	233.74
1978	20.92	318.44
1979	42.53	468.71
1980	65.50	706.70
1981	127.80	1,382.09
1982	252.67	2,733.27
1983	984.00	7,012.99
1984 (August)	2,102.00	14,619.90

Source: Central Bank of Brazil.

rescheduling program. Prior to the maxidevaluation the cruzeiro had stood at 292.5 to the U.S. dollar; afterward it stood at 380.5. The minidevaluation policy since then, in line with inflation, brought the rate to 984 cruzeiros to the U.S. dollar by late 1983, and 2,102 to the U.S. dollar by the end of August of 1984. Given the usually much higher rate of inflation in Brazil relative to that of its trading partners, the country would become increasingly uncompetitive in world markets if there were no adequate adjustment in the cruzeiro exchange rate. Thus, in order to diminish its reliance on external savings, Brazil — under the terms of the IMF stabilization agreement — had adopted an aggressive exchange rate policy: it would devalue the cruzeiro fifteen days after each quarter at a rate equal to "general price inflation without accidental factors" during the preceding three months. For purposes of this policy, accidental factors were defined to include the reduction of subsidies, rises in international prices, poor crops, and similar events.

In 1983 and in the first half of 1984 Brazil had had no difficulty in complying with its commitment. Furthermore, since the U.S. dollar had been rising in relation to other currencies, the government was inclined to accelerate the pace of devaluation in order to back up the competitiveness of Brazil's exports in European and Asian markets. While prices for Brazilian goods in the United States rose only 2.6 percent from the middle of 1983 through the middle of 1984, prices for such goods rose 12.7 percent in West Germany, 15.1 percent in France, and 17.1 percent in Italy.

The Brazilian financial system was reasonably well equipped to handle a full range of banking activities, especially in the large cities. However, by virtue of government regulations, lines of credit were not always easy to obtain. In particular, foreign companies' affiliates frequently had to struggle for funds, using newly developed financing methods. While several factors might be held responsible for high interest rates in Brazil, the most direct was probably expectation of high inflation, as reflected in the periodic adjustment of the price index. Another related major factor that contributed to high interest rates was the frequent "squeeze" of the price index. In Brazil, indexing or monetary correction[3] might be safely regarded as the fundamental interest rate factor in the economy, since it accounted

[3] The index of monetary correction was given by the percent change in the par value of the Obrigacoes Reajustaveis do Tesouro Nacional (National Treasury Indexed Bonds), ORTNs, and was set by the government on a monthly basis. The ORTNs were created in October 1964 with an initial par value of CR$10. They had been issued since then by the Bank of Brazil for the Treasury, and the month-to-month index change was used in a wide variety of contracts in Brazil, notably in financial instruments. For example, the par value of one ORTN was Cr$7,012.99 in December 1983 and Cr$14,619.90 in August 1984. Thus the indexing or monetary correction for the first eight months of 1984 was 108.5 percent (14,619.90/7,012.99). The monetary correction rate for the last 12 months stood at 200.2 percent.

for the major part of the cost of a bank loan, of the yield on a certificate of deposit (CD), of the return on a savings account, and of a typical cruzeiro devaluation, and thus of the cost of a loan denominated in foreign currency (Exhibit 5). It also provided guidelines for overnight transactions in the money market. As may be seen from Exhibits 4 and 5, however, the monetary correction factor did not always equal the inflation or devaluation rate, perhaps as a result of the Bank of Brazil's effort to bring down inflation. Therefore, when investors believed that the monetary correction might be lagging or underestimated the high inflation, they attempted to compensate for this by requiring very high interest rates over monetary correction, which caused a further increase in the cost of bank funding and, in turn, bank lending rates.

Finally, there was the strain put on the financial system by excessive government borrowing in the money market. The sale of new government bonds exhausted bank reserves and drove up the overnight rate on open-market transactions, which in turn pushed up the bank's marginal cost of funding and therefore the lending rates.

Externally, the cruzeiro was not convertible. There was no active forward market for the cruzeiro and cover was usually not obtainable. Foreign currency could officially be obtained only for transactions specifically sanctioned by the government, from institutions authorized to operate with foreign exchange. All transactions had to be supported with appropriate, and often onerous, documentation and were closely monitored by the Central Bank, which performed a daily inspection of transactions made through each registered broker.

There was also an illegal but highly organized parallel market for U.S. dollars (mostly cash in the form of U.S. one-hundred dollar bills), but companies were advised not to participate in it since transactions in this market were not endorsed by the Brazilian government. Nevertheless the daily black market rate was quoted prominently in the major newspapers. In late August the parallel market rate stood at Cr$2,445 per U.S.$1.

THE FINANCING ALTERNATIVES

After a few phone calls to Brazil and discussions with financial officers of other multinational corporations operating under similar conditions, several options to meet the financing needs of Morris de Minas had emerged. In order to make his task easier, Albuquerque divided the alternatives into those not involving exchange risk and those doing so. Two options, a Euro-dollar loan to Morris de Minas and the establishment of a financing subsidiary, fell into the latter category, while another, a back-to-back loan, bore only partial exchange risk. Albuquerque thought he should begin with two widely used financing techniques that involved no foreign exchange risk.

1. DISCOUNTING OF RECEIVABLES AT BRAZILIAN COMMERCIAL BANKS

Traditionally, the most prevalent form of short-term financing for a company such as Morris was to discount receivables, with recourse, at Brazilian commercial banks.

The normal range of terms on trade bill discounts was 30 to 120 days, although occasional 180-day operations were observed. The range of nominal rates was 9 to 11 percent per month, including a 0.125 percent tax on financial transactions, all of which would be tax deductible. However, with the prevailing practice of charging upfront commitment fees and requiring compensating balances of 25 to 35 percent, the effective rate was approximately 395 percent per annum. Given the fact that firms need some balances to back up their day-to-day operations, the effective rate of interest would be less because the actual required compensating balance was not quite as high as it seemed to be.

The major drawback with this method, however, was that local banks did not have an abundant supply of cruzeiros. Because of the tight monetary policy of the Brazilian government, both in the form of a 35 percent reserve requirement and other restrictions on the use of demand deposit funds, commercial banks often had a limited amount of funds they could make available to a client for the discounting of receivables. Compounding the problem was the fact that foreign-owned subsidiaries in Brazil faced official restrictions on lending, since the Brazilian government reserved 75 percent of commercial bank loan portfolios for privately owned local firms, which forced foreign-owned companies to compete with state agencies for the remaining 25 percent of the domestic credit supply. As a result, firms with large sales volumes and large working capital needs, as in the Morris de Minas case, would find it extremely difficult, if not impossible, to set up such large discount lines, even considering the use of a large number of banks. Adding to this, Albuquerque felt that the local subsidiary should not enter into discount agreements with more than twenty local banks because of the complications that almost certainly would arise from this expedient. In consequence, he felt that the firm should not count on raising more than half the required amount in this manner.

It was also possible to discount Morris' receivables with recourse at local private finance companies, which were the normal sources of credit to consumers, and which were somewhat less constrained by government regulations.

Albuquerque's assistant had computed the cost of discounting the receivables to be, on the average, approximately equal to 494 percent per annum. All of this cost would be deductible in computing profits subject to Brazilian corporate taxes, which for Morris de Minas would be approximately 45 percent.

2. LOAN FROM LOCAL INVESTMENT BANKS

As another alternative without currency risk, the Brazilian subsidiary would borrow its cruzeiro requirement from local investment banks. The six-month investment bank loan rate was regarded as the Brazilian prime rate and was related to the banks' CD rate, which had a minimum term of six months, according to Central Bank regulations.

A legal rate control imposed by the Central Bank of Brazil prevented large banks from charging more than 20 percent per annum over monetary correction on a six-month loan. Taking into account semiannual compounding, this came to 9.54 percent for six months. For small banks, the limit was 24 percent per annum. But as in other high-inflation countries, it was very difficult, if not impossible, to control interest rates in Brazil. Bankers were accustomed to living with interest rate controls and had quickly developed a number of ingenious ways to circumvent them on both CDs and term loans, such as discounts for CDs and commitment fees and/or compensating balances for loans. Thus the old trick of charging a commitment fee up front had became general practice in recent years. Although fees varied, the most common charge was 5 percent for a six-month loan. There was also an upfront financial transactions tax of 0.125 percent per month on principal plus interest. Therefore, in order to obtain 100 cruzeiros, for example, one would have to borrow approximately 106 cruzeiros. Albuquerque's assistant calculated this as follows:

$$
\begin{aligned}
\text{Borrowing} \\
\text{requirement} \\
\text{for CR\$100}
\end{aligned}
= \frac{100}{1\text{-Upfront fee (\%)} - \text{Upfront taxes (\%)}}
$$

$$
= \frac{100}{1\text{-Upfront fee (\%)} - (\text{Prin.} + \text{Interest}) \times \text{F.T. tax}}
$$

$$
= \frac{100}{1 - .05 - (1 + .0954) \times 6 \times .125/100}
$$

$$
= 106.18
$$

From this, the effective loan rate, before indexing, could be calculated by figuring that for each Cr\$100 obtained, Morris would have to pay the 9.54 percent interest rate on Cr\$106.18. This effective interest charge, plus the ORTN monetary correction, would be fully deductible in computing profits subject to Brazilian corporate taxes.

However, because of current tight local credit conditions, Morris might have to use a large number of banks, perhaps ten, to meet its working capital needs in full.

3. RESOLUTION 63 EURODOLLAR LOAN[4]

The first of the alternatives bearing currency risk would be a Eurodollar loan under Resolution 63 of the Central Bank of Brazil. In general, the cost of a six-month Resolution 63 loan included the six-month LIBOR (London Interbank Offered Rate), which in late August was quoted at 12.25 percent per annum, plus a spread of 2.25 percent per annum over LIBOR, plus an upfront local commission of 7 percent per annum, and plus an upfront tax (Financial Transactions Tax) of 0.25 percent on principal plus financial charges. The remittance of interest on foreign loans was subject to an effective withholding tax of 20 percent of the sum of LIBOR plus any spread. Financial charges (including any foreign exchange losses) on Morris de Minas borrowing, however, were deductible in computing profits subject to the Brazilian corporate profits tax.

4. BACK-TO-BACK LOAN[5]

A second alternative involving minimal exchange risk was a back-to-back loan, also known as a cash-collateralized loan. The back-to-back loan was a financial arrangement between the Bank of Brazil and the United States parent company. Morris (USA) would make a dollar deposit equal to Morris de Minas' funds needs in the New York Branch of the Bank of Brazil. In return, the Brazilian bank would lend the countervalue in cruzeiros, at the prevailing exchange rate, to Morris de Minas.

At the maturity of the loan, the parent company's dollar funds would

---

[4] Resolution 63 loans were medium to long-term foreign currency credits extended by a foreign bank to a Brazilian bank, which passed them on to local borrowers, in cruzeiros, as foreign currency-denominated loans. As for all incoming foreign loans, the term and rate structure of Resolution 63 loans were regulated by the Central Bank of Brazil. In August 1984 these repass loans had a minimum term of three months, whereas the minimum term of credits granted by a foreign bank was eight years. While the Brazilian bank was liable for the foreign credit and bore the credit risk when it passed the funds on, the ultimate borrower, among other costs, assumed the foreign bank's credit charges and the exchange risk as well. The Central Bank of Brazil, however, assured that exchange was available when needed for paying off the loan.

[5] This exchange financing technique is generally used, when possible, to extend financing to a company's affiliates in countries that have high interest rates and/or restricted capital markets.

be returned simultaneously with the repayment of the loan in cruzeiros by the Brazilian subsidiary. The exchange risk would be borne by the Bank of Brazil, because the exchange rate of cruzeiros for dollars would remain the same both when the parent currency is converted for local lending and when it is returned to the parent at maturity.

The parent company's dollar deposit in New York would earn interest at the prevailing market rate of 11 percent per annum. On the other hand, the Bank of Brazil would charge an interest rate equivalent to 20 percent p.a. over indexing on the loan in cruzeiros. Interest and monetary correction on this cruzeiro loan to Morris de Minas would be tax deductible.

It was the Morris (USA) policy to charge 13 percent p.a. payable in dollars on all loans made to its subsidiaries. Since the back-to-back loan would tie up Morris dollar funds, a 13 percent interest charge per year, payable in dollars, would be required of Morris de Minas on the dollars deposited in New York. However, since the parent company would receive interest of 11 percent p.a. on its dollar deposit with the Bank of Brazil, the Brazilian affiliate would only be charged for the remaining 2 percent p.a. interest. This interest payment would not be tax deductible in Brazil because the dollar deposit was not loaned directly to Morris de Minas. In addition, it would be subject to a 20 percent withholding tax applied to all interest remittances on foreign loans.

Another alternative, possibly cheaper, would be a direct loan from the parent company, Morris (USA). In recent months Morris (USA) had made similar dollar-denominated loans to foreign subsidiaries at an interest rate of 13 percent p.a. However, Brazilian regulations stipulated a minimum term of eighteen months on such foreign loans made directly by foreign companies to its affiliates in Brazil, and there was no assurance that the foreign exchange would be available to repay the loan, or at what price. For this reason Albuquerque felt that a surcharge of perhaps 2 percent would have to be added to the rate normally charged for subsidiary loans.

5. A WINDOW: RESOLUTION 63 LOAN WITH NO EXCHANGE RISK[6]

Yet another alternative was a variation on the Resolution 63 loan. In this type of financing, the Circular 767 of the Central Bank of Brazil allowed the lending bank to charge a fixed rate for the expected devaluation of the cruzeiro against the U.S. dollar as a part of the loan's cost. In practice this meant that the bank would charge a sort of "currency premium" in addi-

[6] Financing Foreign Operations (FFO), "Brazil: Financial Update Bulletin", October 1984.

tion to monetary correction. Because the bank would substitute a fixed charge for the actual devaluation of the cruzeiro over the term of the loan, the foreign exchange risk was shifted away from the borrower towards the lending bank. Furthermore, reflecting the aggressive Brazilian foreign exchange policy of devaluating the cruzeiro at the same rate as inflation, which made unnecessary a one-shot maxidevaluation, the effective cost, including the premium, over monetary correction was as low as 20 percent per annum, compared with common cruzeiro denominated loans costing 35.3 percent per annum over monetary correction.

However, this window might not continue open for long because banks were getting increasingly concerned about the government policy towards inflation, devaluation, and monetary correction after the January 1985 presidential election. To use it, the firm would have to move quickly.

6. ESTABLISHING A FINANCE COMPANY IN BRAZIL[7]

The final alternative consisted of establishing a finance company (financeira) in Brazil to assure consumer sales financing. There were four types of finance companies operating in Brazil: financeiras pertaining to financial conglomerates, financeiras related to industrial groups, financeiras linked to retail groups, and independent financeiras. All of them were subject to the same government regulations, which were fairly loose. They differed basically in terms of the market segment they attended. Funding was obtained through the issuance and sale of "letras de cambio"[8] in the money

[7] Authorization for the establishment of finance companies in Brazil was granted by the federal government, through the Central Bank, via the issuance of a "carta patente" (registration certificate). Since no new cartas patente had been issued for a number of years, the market value of an existing registration certificate was very high. Assuming that Morris de Minas could find a registration certificate for sale in the Brazilian financial market, it would have to pay about US$3 million for it. Furthermore, because the foreign ownership of financial institutions was restricted and carefully supervised in Brazil, Morris de Minas would still have to get the necessary Central Bank approval of the purchase, what should only be expected if it could convince the Brazilian authorities that its entry would bring very expressive benefits to the financial market in general. The Central Bank's manner of thinking towards this issue could be inferred from its manifest preference to intervene in failed institutions, assuming their losses, but keeping their control in hands of nationals, or even to liquidate the institution rather than authorizing the transfer of their control to foreigners. Nevertheless, if the purchase of the registration certificate by Morris de Minas were carried out successfully, all of the US$3 million investment (plus capital gains if any, from the resale of the carta patente) would be repatriated when the finance company was eventually collapsed always assuming that the authorities would continue to allow such funds to be remitted.

[8] A letra de cambio was a form of draft. It was an instrument in which the finance company promised to pay a certain sum of money to the bearer at a definite future time. In August 1984, the minimum term of a letra de cambio was six months. In general, letras de cambio were sold at a discount.

markets. However, contrary to the common practice, financing would have to be extended to consumers prior to the sale of the drafts in the market.

In a typical consumer sales financing transaction, the customer signs promissory notes and a credit contract with the finance company, which would pay cash directly to the seller. The finance company, then, would issue letras de cambio which would be sold to investors on the Brazilian money market, where such drafts were actively traded. Presently, six-month letras de cambio were being discounted at a rate equivalent to 295 percent per annum in Belo Horizonte.

Despite the minimum required investment of approximately U.S.$3 million in the proposed finance company, which would issue and guarantee the letras de cambio, it was felt that Morris might not be able to obtain the total amount of funds to attend its immediate working capital needs due to factors such as timing, and most important, legal constraints on the ratio "outstanding loans (and consequently, outstanding letras de cambio) to equity" of finance companies in Brazil. Since the company would exist on paper only, Albuquerque felt that the cost of running it would be minimal, apart from start-up legal expenses.

As usual, Morris de Minas would have to pay 13 percent p.a. to its U.S. parent for the investment in the finance company which would tie Morris (USA) funds. In addition, Morris de Minas would incur the cost related to the discounting of the letras de cambio. All these costs were assumed to be tax deductible, since the funds would be advanced to Brazilian corporations. As before, the remittance of interest on foreign loans would be subject to a withholding tax of 20 percent.

FINAL REMARKS

Having gathered all the background information needed to properly evaluate the various financing methods that had been identified, David Albuquerque began to work on his plan. He knew that anticipations about Brazilian inflation and its effects on the behavior of exchange rates would be the key variables in the choice of the appropriate financing strategy. But overall he wanted to make a recommendation that would meet the company's needs, enable Morris to overcome government and monetary regulations, and minimize costs and risks while leaving the door open to future Morris visits to the Brazilian money markets.

Gunter Dufey

Case 20

FX Risk? In Texas?

S.T. Sheridan, Jr. had been a customer of the middle market/private banking unit of C-Bank in San Antonio, Texas, for some years.

The son of a wealthy doctor, he had great difficulty in his younger years focusing on a career. After flunking out of several colleges, he traveled widely in Europe and even worked for a while in Germany as an orderly in a U.S. Army hospital. S.T. finally returned home to Dallas, made peace — sort of — with his dad and finished college at South Texas State. By then he was 26 and it was time to settle on a career. With his academic record, no respectable U.S. medical school was going to admit him. S.T. Sr. revived his hopes of having his son follow him in the medical profession and provided the wherewithal to get Jr. into a medical school somewhere south of the border.

After two years, S.T. Jr. gave up. The curriculum was demanding, he was ill-prepared, and his chances of ultimately passing the U.S. medical boards were simply too remote. Also, during his last six months at medical school he was severely distracted as he had met Colleen, a fellow student whose parents lived in Waco, Texas. Colleen was not too serious about her studies either. Some of her fellow students suspected she was more interested in finding a husband than a career.

In any case, they got married and settled in San Antonio. Colleen was soon expecting their first child and S.T. Jr. finally started to concentrate his energies on making a living. Through a referral of his father, he found a job as a salesman with a medical supply company and to everybody's surprise did rather well. His pleasant manner and knowledge of the medical profession made him a success. After two years, he and Colleen took a brief vacation in Europe, and to make it tax deductible, he visited some German manufacturers of medical equipment. On the flight back to Dallas he decided to strike out on his own. With a small stake provided by both his father and father-in-law, he set up his own firm in early 1978 to import, sell, and service German medical equipment, which was expensive but superior in styling and quality to competing American brands.

By now S.T. Jr. had developed ambition; he worked hard and success came quickly. It was then that he became a customer of C-Bank. He required L/Cs that the German suppliers demanded in the initial stages of their relationship.

In the first year S.T. almost went broke. His DM denominated payables turned out to be very expensive when the Deutsche mark moved from 2.10 in May 1978 to 1.72 in October. S.T. talked to the bank and his account officer suggested he buy DMs three months forward to cover his payables. As the account officer explained, he would even be making money when the DM would begin to appreciate!

In 1980 S.T.'s relationship with his banker began to be strained. He systematically lost money on his forwards as the DM started to drop in value via the U.S. dollar. Fortunately, S.T.'s business started to boom. The German equipment became extremely price competitive: where it used to be just a quality advantage, with the strength of the dollar it became a price advantage too! S.T.'s fortunes soared and he was soon able to repay the small working capital loan from the bank, and return the funds received from his father-in-law as well as his dad with interest.

By 1984 S.T.'s company had made so much money that he now did business with the investment department of C-Bank; they ran his (conservative) portfolio which consisted of stripped Treasury Notes acquired when interest rates were well in the double digits. By the spring of 1985 things changed. The dollar started to drop precipitously and margins in S.T.'s import business deteriorated rapidly. He had to make a difficult choice: either reduce the volume of his business operations, or incur losses, or a combination of both.

At that point he came to the bank to ask for an introduction to Deutsche Bank which, he learned, had opened a small branch in Houston. His idea was to get a DM line of credit to finance his inventory and benefit from the lower cost of DM financing to improve his profitability.

Question:

Analyze S.T. Jr.'s FX problems. What would you recommend? Which business opportunities do you see for a bank? Would your recommendation change if and when S.T. decided to represent Dysanics, a small U.S. producer of a line of scanners and X-ray machines that competed with Siemens AG and Philips NV products?

Relevant Market Data for July 8, 1985	
U.S. Prime	9.25%
3 month E$	7.75%
3 month EDM	5.31%
Spot DM	3.0280
FWD 90 DM	3.0098
FWD 180 DM	2.9898

Ian H. Giddy

Case 21

Scott Paper

As Director of Planning for Scott Paper Company, Dick Thompson does not typically have to get into arguments with the firm's accountants. Recently, however, his efforts to give Scott's manufacturing subsidiaries in Europe and Japan more financial independence had been frustrated by the VP Finance, who pointed to the losses these subsidiaries had sustained during the past six months. The reason was not in dispute: because of the U.S. dollar's rise of almost 7 percent against most other currencies, the translated value of the foreign subsidiaries had fallen.

Dick's argument was that the loss was fictional, a "paper loss" resulting from the firm's accountants ignoring the value of the overseas operations' fixed assets and future revenues. "Because of purchasing power parity," he said, "foreign prices tend to rise, relative to U.S. prices, by an amount sufficient to offset the currency change. For example, if you were to take a few representative goods in the United States, and compare the prices of identical goods in Japan and Europe, translated into U.S. dollars at the current rate, you'd find they're similar."

"Is that so? Prove it!" retorted the chief accountant. "I'd bet that if you compared the price of a Big Mac, or a gallon of gasoline or any other comparable commodity in a couple of different countries, you'd find that there's no practical relationship between prices and exchange rates."

Who is right? Can you identify the prices of one or more comparable consumer goods in at least three different countries? Are their prices the same in U.S. dollars, and if not, what is the percentage deviation from the "law of one price?" Please identify your sources!

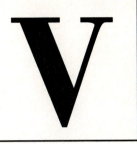

Instruments
and Techniques

Ian H. Giddy

Case 22

Bookwell's Financing Choices

It was 9:30 on a cold Wednesday morning, and John Ackton had a problem. At 10:30 A.M. the company's financial staff had a meeting and John was expected to make recommendations on how to finance the firm's expanding working capital.

John Ackton was Assistant Treasurer of Bookwell's Ltd., a newly acquired British subsidiary of Bookrite, the New York publishing firm. Based in Oxford, Bookwell's was a publisher and distributor of academic books; at the time, their market was primarily in the United Kingdom. In their last budget, Ackton and his colleagues had estimated additional working capital needs of £2 million for the next six months.

John Ackton's inclination was to take out a £2 million, six-month sterling loan from Barclay's Bank in London, with whom the company had done business for years. He was keen to make a good show, however, of evaluating all possibilities, so he had posed himself three questions.

First, should Bookwell's borrow in England, as in the past, or should it borrow in the Euromarket? What was the risk of the latter?

183

John had been able to obtain the following information about six-month interest rates:

Deposit rates (per annum)		*Loan rates* (per annum)	
Domestic bank deposits	10.56%	Domestic bank loan	13.00%
Eurosterling deposits	11.06%	Eurosterling loan	11.92%

Second, should the company obtain short-term or longer-term debts? John knew he could borrow at fixed rates for one to twelve months, and although he had not yet obtained quotes for all maturities, his Reuters screen revealed the following Eurodeposit rates:

Eurosterling deposits

3 months	10.94%
6 months	11.06%

John had a feeling that U.K. interest rates might be brought down a bit, so he wondered whether it might be advisable to take the shortest possible maturity in hope of rolling it over at a lower cost.

Third, and most important, was the question of in which currency to borrow. John knew that the Eurodollar market had the greatest availability of funds and lower interest rates than the sterling market, but he feared the exchange risk involved in borrowing in dollars. According to forecasts, sterling could rise if U.S. interest rates came down. One possibility worth considering was to borrow abroad and hedge the exchange risk in the forward market. But how to evaluate these choices? He had only the following information (for six-month loans):

Eurodollar loan rate	10.50%
Eurosterling loan rate	11.92%
$/£ forward premium (cost of cover)	2.39%

Exchange rates	**Dollars per pound**	**Pounds per dollar**
Spot rate today	$1.71	£ .585
6-month forward rate	$1.69	£ .592
Forecast of $/£ spot in 6 months	$1.72	£ .581

(Note: The "pounds per dollar" is simply the inverse of the "dollars per pound," e.g., .585 = 1/1.71)

Can you help John Ackton make recommendations on these three decisions? Consider carefully the principles behind each choice.

Ian H. Giddy

Case 23

Wooden Stake

Metrobank's Bucharest office recently arranged a swap deal in which the bank intermediated between the Wooden Stake Corporation, a northwestern U.S. lumber firm that wanted six-year fixed rate sterling funds, and the Bank of Transylvania, which wanted floating-rate dollar funds. Wooden Stake obtained a floating-rate loan linked to LIBOR while Bank of Transylvania issued a fixed rate Bulldog bond; each effectively paid the other's interest with Metrobank coming in between.

1. Show, by means of diagrams, the initial, annual and final cash flows arising from this swap.
2. Show what flows (if any) might have occurred if Wooden Stake had wanted dollar funds instead.

185

3. What conditions are necessary for such a swap to occur?
4. Assume that dollar and sterling six-year interest rates were 10% and 11% and that the sterling/dollar exchange rate was $1.50 at the initiation of the swap. Eurodollar LIBOR was 8½% at that time. Five years later, sterling has fallen by 2% and sterling rates by 1%. What position would Metrobank be in if Transylvania went under?

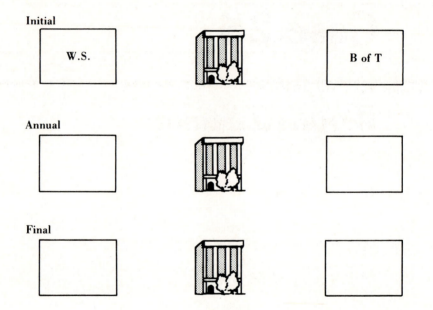

Ian H. Giddy

Case 24

Grupo Zuliano

Jose Luiz Bermudez was the Director of Finance of Grupo Zuliano, a petro-chemical company located in Maracaibo, Venezuela. Recently, he had been considering ways to finance a naphtha processing facility that was expected to cost $60 million. Most of the equipment was to be imported from the United States. However the driving force behind the project was a long-term contract with Ciba-Geigy, the Swiss agro-chemical company.

Under the contract, Ciba-Geigy would commit to purchasing the bulk of the plant's output at a predetermined price in ECU, the European currency unit. Senior management had suggested Zuliano fund this program by issu-ing a Eurobond denominated in ECU (to match revenues), but Bermudez found that this was not feasible — Eurobond investors were simply not famil-iar with the company and were uncertain about political risk in Venezuela.

Following discussions with several U.S. banks, however, Bermudez found that Grupo Zuliano could borrow five-year Eurodollars locally at semi-annual LIBOR + ¾ percent, and Chemical Bank agreed to enter into a currency swap with the company. LIBOR was 3.9375 percent at the time. Chemical's swap quotations are shown below.

a. Diagram the swap with little boxes.
b. What would Zuliano's cost of capital be if it did the swap?
c. How would a 0.75 percent up-front commitment fee affect Zuliano's cost of capital?

CHEMICAL BANK SWAP QUOTATIONS	
Years	**Swap Rates, ECU Fixed Annual vs 6-Mo US Dollar LIBOR**
2	7.00 – 7.10
3	7.00 – 7.10
4	7.20 – 7.30
5	7.20 – 7.35
7	7.25 – 7.35
10	7.40 – 7.50

Gunter Dufey

Case 25

An Interest Rate Swap: Will It Work?

Doug Sharp, Metrobank's chief swap dealer, had received a call from his loan production office in Miami where the local representative had worked for months on a seven-year, fixed-rate funding deal for the holding company of Basket Corporation, a Miami S&L intent on stretching the duration of its liabilities. In the end, Metrobank's credit committee had decided not to participate in the syndicated loan because the risk/reward ratio did not quite meet its new and improved standards.

Basket Corporation had approached the investment bank of Drixel, Milk, et al. which proposed to issue a seven-year note in the domestic market at an all-in cost of 12⅝ percent. As a final alternative, Basket Corporation was considering going into the commercial paper market. To back it up, the bank had found a Japanese institution with an AA rating that was willing, incredibly, to write an L/C at a .5 percent fee, payable semiannually, which made the dealers believe the paper could be placed at 9⅝ percent currently.

"Will you people consider at least doing a swap?" the representative asked, "so all my efforts aren't completely for naught."

"If your division takes the credit risk," Doug Sharp replied, "we'll definitely look at it."

Shortly thereafter he got a call from an investment bank, Goldman Brothers, asking whether the bank would be willing to do a swap for an AA rated Japanese institution, Sushi Bank, whose N.V. subsidiary was about to go to market with a seven-year Eurobond issue at 12 percent. That bank had a target of LIBID –⅛, in order to fund its LIBOR priced international assets.

Doug leaned back and started to play on the keyboard of his work station. The Reuter's screen showed current LIBOR rates for O/N at 9 percent, seven days 9⅛, one month 9¼, three months 9⅜, six months 9⅝, and for one year LIBOR stood at 9⅞. The broker screen for swaps showed that basis swaps CP against LIBOR were quoted at CP + 25; seven-year swap indications were T + 80/87.

"It's all a matter of how greedy Basket Corporation is," Doug thought, "especially since we need at least 12 basis points for a deal like this."

Questions:
1. Could Metrobank do the swap? How much could Metro give to Basket Corporation?
2. What are the risks to Basket Corporation, to Sushi, and, most importantly, to Metrobank?

Case 26

U.S. Dollars vs Australian Dollars: Money to be Made?

Jim Beltram, the Assistant to the Treasurer of a large regional bank in the western part of the United States, is contemplating a deal. Normally, the bank raises U.S. dollar funds at LIBOR –⅛ in the interbank market to LIBOR –¼ when funds are obtained from corporations or large individual investors through the London and Nassau operations.

However, several competitors have recently issued five year notes in Australian dollars (A$), yielding between 13 and 13.5 percent. There is apparently good demand for this paper from wealthy individual investors in the United States, offshore accounts, and some "high-yield" bond funds.

Since none of the regionals had ambitions to enter the overcrowded Australian banking market, they must have swapped these funds into sub-LIBOR U.S. dollars, the type of liability a U.S. bank needs. Jim had heard that in the competitive swap market, intermediaries required at least 30 BP (in U.S.$) for a currency/coupon deal. "I wonder how they do it," Jim thought, turning to his Reuter's screen to pull up some rates. The U.S. market page showed the following indications:

> T-Bills, 6 month: 7% (bond equivalent yield)
> U.S. Treasury Notes, 5 year: 10% (semi-annual)
> 6 month LIBOR: 8%

On the Australian dollar page, West Pac's New York office quoted the following indications:

> Commonwealth of Australia, 5 year: 14% (yield/annual payments)
> Australian Corporate Issues, AA equivalent (Domestic): 14.5%
> (secondary market yield to maturity/annual coupons)
> Note: Australia levies a withholding tax of 10% on interest paid to
> nonresidents

"Can something be done here?" he mused, and started to punch numbers into his trusty calculator.

Questions:

How much **arbitrage profit** (before fees and expenses) is available in the market, if the investment banker can sell his bank's A$ paper to yield 13 percent (before commissions) and AA corporates raise U.S. dollar funds in the international market for syndicated loans at ¼ percent over LIBOR? If Jim's bank succeeds in obtaining funds simply at LIBOR –⅛, is there any other advantage gained that might justify the underwriting cost of 2 percent up front (in U.S. dollars)?

Ian H. Giddy

Case 27

Sasol

Sasol is the state-owned oil company of South Africa. In the winter of 1992 the firm was considering alternative ways to finance an expansion of Sasol's successful oil-from-coal production capacities. For the first time in many years South Africa's state companies were able to issue public bonds in the Euromarket.

A recent presentation from Swiss Bank Corporation had indicated that investors would give a good reception to a three year, $75 million Sasol Eurodollar bond. The indicated all-in cost, taking into account fees, was 5.9 percent per annum. Jan van Heerden, Sasol's director of financing, favored taking this opportunity to obtain funds as quickly as possible.

On the other hand there were those within the company who favored an alternative proposal, suggested by the New York investment bank Salomon

193

Brothers, to do a private placement of a $75 million, three year note whose principal was linked to the price of oil. This group argued that South Africa nowadays had to compete in the world market for oil — the "laager" days were over, and Sasol was vulnerable to world prices like other oil companies.

The Salomon proposal was more expensive; the interest rate would be 9.3 percent. But the deal would offer Sasol a substantial protection against any fall in oil prices. The price of a barrel of West Texas Intermediate was now $21.80. If the deal were done today, the amount of principal that had to be repaid in three years would be reduced by any drop in the WTI price. For example, if WTI had fallen by $5 to $16.8 by the maturity date in August 1995, the amount due would be only $57,798,165. The investor would be hedged by Salomon against fluctuations in the price of oil. The Sasol economics department had prepared a brief memo on commodity-linked bonds such as this one (Exhibit 1).

van Heerden agreed that Sasol should begin hedging itself against fluctuations in the world market price of oil. However his view was that the hedging should be done separately. Indeed he had sought out quotations on long-term forward contracts from several banks and commodities firms. He was disappointed that some had been unwilling to give firm quotations, being reluctant to make long term commitments given Sasol's perceived credit risk and the political situation in South Africa. One bank, Bankers Trust, had given van Heerden an indicative quotation, subject to approval by the bank's credit committee. The Bankers Trust quotation was for a three year forward contract at $17.54 per barrel of Brent crude oil, on a notional principal amount of $75 million. (Spot Brent was $20.45.) In this contract no oil would be delivered; instead Sasol would take a "short" position, and Bankers a "long" position in Brent crude. If the price in three years were below $17.54, Bankers Trust would pay Sasol the difference, expressed as a fraction of $17.54 times $75 million. For example, if Brent fell by five dollars Bankers would pay Sasol $8,948,636. Of course if Brent remained above $17.54, Sasol would pay Bankers Trust.

As South Africa's credit improved, van Heerden thought, more opportunities would become available. Another possibility he had been looking into was a commodity swap. He had prepared a memo on this technique (Exhibit 2). And a final possibility was simply to use oil futures, such as those quoted in the *Financial Times* (Exhibit 3), to hedge Sasol's oil revenues.

Which of these alternatives do you think is best for Sasol?

Source: Reuters, Ltd. July 31, 1992. Reprinted with permission.

Exhibit 1 Commodity-linked bonds

Commodities are playing an increasingly important role in the international capital market. As the international financial community grows more comfortable with the notion that commodities can be used in many of the same hedging and arbitrage transactions as financial instruments, so commodities or commodity indices are being incorporated into bonds and other financial instruments. Today there are even bank deposits whose values are linked to gold.

In the Eurobond market, issues whose interest or principal or both are linked to a commodity such as gold, silver or oil are becoming common. Companies have two very different motivations for issuing bonds of this kind.

The first is exemplified by PEMEX, the Mexican state oil company, which issued oil-linked bonds starting in the early 1980s. In issuing its *Petrobonos*, PEMEX sought to hedge the mismatch between its debt servicing costs and its revenues. This kind of commodity-linked bond, because it is issued by companies for whom the commodity linkage provides a hedge for their *natural business*, will have the linkage tailored to the issuer's needs.

The second motivation is based on a kind of arbitrage. Some companies and financial institutions issue commodity-linked bonds even though they may have no business in that commodity. These are typically tailored to *investors' requirements*. The commodity linkage is 100 percent offset by a commodity swap or forward contract, as a rule provided by the same bank or banks that arranged the bond issue. The banks offer the issuer a package designed to provide cheaper funding costs. This is possible because investors are in effect willing to accept a lower return for the combination of a bond and a long-dated commodity contract (forward, swap or option) that the investor could not readily obtain elsewhere. Such was the motivation for a Union Bank of Finland Oil Indexed Note whose interest rate was linked to the price of oil.

Exhibit 2 Commodity swaps

A commodity swap involves the exchange of fixed and floating cash flows pegged to the price of a commodity, just as an interest rate swap involves the exchange of fixed and floating interest rate flows. Indeed the commodity swaps market began its growth in the late 1980s, when dealers in swaps and options applied their technology to commodities.

Variations include options (which give buyers the right to buy or sell a notional commodity at some future date), caps and floors on commodity prices, and swaps linked to the provision of loans or the issuance of bonds.

In a typical commodity swap, the company may issue floating rate debt based on LIBOR. Then it would enter into a swap where the swapper pays the company's floating rate in exchange for a fixed rate, where the fixed rate is adjusted for changes in the price of a commodity. In many ways the commodity swap is little more than a long-dated, over-the-counter forward contract in a commodity, with settlement in cash rather than physical delivery of the commodity itself.

The oil industry accounts for the bulk of the commodity swap market, with the remainder largely made up of industrial metals like copper, aluminum, zinc and platinum. A few are done on soft commodities such as pulp, paper and orange juice concentrate. Commodity swaps tend to flourish in those markets where there is already an exchange-traded contract, for the market makers require a place to hedge their exposure. Yet the great bulk of the commodity swap market is in the oil business, where there is liquidity in only two or three oil instruments. A freight company, for example, may want a hedge against price fluctuations in diesel fuel. The bank providing such a hedge might protect itself using the short-term futures contracts in crude oil. There can be substantial "basis risk" between the short-term price of crude and the longer term price of diesel. Some banks offer commodity swaps out as long as ten years.

Exhibit 3 *Commodity futures quotations from the* **Financial Times**

New York

GOLD 100 troy oz.; $/troy oz.

	Close	Previous	High/Low	
Aug	356.5	356.5	356.9	356.0
Sep	357.5	357.3	0	0
Oct	358.6	358.4	358.9	358.0
Dec	360.6	360.4	361.0	360.1
Feb	362.5	362.3	362.4	362.4
Apr	364.3	364.1	363.8	136.8
Jun	366.2	366.0	365.8	365.8
Aug	368.1	367.9	0	0
Oct	370.2	370.0	0	0

PLATINUM 50 troy oz; $/troy oz.

	Close	Previous	High/Low	
Oct	377.7	374.0	378.0	375.0
Jan	375.7	372.0	375.5	372.5
Apr	375.8	372.0	375.0	373.0
Jul	376.8	373.0	0	0

SILVER 5,000 troy oz; cents/troy oz.

	Close	Previous	High/Low	
Aug	392.1	389.2	0	0
Sep	393.2	390.3	393.5	390.0
Dec	397.2	394.3	397.5	394.0
Jan	398.6	395.7	0	0
Mar	401.4	398.4	400.0	399.5
May	404.2	401.2	0	0
Jul	406.8	403.8	0	0
Sep	409.7	406.6	408.0	408.0
Dec	414.2	411.1	414.5	412.0

HIGH GRADE COPPER 25,000 lbs; cents/lbs

	Close	Previous	High/Low	
Aug	113.10	113.55	113.50	112.90
Sep	113.35	113.95	113.85	113.15
Oct	113.25	113.80	113.25	113.25
Nov	113.05	113.60	0	0
Dec	113.10	113.65	113.40	112.90
Jan	112.70	113.20	0	0
Feb	112.35	112.85	0	0
Mar	112.05	112.50	112.30	111.80
Apr	111.40	111.80	0	0
May	110.90	111.25	0	0

CRUDE OIL (Light) 42,000 US galls $/barrel

	Close	Previous	High/Low	
Sep	21.83	22.00	21.92	21.80
Oct	21.72	21.88	21.80	21.70
Nov	21.63	21.78	21.71	21.61
Dec	21.54	21.68	21.60	21.52
Jan	21.40	21.53	21.48	21.40
Feb	21.25	21.37	21.32	21.25
Mar	21.11	21.22	21.15	21.12
Apr	20.98	21.08	21.05	20.98
May	20.86	20.96	20.95	20.95
Jun	20.74	20.84	20.82	20.74

HEATING OIL 42,000 US galls, cents/US galls

	Close	Previous	High/Low	
Aug	6036	6089	6075	6025
Sep	6096	6135	6120	6080
Oct	6188	6235	6225	6180
Nov	6288	6335	6315	6280
Dec	6373	6422	6420	6370
Jan	6393	6446	6430	6400
Feb	6293	6346	6345	6300
Mar	6053	6101	6110	6065
Apr	5833	5876	5900	5860
May	5658	5701	5715	5675

COCOA 10,000 tonnes; $/tonnes

	Close	Previous	High/Low	
Sep	1035	1027	1048	1027
Dec	1094	1087	1108	1087
Mar	1145	1136	1148	1138
May	1174	1165	1177	1174
Jul	1203	1194	1206	1202
Sep	1233	1224	0	0
Dec	1268	1259	0	0
Mar	1304	1295	1310	1300
May	1332	1323	0	0

COFFEE "C" 37,500 lbs; cents/lbs

	Close	Previous	High/Low	
Sep	57.95	55.55	58.00	55.75
Dec	60.10	58.35	60.10	58.50
Mar	62.80	61.10	62.85	61.00
May	66.55	65.15	66.70	65.15
Jul	68.70	67.00	68.70	68.70
Sep	70.85	69.50	0	0
Dec	74.40	73.50	0	0

SUGAR WORLD "11" 112,000 lbs; cents/lbs

	Close	Previous	High/Low	
Oct	9.48	9.39	9.50	9.36
Mar	9.24	9.20	9.26	9.16
May	9.18	9.16	9.22	9.10
Jul	9.12	9.08	9.17	9.10
Oct	9.05	8.96	9.12	9.05

COTTON 50,000; cents/lbs

	Close	Previous	High/Low	
Oct	61.82	61.63	62.15	61.47
Dec	60.27	60.35	60.30	60.25
Mar	61.44	61.56	61.70	61.30
May	62.20	62.40	62.30	62.05
Jul	62.75	62.77	62.95	62.75
Oct	63.00	63.03	0	0
Dec	63.30	63.38	63.30	63.26

Exhibit 3 (Cont.)

New York

ORANGE JUICE 15,000 lbs; cents/lbs

	Close	Previous	High/Low	
Sep	118.15	118.70	119.00	117.75
Nov	114.10	114.40	114.90	114.00
Jan	113.60	113.75	114.00	113.30
Mar	113.65	113.85	114.10	113.60
May	113.85	113.85	114.05	113.90
Jul	113.65	113.45	114.00	114.00
Sep	113.65	113.45	0	0
Nov	113.65	113.45	0	0

INDICES

REUTERS (Base: September 18 1931 = 100)

Jul 30	Jul 29	mnth ago	yr ago
1543.2	1548.6	1545.8	1692.5

DOW JONES (Base: Dec. 31 1974 = 100)

	Jul 29	Jul 28	mnth ago	yr ago
Spot	116.52	116.79	118.74	120.84
Futures	117.94	118.36	119.87	123.71

London Markets

SPOT MARKETS

Crude oil (per barrel FOB)		+ or –
Dubai	$18.25–8.30	–0.15
Brent Blend (dated)	$20.45–0.55	–.175
Brent Blend (Sep)	$20.45–0.55	–.175
W.T.I (1 pm est)	$21.80–1.85	–0.25

Oil products (NWE prompt delivery per tonne CIF)		+ or –
Premium Gasoline	$226–229	
Gas Oil	$182–183	–3.5
Heavy Fuel Oil	$85 –87	
Naphtha	$194–195	–2

Petroleum Argus Estimates.

Other		+ or –
Gold (per troy oz)♣	$356.60	–0.25
Silver (per troy oz)♣ §§	392.0c	–2.0
Platinum (per troy oz)	$376.25	+3.75
Palladium (per troy oz)	$89.50	+1.15
Copper (US Producer)	118.42c	–0.70
Lead (US Producer)	39.5c	
Tin (Kuala Lumpur market)	16.89r	–0.16
Tin (New York)	314.5c	–7.5
Zinc (US Prime Western)	62.0c	
Cattle (live weight)†	112.69	–0.60*
Sheep (live weight)†♦	74.49p	–1.65*
Pigs (live weight)†	83.79p	–0.63*
London daily sugar (raw)	$263.0w	–13.0
London daily sugar (white)	$293.0w	–6.0
Tate and Lyle export price	£246.0	–6.5

Barley (English feed)	£109.5z	
Maize (US No. 3 yellow)	£151.5	
Wheat (US Dark Northern)	Unq	
Rubber (Sep)♥	50.50	
Rubber (Oct)♥	50.50p	
Rubber (KL RSS No 1 Jul)	222.0r	
Coconut oil (Philippines)§	$500.0t	
Palm Oil (Malaysian)§	$367.5y	
Copra (Philippines)§	$337.5	+2.5
Soyabeans (US)	£138.0z	+3.0
Cotton "A" index	64.30c	+0.05
Wooltops (64s Super)	380p	–3.0

£ a tonne unless otherwise stated. p-pence/kg. c-cents/lb. r-ringgit/kg. t-Oct/Nov w-Aug/Sept y-Sep z-Aug. †Meat Commission average fatstock prices change from a week ago ♥London physical. §CIF Rotterdam. ♣Bullion market close. m-Malaysian cents/kg. ♦ Sheep prices are now live weight prices. §§Correction for 16/7/92 394.0c.

Compiled from Reuters

SUGAR — London FOX $ per tonne

Raw	Close	Previous	High/Low	
Aug	245.00	245.00	222.60	222.00
Oct	213.00	210.80	211.00	210.0
Dec	207.00	199.60	204.00	
Mar	204.80	204.80	204.40	204.20
May	203.40	204.40	202.00	

White	Close	Previous	High/Low	
Oct	266.50	266.00	268.00	265.00
Dec	262.50	261.50	263.00	261.00
Mar	267.30	267.50	267.50	265.80
May	271.00	270.50	271.00	269.10
Aug	274.50	274.00	275.50	273.50
Oct	267.00		268.50	267.00
Dec	266.90		268.00	267.00

Turnover: Raw 826 (222) lots of 50 tonnes. White 1574 (1760) Paris- White (FFr per tonne): Oct 1344.57 Dec 1338.62

CRUDE OIL — IPE $/barrel

	Close	Previous	High/Low	
Sep	20.46	20.66	20.60	20.46
Oct	20.43	20.58	20.55	20.43
Nov	20.38	20.51	20.45	20.37
Dec	20.29	20.40	20.32	20.29
Jan	20.14	20.28	20.18	20.14
Feb	20.02	20.15		
Apr	19.75	19.85	19.75	
May	19.64		19.65	
IPE Index	20.65	20.76		

Turnover 22967 (15822)

Exhibit 3 *(Cont.)*

GAS OIL — IPE			$/tonne
	Close	Previous	High/Low
Aug	185.75	188.00	187.00 185.50
Sep	188.00	190.50	189.50 187.75
Oct	190.50	193.00	191.75 190.25
Nov	192.50	194.75	193.50 192.00
Dec	193.75	196.00	194.75 193.50
Jan	192.50	194.50	193.50 192.50
Feb	188.50	190.25	189.00
Mar	184.50	186.25	185.50 184.50
Apr	181.00	183.00	181.00

Turnover 12826 (12086) lots of 100 tonnes

FRUIT & VEGETABLES

Seedless grapes are abundant at 90–£1.20 a lb (90–£1.50), along with Spania plums at 45–55p a lb (40–60p). New season English Discovery apples are in the shops at 60–65p a lb (40–50p). Top quality cabbage is this week's best vegetable buy, with English Primo and Savoy cabbages at 20–25p a lb (30–35p each). Potatoes remain good at 10–15p a lb (10–15p). Homegrown celery at 40–45p a head (50–55p) is in good supply. Other good salad buys include tomatoes at 45–50p a lb (40–50p), peppers at 80p–£1.00 a lb (70p–£1.00) and round lettuce at 20p–25p each (25–30p). (Last weeks prices shown in brackets).

COCOA — London FOX			£/tonne
	Close	Previous	High/Low
Jul	604	600	580
Sep	616	612	623 609
Dec	645	642	653 638
Mar	673	672	681 671
May	693	690	696 688
Jul	711	708	715 711
Sep	730	727	737
Dec	757	754	760 756
Mar	784	782	791 780

Turnover: 6959 (4172) lots of 10 tonnes
ICCO indicator prices (SDRs per tonne). Daily price for Jul 29 786.45 (771.76) 10 day average for Jul 30 757.57 (755.59)

COFFEE — London FOX			$/tonne
	Close	Previous	High/Low
Jul	736	712	712 698
Sep	746	727	754 718
Nov	765	742	770 735
Jan	790	758	783 756
Mar	800	777	792 774
Jul	822	808	822

Turnover: 1528 (794) lots of 5 tonnes
ICO indicator prices (US cents per pound) for Jul 29; Comp. daily 46.55 (46.87) 15 day average 49.17 (49.31)

POTATOES — London FOX			£/ tonne
	Close	Previous	High/Low
Apr	69.5	70.6	70.0

Turnover 22 (101) lots of 20 tonnes.

SOYAMEAL — London FOX			£/tonne
	Close	Previous	High/Low
Aug	120.50		120.50 120.00
Oct	120.00		120.00
Dec	122.50	121.00	122.50 120.50

Turnover 510 (40) lots of 20 tonnes.

FREIGHT — London FOX			$10/Index point
	Close	Previous	High/Low
Aug	1050	1066	1063 1050
Sep	1065	1112	1102 1079
Oct	1175	1195	1190 1175
Jan	1205	1220	1220 1205
Apr	1255	1270	1260 1255
BFI	1088	1093	

Turnover 218 (139)

GRAINS — London FOX			£/tonne
Wheat	Close	Previous	High/Low
Sep	111.40	112.00	111.75 111.40
Nov	114.75	115.30	115.10 114.75
Jan	118.60	119.10	118.80 118.55
Mar	121.70	121.85	122.00 121.70
May	124.75	125.10	124.85 124.75
Barley	Close	Previous	High/Low
Sep	109.40	109.55	109.40

Turnover: Wheat 369 (104), Barley 5 (148).
Turnover lots of 100 Tonnes.

PIGS — London FOX		(Cash Settlement)	p/kg
	Close	Previous	High/Low
Aug	106.0	105.5	105.5 104.9
Oct	105.2		105.2
Nov	104.8		104.3

Turnover: 5 (5) lots of 3,250 kg

LONDON METAL EXCHANGE

	Close	Previous	High/Low
Aluminium, 99.7% purity ($ per tonne)			
Cash	1310–1	1313–4	
3 months	1333.5–4.0	1337–8	1335/1325
Copper, Grade A (£ per tonne)			
Cash	1308.5–9.5	1320.5–1.5	1309/1308
3 months	1334–4.5	1344.5–5.5	1338/1334

Exhibit 3 *(Cont.)*

Lead ($ per tonne)			
Cash	353–4	336–7	
3 months	363–4	346–7.5	346/347.5

Nickel ($ per tonne)			
Cash	7420–30	7495–505	7440
3 months	7490–5	7560–70	7525/7485

Tin ($ per tonne)			
Cash	6770–80	6825–35	6775
3 months	6810–20	6868–70	6890/6780

Zinc, Special High Grade ($ per tonne)			
Cash	1352–3	1345.5–6.5	1353
3 months	1361–2	1353–4	1367/1345

LME Closing £/$ rate:
SPOT: 1.9190   3 months: 1.8881

LONDON BULLION MARKET
(Prices supplied by N. M. Rothschild)

Gold (troy oz)

	$ price	£ equivalent
Close	356.50–356.70	
Opening	356.40–356.80	
Morning fix	356.75	186.409
Afternoon fix	356.75	186.215
Day's high	356.85–357.15	
Day's low	356.30–356.60	

Loco Ldn Mean Gold Lending Rates (Vs US $)			
1 month	2.73	6 months	2.74
2 months	2.74	12 months	2.77
3 months	2.74		

Silver Fix	p/troy oz	US cts equiv
Spot	204.30	319.50
3 months	209.40	394.60
6 months	214.60	398.00
12 months	225.45	406.40

GOLD COINS

	$ price	£ equivalent
Krugerrand	355.00–357.00	185.00–187.00
Maple leaf	366.90–369.25	
New Sovereign	85.00– 87.00	44.00– 46.00

TRADED OPTIONS

Aluminium (99.7%)	Calls		Puts	
Strike price $ tonne	Sep	Dec	Sep	Dec
1300	39	74	15	30
1350	15	47	41	52
1400	4	28	80	82

Copper (Grade A)	Calls	Puts		
2450	89	113	15	44
2500	56	86	32	76
2550	31	63	57	103

Coffee	Sep	Nov	Sep	Nov
650	96	120		5
700	51	79	5	14
750	18	48	22	33

Cocoa	Sep	Dec	Sep	Dec
575	44	79	3	9
600	25	61	9	16
625	12	46	21	26

Brent Crude	Sep	Oct	Sep	Oct
2000	57		9	34
2050	28		25	51
2100	9	28		

Source: *Financial Times,* July 31, 1992.

Ian H. Giddy

Case 28

Leroy Merz's Options

Wearing shorts is not normally encouraged at the world headquarters of International Computers and Telegraphics, but at 9:30 on a Sunday morning in August, who cares? So thinks Leroy Merz, Assistant Treasurer (International) of I.C. & Tel., as he strides bare-legged across Rockefeller Plaza heading for the thirty-fourth floor of the building that dominates the Plaza's west perimeter.

As Merz had expected, the air conditioning had been off since Friday evening and his office almost drips with New York's summer humidity. "I must get this options memo done," thinks Merz, "and get out of here. Foreign exchange options? A year ago nobody had heard of them, now everyone at the Foreign Exchange Managers Club claims that their firm is plunging in . . . so I had better get the story straight before someone in the

201

Finance Committee starts asking questions. Let's see, there are two ways in which I can envisage us using options now. One is to hedge a dividend due on December 15th from I.C. & Tel. Germany. The problem is Germany's new capital controls — who knows if we'll get permission from the Bundesbank to repatriate the full amount? The other is to hedge our upcoming payment to Matsumerda for their spring RAM chip shipment. With the yen at 242 and falling I'm glad we haven't covered that payable so far, but now I'm getting nervous and I would like to protect my posterior. An option to buy yen on September 10 might be just the thing. Gee it's hot in here."

Before we delve any further into Leroy Merz's musings, let us learn a bit about I.C. & Tel., and about foreign exchange options. International Computers and Telegraphics is a $7 billion sales company engaged in, among other things, the development, manufacture, and marketing of microprocessor-based equipment. Although 30 percent of the firm's sales are currently abroad, the firm has full-fledged manufacturing facilities in only three foreign countries, Germany, Canada, and Brazil. An assembly plant in Singapore exists primarily to solder Japanese semiconductor chips onto circuit boards and to screw these into Brazilian-made boxes for shipment to the United States, Canada, and Germany. The German subsidiary has developed half of its sales to France, The Netherlands, and the United Kingdom, billing in local currency, but since the German authorities insist that all export revenues must be converted into Deutsche marks, I.C. & Tel. Hamburg has accumulated a cash reserve of DM899,028, worth US$312,-000 at today's exchange rate. (The Deutsche mark is presently at a premium of 6.25 percent against the dollar in the forward market.) While the Hamburg office has automatic permission to repatriate DM3 million, they have been urged to seek authorization to convert another DM1 million by December 15th. The firm has an agreement to buy three hundred thousand RAM chips at Y4000 each semi-annually, and it is this payment that will fall due on September 10th.

The conventional means of hedging exchange risk are forward or future contracts. These, however, are fixed and inviolable agreements. In many practical instances the hedger is uncertain whether foreign currency cash inflow or outflow will materialize. In such cases what is needed is the right, but not the obligation, to buy or sell a designated quantity of a foreign currency at a specified price (exchange rate). This is precisely what a foreign exchange option provides.

A foreign exchange option gives the holder *the right to buy or sell a designated quantity of a foreign currency* at a specified exchange rate up to or at a stipulated date.

The terminal date of the contract is called the expiration date (or maturity date). If the option may be exercised before the expiration date, it is called an American option; if only on the expiration date, a European option.

The party retaining the option is the option buyer; the party giving the option is the option seller (or writer). The exchange rate at which the option can be exercised is called the exercise price or strike price. The buyer of the option must pay the seller some amount, called the option price or the premium, for the rights involved.

The important feature of a foreign exchange option is that the holder of the option has the right, but not the obligation, to exercise it. He will only exercise it if the currency moves in a favorable direction. Thus, once you have paid for an option you cannot lose, unlike a forward contract, where you are obliged to exchange the currencies and therefore will lose if the movement is unfavorable.

The disadvantage of an option contract, compared to a forward contract, is that you have to pay a price for the option, and this price or premium tends to be quite high for certain options. In general, the option's price will be higher the greater the risk to the seller (and the greater the value to the buyer because this is a zero-sum game). The risk of a call option will be greater, and the premium higher, the higher the exercise price relative to the forward rate; after all, one can always lock in a profit by buying at the exercise price and selling at the forward rate. The chance that the option will be exercised profitably is also higher, the more volatile is the currency, and the longer the option has to run before it expires.

Returning to Leroy Merz in his Rockefeller Center office, we find that he has been writing down some numbers while we have been away. During the past week he had telephoned the foreign exchange departments of several major banks and was able to obtain quotes from two of them. They were close to these rates (reported in the latest issue of *The Wall Street Journal*):

	German D-mark		**Japanese Yen**
Spot	2.8815		241.15
Forward Contracts			
30 day	2.8650		240.03
90 day	2.8365		237.75
Call Option			
Sept.: Strike = 34¢/DM	1.17 (3.37%)	Strike = 0.40¢/Yen	
Dec.:	1.93 (5.56%)		
Sept.: Strike = 35¢/DM	0.51 (1.47%)	Strike = 0.41¢/Yen	0.85 (2.05%)
Dec.:	1.23 (3.54%)		1.61 (3.88%)

	German D-mark		Japanese Yen
Sept.: Strike = 36¢/DM	0.20 (0.60%)	Strike = 0.42¢/Yen	0.36 (0.87%)
Dec.:	0.78 (2.25%)		0.95 (2.29%)

Put Option

	German D-mark		Japanese Yen
Sept.: Strike = 34¢/DM	0.16 (0.50%)	Strike = 0.40¢/Yen	
Dec.:			0.24 (0.58%)
Sept.: Strike = 35¢/DM	0.55 (1.59%)	Strike = 0.41¢/Yen	0.23 (0.55%)
Dec.:	0.91 (2.62%)		0.44 (1.06%)
Sept.: Strike = 36¢/DM	1.28 (3.69%)	Strike = 0.42¢/Yen	
Dec.:	1.54 (4.44%)		

The option prices are quoted in U.S. cents per Deutsche mark. Yen are quoted in hundredths of a cent. Looking at these prices, Leroy realizes that he can work out how much the Deutsche mark or yen would have to change to make the option worthwhile. He has attempted to obtain quotes for buying Japanese yen for the next anticipated payment in March, but has been unable to find a bank willing to sell him a call option on yen that far ahead. That makes him wonder about the depth of this market. "Will I be able to reverse these contracts once I buy them?" he wonders. He scratches his knee. "Perhaps it would be preferable to buy some options on an organized exchange, which will enable me to sell the option if I decide not to use it, and even exercise it before maturity. But everyone tells me these options, now available on the Philadelphia and Montreal exchanges, are quite illiquid and in any case only available in small, standardized quantities. Could I put together enough contracts to make it worthwhile?"

Scraping around on his messy desk, Merz finds *The Wall Street Journal* from which he obtained the above rates. "I'll attach these numbers to my memo," mutters Merz, but the truth is he has yet to come to grips with the real question, which is when, if ever, are currency options a better means of hedging exchange risk for an international firm than traditional forward exchange contracts?

As he is about to put pen to paper, another thought occurs to Leroy. His banker has been arguing persuasively that I.C. & Tel. could take advantage of the German marks they had coming in on December 15, by *writing* a call option on the funds. According to the banker, the firm could receive a premium of about 3 percent for such an option. Then, if the mark falls, I.C. & Tel. would simply keep the premium they receive for the option because the call option would not be exercised. If the mark rises, and the option is exercised, I.C. & Tel. would simply deliver the currency at the prearranged exchange rate — the strike price — which could be set equal to the forward rate if desired. This "covered option writing" idea seems so attractive that Leroy wonders why none of his colleagues at the club have tried it.

Ian H. Giddy

Case 29

How to Advance Your Career

You are the cleaning lady at the Empire State Building. One afternoon you are mopping the floor in the trading room of the Empire Financial Group. A phone rings, but everybody's too busy to notice it, so you pick it up.

It is a customer who is interested in selling DM125,000 next December at a guaranteed exchange rate of DM2.78. He's interested in options and futures. This is your big chance. Can you figure out roughly what prices to quote the customer, given the data from *The New York Times*?

Exhibit 1 *Financial futures Wednesday, July 24, 1985*

Commodity research bureau index

Today 221.2		Previous day 222.5			Year Ago 252.7	

Season						Open
High	Low	High	Low	Close	Chg.	Interest

British pound (1MM)

25,000 pounds; $ per pound

1.4450	1.0200	Sep	1.4010	1.3875	1.3995	+10	35,088
1.4040	1.0200	Dec	1.3900	1.3770	1.3895	+5	6,434
1.3915	1.0680	Mar	1.3800	1.3740	1.3835	—	962
1.3795	1.1905	Jun	—	—	1.3765	—	37

Last spot 1.4045, off 45.
Est. sales 11,747. Prev. sales 12,785.
Prev day's open int 42,521, up 568.

Canadian dollar (1MM)

100,000 dollars; $ per Canadian dollar

.7585	.7025	Sep	.7389	.7372	.7383	−20	7,145
.7566	.7006	Dec	.7374	.7359	.7364	−22	734
.7504	.6981	Mar	.7365	.7344	.7345	−21	263
.7360	.7070	Jun	—	—	.7331	−21	93

Last spot .7392, off 25.
Est. sales 1,488. Prev. sales 829.
Prev day's open int 8,235, off 62.

West German mark (1MM)

125,000 marks; $ per mark

.3555	.2930	Sep	.3506	.3476	.3501	—	46,730
.3610	.2971	Dec	.3534	.3506	.3530	—	4,602
.3599	.3040	Mar	—	—	.3560	—	931
.3633	.3335	Jun	—	—	.3601	—	2

Last spot .3478, off 17.
Est. sales 26,892. Prev. sales 37,138.
Prev day's open int 52,265, off 1,699.

Japanese yen (1MM)

12.5 million yen; $ per yen

.004268	.003870	Sep	.004198	.004178	.004194	−8	29,813
.004350	.003905	Dec	.004219	.004202	.004217	−8	1,664
.004307	.004035	Mar	.004230	.004228	.004240	−11	39

Last spot .004181, up 01.
Est. sales 10,212. Prev. sales 10,525.
Prev day's open int 31,316, off 760.

Exhibit 1 (continued)

Season							Open
High	Low		High	Low	Close	Chg.	Interest

Swiss franc (1MM)
125,000 francs; $ per franc

High	Low		High	Low	Close	Chg.	Interest
.4830	.3480	Sep	.4283	.4236	.4281	+20	28,420
.4360	.3531	Dec	.4316	.4271	.4316	+22	2,336
.4383	.3835	Mar	.4332	.4315	.4356	+24	59

Last spot .4252, off 07.
Est. sales 25,335. Prev. sales 28,450.
Prev day's open int 30,815, up 651.

Source: From "Carmen's Chance," July 24, 1985. Copyright © 1985 by The New York Times Company. Reprinted with permission.

Exhibit 2 Treasury bills

Date —1985—		Bid	Ask	Chg.	Yield
Aug	1	6.87	6.81	−0.13	6.91
Aug	8	7.22	7.18	—	7.30
Aug	15	6.90	6.86	−0.10	6.98
Aug	22	6.89	6.85	−0.06	6.98
Aug	29	6.90	6.86	−0.02	7.00
Sep	5	7.06	7.02	−0.08	7.17
Sep	12	7.06	7.02	−0.07	7.18
Sep	19	7.05	7.01	−0.09	7.18
Sep	26	7.03	6.99	−0.04	7.17
Oct	3	7.24	7.20	−0.05	7.40
Oct	10	7.24	7.20	−0.04	7.41
Oct	17	7.24	7.20	−0.03	7.42
Oct	24	7.24	7.20	−0.02	7.43
Oct	31	7.23	7.19	−0.04	7.43
Nov	7	7.25	7.21	−0.02	7.47
Nov	14	7.25	7.21	−0.01	7.48
Nov	21	7.27	7.23	−0.01	7.51
Nov	29	7.27	7.23	−0.03	7.52
Dec	5	7.28	7.22	−0.03	7.52
Dec	12	7.28	7.24	−0.03	7.55
Dec	19	7.28	7.22	−0.01	7.54
Dec	26	7.23	7.19	−0.02	7.52
—1986—					
Jan	2	7.30	7.26	−0.02	7.61
Jan	9	7.32	7.28	−0.03	7.64
Jan	16	7.36	7.32	−0.01	7.69
Jan	23	7.37	7.35	+0.01	7.74

Date —1986—		Bid	Ask	Chg.	Yield
Feb	20	7.38	7.32	—	7.71
Mar	20	7.38	7.34	−0.02	7.75
Apr	17	7.43	7.39	−0.02	7.83
May	15	7.46	7.44	−0.03	7.91
Jun	12	7.47	7.43	−0.01	7.93
Jul	10	7.48	7.46	—	8.00

Source: From "Carmen's Chance," July 24, 1985. Copyright © 1985 by The New York Times Company. Reprinted with permission.

Exhibit 3 *Financial options*

U.S. Treasury bonds (CBOE)

Option & Underlying	Strike Price	Calls—Last			Puts—Last		
		Sep	Dec	Mar	Sep	Dec	Mar
Treasury Notes $100,000 9⅞s 1990-points and 32nds.							
TNote100a	100	0.15	r	r	r	r	r
	101	0.10	r	r	r	r	r
Treasury Bonds $100,000 11¼s 2015-points and 32nds.							
TBnd 1001	106	1.08	r	r	r	r	r
	108	r	1.05	r	r	r	r
	110	0.08	r	r	r	r	r
Treasury Bonds $100,000 11¾s 2014-points and 32nds.							
TBnd100u	110	0.20	1.11	s	r	r	s
Total call vol.			704	Call open int.			15,746
Total put vol.				Put open int.			11,340

Foreign currencies (PHIL)

		Sep	Dec	Mar	Sep	Dec	Mar
12,500 British Pounds—cents per unit.							
BPound	105	r	35.00	r	r	r	r
140.88	110	30.10	r	r	r	0.25	r
140.88	115	25.20	r	r	r	r	r
140.88	120	20.20	r	r	0.10	r	r
140.88	125	15.50	15.50	r	0.30	1.70	r
140.88	130	10.70	r	r	r	3.00	5.00
140.88	135	6.15	r	r	1.90	r	7.20
140.88	140	3.60	5.90	7.85	3.90	r	r
140.88	145	1.80	4.25	r	r	r	r
140.88	150	0.75	2.90	r	r	r	r

Exhibit 3 (*continued*)

Option & Underlying	Strike Price	Calls—Last			Puts—Last		
		Sep	Dec	Mar	Sep	Dec	Mar
50,000 Canadian Dollars—cents per unit.							
CDollr	71	r	r	r	r	0.21	r
73.96	73	1.16	r	r	0.22	r	r
73.96	74	0.51	r	r	r	r	r
73.96	75	0.15	r	r	r	r	2.35
62,500 West German Marks—cents per unit.							
DMark	30	4.80	r	r	r	r	r
34.89	31	3.81	r	r	r	0.17	r
34.89	32	2.95	3.44	r	0.07	0.32	r
34.89	33	1.97	2.66	3.20	0.19	0.58	r
34.89	34	1.41	2.04	2.46	0.46	r	r
34.89	35	0.72	1.50	2.03	0.78	1.32	r
34.89	36	0.40	1.00	1.53	r	r	r
34.89	37	0.17	0.73	r	r	s	r
125,000 French Francs—10ths of a cent per unit.							
FFranc	115	2.00	r	r	r	r	r
6,250,000 Japanese Yen—100ths of a cent per unit.							
JYen	38	r	4.05	r	0.01	r	r
41.85	39	r	3.17	r	r	r	r
41.85	40	1.90	2.31	r	r	r	r
41.85	41	1.12	1.54	r	r	r	r
41.85	42	0.59	1.03	r	0.63	r	r
41.85	43	0.21	0.72	r	r	r	r
41.85	44	0.10	r	r	r	r	r
62,500 Swiss Francs—cents per unit.							
SFranc	33	r	r	r	r	0.01	r
42.62	34	r	r	r	0.01	r	r
42.62	35	7.46	r	r	0.01	r	r
42.62	36	r	r	r	0.01	0.08	r
42.62	37	r	5.80	r	r	r	r
42.62	38	r	r	r	0.04	0.25	r
42.62	39	3.48	4.03	r	r	r	r
42.62	40	2.65	3.30	r	0.16	r	r
42.62	41	1.83	2.62	r	0.34	0.81	r
42.62	42	1.38	r	r	0.80	1.30	r
42.62	43	0.85	1.60	r	1.10	r	r
42.62	44	r	1.23	r	r	r	r
Total call vol.			6,712	Call open int.			178,827
Total put vol.			5,969	Put open int.			124,695

Gunter Dufey

Case 30

Options Trip

Janet Rabson had labored for many years in the accounting department of a medium sized construction company. Through hard work, intelligence and a bit of luck she worked her way up to the newly created Treasurer's job, a responsibility split off from those of the V.P. Finance and Controller. The company not only promoted her, but also agreed to pay for her training, especially since the company began to look seriously at construction projects overseas.

A great deal of Janet's time was taken up by haggling with bankers, and she was determined not to be taken advantage of, especially when it came to using new financial instruments. Thus she readily accepted the invitation of the Royal Bank of Scotland to a two-day seminar on options to be held in London.

The seminar, for which the bank hired an instructor from a U.S. business school, gave Janet lots of useful information about the use and abuse of options in corporate risk management. On the plane on the way home, the flight attendants handed out the *International Herald Tribune* and Janet, eager to catch up on the business news, saw an article that caught her attention. "Oh, how timely," she thought, "let's see whether we can't learn a trick or two from the clever Japanese!"

Exhibit 1 **Options Trip Japanese Exporters**
Price of "Zero-Cost" Dollar Tactic Was Lost Opportunity

Reuters

TOKYO — Japanese exporters lost out on the chance to make big profits when the dollar rose to 135 yen because they were forced to sell at much lower levels to cover currency option commitments, according to currency analysts.

What are called foreign exchange opportunity losses occurred in June, when the dollar rose above 127 yen on news of an unexpectedly small April U.S. trade deficit.

The rise triggered the exercising of dollar call options sold by exporters as part of a strategy called "zero-cost." The option holders required them to sell dollars below market prices.

"Japanese corporations lost the chance to sell dollars at higher levels, but real losses were probably few," said Tetsufumi Fujisawa, head option trader at Sumitomo Bank Ltd.

In a typical zero-cost option transaction to hedge against a falling dollar, an exporter buys a $10 million put option. This gives the exporter the right to sell dollars at a specified price, no matter how low the currency falls.

But the exporter must also sell a $30 million call option under this strategy. This option gives the other party, usually a bank, the right to buy dollars from the exporter, also at a predetermined price. This three-to-one ratio enables the party that sells the riskier put option to dispense with the premium that the buyer would normally pay, thus giving rise to the name "zero-cost."

Japanese exporting companies, especially car makers and electronics companies, which receive dollars from overseas sales, had been using zero-cost options heavily since February to hedge against a lower dollar, option traders said.

As long as the dollar was unchanged or falling, exporters could sell portions of their incoming dollars for yen at favorable prices.

Many Japanese exporters sold dollars aggressively after the release of good U.S. trade deficit numbers to keep the dollar from rising over the call option strike price, at which they would have to sell dollars cheaply, traders said.

"This strategy was quite successful until June, but in June a lot of the corporates got caught," said Arie Assayag, a currency options trader at Société Générale's Tokyo branch.

In June, dollar bullishness after a smaller-than-expected $10.3 billion April U.S. trade deficit overpowered sales of the currency by Japanese exporters.

The dollar, which traded around 125 yen on June 14, rose to close on June 22 above 127.50 yen for the first time in Tokyo in three months. It continued to soar and ended at the year's high for Tokyo of 135.15 yen on July 18.

Many exporters rushed to buy dollars in the spot market to cover option commitments.

This sudden rush for dollars helped add momentum to the currency's upward surge, traders said.

"When the dollar went up, a lot of people said, 'Hell, I want to change my mind,' but they couldn't," said an options specialist at a U.S. investment banking firm in Tokyo.

Japanese exporters "got a little cocky toward the end and probably ended up eroding some of the gains they had made on earlier transactions" in options, the specialist said.

Ironically, zero-cost options were originally designed by banks in part to induce Japanese corporations, which dislike paying premiums, to use options, traders said.

Many Japanese exporters calculate their break-even levels on a 125 yen dollar, so few companies actually lost money, traders said. With the dollar trading above 130 yen, exporters have been able to profit by selling dollars forward.

In addition, many companies had matched their call option commitments with dollar proceeds from overseas sales. Many exporters who were not matched evenly went to the currency swap market to borrow dollars owed on option commitments.

Other exporters hedged by buying dollars or straight-out call options to cover their positions, traders said.

"It's true that there were opportunity losses, but actual profits were much bigger," said Masao Kotani, vice president at Citibank's Tokyo branch.

Still, options traders said that zero-cost option trading, which until June accounted for 60 percent of the $6 billion to $10 billion monthly volume in the Tokyo over-the-counter corporate cash currency option market, declined sharply in July and August.

Japanese importers, seeing the possibility that the dollar may rise further, are starting to use zero-cost options to hedge against the currency's upside movement.

Source: Reuters, August 16, 1988.
Reprinted with permission.

"Hmm," Janet frowned, "What are they doing?! It doesn't make sense to me. I'd better draw some hockey sticks like we learned in the seminar! Then perhaps I can understand what's actually going on."

Ian H. Giddy

Case 31

An Order of French FRAs

Paris is an exciting place, especially since on your second day on the job in your bank's French affiliate, you have been asked to respond to a customer's request for a fifteen-month fixed rate French franc loan. Of course the bank is perfectly willing to make this loan. The only thing is that the French unit has had trouble accessing the interbank market for funds that far out: the best they can get at a reasonable cost — 14 percent to be precise — is a nine-month interbank placement. It seems that everyone is worried about another franc–D mark realignment beyond that period. So the Treasurer decided to go ahead and make the loan at a fixed fifteen-month rate, and fund only the first nine-month leg.

Where's the other leg? It's been dumped in your lap, of course, along with an article about Future Rate Agreements. All you know is that an

FRA is a sort of interbank interest rate futures contract, one where two parties agree to fix a future interest rate at a specified level for a specified future period. If, at the start of the specified period, the market rate (in this case French franc LIBOR) turns out to be different from the fixed-in-advance rate, the losing party compensates the winning party in cash.

Your boss knows this; but he wants to appear smarter than he actually is when he meets with the Treasurer, so he's asked you to find out:

(1) How exactly could a French FRA be used to fix the bank's cost of funding for the second leg of the loan?

(2) What would be reasonable quotes for a suitable FRA? Why?

(3) If the bank hedged its cost with an FRA at *x* percent, what would be the minimum rate it could charge on the loan and still make a ¾ percent spread?

(4) Should the customer be charged a fee up front for the cost of hedging? Why or why not?

(5) What would happen if after nine months' time, the six month interest rate is 2 percent lower than the rate agreed upon at the time the FRA was negotiated?

(6) What credit risk, if any, would the bank face if it hedged with one of these agreements?

Being a trader, your first reaction is to stare at the Reuters screen quotations of Euro French franc rates. You figure these rates would be available to your bank at least for up to nine months. But from there on in, you're on your own.

Exhibit 1 *Noonan Astley Eurocurrency Rates*

	US DLR	UK STLG	FR FRANCS	D MARKS
Call	10 – 10-1/8	10 – 10-1/8	—	—
2 Days	12-5/8 – 12-3/4	12-5/8 – 12-3/4	—	6-1/4 – 6-3/8
1 Week	11-3/4 – 11-7/8	11-3/4 – 11-7/8	12-1/8 – 12-1/4	7 – 7-1/8
1 Mo	11-3/8 – 11-1/2	11-7/8 – 12	12-1/8 – 12-1/4	7-1/4 – 7-3/8
3 Mo	11 – 11-1/8	12-1/4 – 12-3/8	13 – 13-1/8	7 – 7-1/8
6 Mo	10-1/2 – 10-5/8	12-1/2 – 12-5/8	14-1/4 – 14-3/8	6-1/2 – 6-5/8
9 Mo	10-1/4 – 10-3/8	12-1/2 – 12-5/8	13-7/8 – 14	6-1/2 – 6-5/8
12 Mo	10-1/4 – 10-3/8	12-1/2 – 12-5/8	13-5/8 – 13-3/4	6-1/2 – 6-5/8
15 Mo	10 – 10-1/8	—	13-1/4 – 13-3/8	6-1/4 – 6-3/8
18 Mo	9-3/4 – 9-7/8	—	13 – 13-1/4	6-1/4 – 6-3/8

REUTERS

Ian H. Giddy

Case 32

Banque Federale de Paris and the Cap Floater

In early 1990 Alexandre Fuchs, working at Banque Federale de Paris's London subsidiary, thought that the time was ripe for a revival of the "cap floater" concept. French rates were at painfully elevated levels and the vast majority of commentators seemed to think they had to come down. Alex had heard BFP's fixed-income salespeople echo this view, saying their clients either shared that outlook or at least did not think French rates could go much higher. And Fuchs had a customer, Svenske Skandelsbank, who, after opening a Paris office, wanted to obtain long-term French franc money to fund its EuroFF loan portfolio. Hence Alex and his colleagues had been making enquiries among the French institutional investor community about the possibility of underwriting a EuroFF floating rate note with a cap.

The cap floater first appeared in the Eurodollar floating rate note market in the mid-1980s. A borrower would issue an otherwise ordinary Eurobond with a floating rate that was reset periodically at a spread over six-month LIBOR (or sometimes three-month LIBOR). The floating rate note would pay a spread over LIBOR slightly higher than comparable uncapped floaters, but the rate would be subject to an absolute ceiling. For example, if LIBOR were 9 percent at the time of issue, the cap might be set at 13 percent. The investor's return would be limited by the cap, but if the cap were far enough above the current LIBOR level, he would not object too much. Indeed certain investors found the 25-50 basis points above comparable FRNs that the "cap floaters" offer very appealing.

Next, through an investment bank, the issuer would sell his interest rate insurance for an annual or upfront fee to another borrower who needed ceiling rate protection — and was willing to pay for it. This was called "stripping the cap from the floater".

BFP's Eurobond people had concluded that SSB could successfully issue FF 300 million ten year FRNs with a cap of 11 percent and an interest rate of ½ percent above three-month PIBOR, about 60 basis points more than SSB would ordinarily pay on a floater of this tenor. (Three month FF LIBOR was presently 8¾ percent, the six month rate was 9 percent. Indicative longer term rates were 9.5 percent for one year, 10 percent for three years, 11 percent for five and 11.5 percent for seven years and longer.) This was where the bank's vast distribution in the French domestic market was useful. The Swedish bank was willing to issue such a note and to sell the cap to BFP or another suitable counterparty. Selling the cap entailed an agreement to pay out the difference between PIBOR and 10½ percent, should the rate exceed that level. (The 10½ percent, rather than 11 percent, reflected the 50-basis point spread over LIBOR that SSB was paying on the FRN.)

This could be my first big deal, Alex thought, as long as our corporate finance people can find a French client who would want to buy the interest rate hedge. But before I push them, I had better figure out what price for the cap would make the deal profitable for all concerned, including BFP.

How should the deal be priced? Alex mused over the attached EuroFF cap and floor pricing sheet that BFP's interest rate products group was circulating at the time. Alex decided to diagram exactly how it worked, and who bore what risk when, before deciding on a minimum price for the cap to be sold.

Exhibit 1 BFP Euro-FF Cap and Floor Quotation Sheet

Caps	8.0%	8.5%	9.0%	9.5%	10.0%	10.5%	11.0%	11.5%	12.0%	12.5%
1 yr	0.52	0.37	0.27	0.21	0.16	0.13	0.11	0.09	0.08	0.07
2 yr	1.88	1.47	1.16	0.88	0.69	0.54	0.43	0.34	0.26	0.20
3 yr	3.79	3.12	2.56	2.10	1.71	1.40	1.14	0.92	0.76	0.62
4 yr	5.77	4.85	4.08	3.43	2.89	2.43	2.04	1.71	1.44	1.21
5 yr	7.74	6.63	5.67	4.86	4.15	3.55	3.03	2.59	2.23	1.91
6 yr	9.91	8.61	7.47	6.48	5.62	4.88	4.24	3.67	3.20	2.78
7 yr	12.06	10.59	9.29	8.15	7.16	6.29	5.52	4.85	4.27	3.78
8 yr	14.00	12.38	10.93	9.67	8.56	7.58	6.72	5.95	5.29	4.71
9 yr	15.73	13.99	12.43	11.05	9.83	8.76	7.81	6.96	6.22	5.57
10 yr	17.34	15.47	13.81	12.34	11.03	9.87	8.84	7.93	7.12	6.41
Floors	**6.00%**	**6.25%**	**6.50%**	**6.75%**	**7.00%**	**7.25%**	**7.50%**	**7.75%**	**8.00%**	**8.25%**
1 yr					0.01	0.06	0.10	0.18	0.26	0.37
2 yr			0.01	0.06	0.14	0.24	0.37	0.52	0.68	0.88
3 yr			0.07	0.16	0.26	0.40	0.59	0.08	1.02	1.30
4 yr		0.01	0.13	0.26	0.42	0.62	0.83	1.09	1.41	1.76
5 yr		0.08	0.24	0.42	0.65	0.91	1.19	1.54	1.90	2.33
6 yr	0.02	0.18	0.37	0.60	0.87	1.16	1.49	1.89	2.34	2.81
7 yr	0.13	0.30	0.55	0.79	1.10	1.46	1.86	2.29	2.79	3.34
8 yr	0.23	0.46	0.73	1.03	1.39	1.79	2.24	2.74	3.30	3.90
9 yr	0.46	0.72	1.03	1.38	1.77	2.22	2.72	3.27	3.88	4.54
10 yr	0.71	1.00	1.34	1.73	2.17	2.66	3.21	3.81	4.47	5.19

Gunter Dufey

Case 33

Desperately Seeking L/C
An article from Business Week

Turning to Japan for Cut-Rate Loans

Japan's fears of losing control over its currency have virtually barred overseas borrowers in recent years from the country's capital markets, where the prime rate is 6.75 percent for short-term money and 8.9 percent for long-term. But a few U.S. airlines have zeroed in on a financing scheme that has opened the yen-lending window — at least for the moment. Unless the Japanese government changes the rules, the new device — called a deferred-purchase agreement — seems sure to spread. It could offer cut-rate financing for oil rigs, ships, and other costly equipment, as well as airplanes.

Moreover, Japan is considering opening a second cheap-money win-

Source: Reprinted from the November 23, 1981 issue of *Business Week* by special permission, © 1981 by McGraw-Hill, Inc. Adapted for case discussion by Gunter Dufey, The University of Michigan, 1981.

dow by resurrecting the dollar-denominated "Samurai lease." That was a 1978 ploy to cut Japan's trade surplus with the United States and dump excess dollars.

Trying for more. Only two of the new deferred-purchase agreements have been struck so far: the first by Continental Airlines, Inc. in May and the second by PSA Inc. in August. In both cases, a group of Japanese trading companies led by Marubeni Corp. bought airplanes, which Continental and PSA had on order, from U.S. manufacturers. The airlines then bought the planes from the trading companies on ten-year, yen-denominated credit with 20 percent down. The Japanese required the carriers to buy letters of credit from U.S. banks guaranteeing repayment. After all costs and a lending spread for the Japanese companies, Continental is paying a fixed rate of 11.2 percent on its $58 million in yen debt, and PSA is paying 10.5 percent on $78 million. The carriers would be paying 17 percent or more for U.S. financing.

Continental is so ecstatic about its deal that, although it has no more planes on order, it is negotiating to refinance $40 million of its existing planes in Japan. That would cut $2.5 million from 1982 interest costs, figures the airline's financial vice-president, Roy M. Rawls. Flying Tiger Line Inc., a big freight airline, hopes to sign a yen refinancing deal reportedly valued at $80 million in a few weeks. Hawaii's Aloha Airlines Inc. is negotiating a $27 million deal.

The debts must be repaid in yen, so the risk is that the costs of repayment could soar if the yen surges against the dollar. Because Continental and Flying Tiger generate ample yen revenue from flying Pacific routes, they need not worry much about exchange rates. PSA is another story. The West Coast airline receives only modest yen revenue, so it must buy the bulk of its semiannual debt payment of 1.4 billion yen (about $6.2 million at current exchange rates) in the open market. PSA does not plan to hedge in the futures market because the company believes the cost would cancel the interest rate advantage. Its vulnerability to exchange rates prompted Bank of America and Crocker National Bank to refuse to issue PSA the required letter of credit. On its third try, PSA got one from a group of four banks led by First National Bank of Chicago. "PSA is betting the company," chides one banker, noting that the airline yen debt equals 54 percent of its $145 million net worth.

PSA insists it is not taking undue risks. Its president, Paul C. Barkley, accepts the general belief that the yen will strengthen against the dollar. But even under the airline's worst-case assumption — a dollar worth only 160 yen, versus 228 yen at present — Barkley figures the company's yen-borrowing costs should not exceed the cost of borrowing in dollars. If they threaten to do so, PSA might yet hedge in yen futures. The cheap financing, meanwhile, would mean savings of about $5 million a year at current rates — a welcome economy for a carrier that has been operating at a loss.

Another source? Meanwhile, Japan's Finance Ministry is mulling the reintroduction of the "Samurai lease." Under a short-lived program in 1978, Japanese trading companies bought U.S. airplanes with dollars borrowed cheaply from the Japanese government. That qualified the planes as U.S. exports to Japan, cutting Japan's trade surplus. Then the Japanese companies leased them at cut rates to European, Canadian, and Asian airlines for payment in dollars. Many U.S. airlines asked for Samurai leases, but Japan decided that importing U.S. planes, then exporting them to the U.S., would be little more than a statistical mirage.

The Finance Ministry — prodded by the Ministry of International Trade and Industry — is considering resurrecting these leases and offering them to U.S. companies. Opinion is split on whether the leases will resurface. However, Aloha Airlines, for one, is postponing signing its deferred purchase deal in the hope of getting a Samurai lease instead.

U.S. equipment buyers hope Japan at least continues to allow deferred purchases. U.S. bankers say there is no reason the device could not be used to finance any capital equipment, including factories, although movable goods are preferred in case of defaults. One hindrance is a Financial Accounting Standards Board rule requiring companies to change the reported value of foreign-denominated debt as exchange rates fluctuate. If the yen strengthens, PSA and Continental must take currency translation write-offs on their entire yen debt, which hurts profits. The FASB is expected to revise the rule by year end, however, and it may limit write-offs to current portions of foreign debt.

The main worry is that Japan's Finance Ministry might ban deferred purchases if they become too widespread. It came close to killing the device in May when Continental Airlines announced that it had secured a "loan" from "three Japanese lenders." Marubeni argued successfully that the deal was not a loan and hence did not fall under the ministry's jurisdiction. Says Continental's Rawls: "As far as I'm concerned, you can call it a 'deferred pig in a poke' as long as the rate is 11 percent."

The article had been passed around and the meeting of senior credit officers at Metrobank's Airlines Division was drawing to a close. Decisions had now to be made on providing letters of credit (L/Cs) to the three U.S. carriers mentioned in the article. All three were seeking L/Cs to back up their forthcoming "deferred-purchase agreements" which apparently provided low-cost yen financing.

"None of these is a top-notch credit," said the first banker, "and a letter of credit has just as much credit risk as a loan, and the Fed is about to apply capital requirements against our L/Cs. I don't like it. On the other hand Coastbank has turned PSA down, which probably means it's a strong credit."

"I know what a letter of credit is," said the second banker. "The point is that we can get a decent fee for once and this financing reduces these airlines' costs. My only concern is about the exchange risk when an American airline borrows yen, especially in Japan where passenger fares are controlled."

"But isn't that just a paper exposure based on currency transaction? And won't that all change when the FASB revises its rules and replaces FAS 8 with FAS 52?" asked the third banker.

There was a moment's silence. Then the rookie credit officer blurted out: "This may be a dumb question, but what routes do these airlines fly, and who is their competition?"

The first banker replied, "Continental Airlines flies routes between Tokyo and Guam, Samoa, and other U.S. possessions, carrying primarily Japanese tourists in competition with Air Nippon. It also flies between Denver, Houston, and Washington, D.C. Flying Tigers carries live cattle from the western U.S. to Japan (the sukiyaki run), while returning with Japanese consumer electronics and similar cargo. It is in competition with NWO, UAL, PANAM, JAL, KAL, and THAI.

"PSA flies primarily between SFO and LAX, and other points on the West Coast. On these routes it carries a goodly number of Japanese businessmen who like the smiling faces on the planes and the friendly flight attendants.

"Let me summarize the issues. First, given that the creditworthiness of all three airlines seems equally precarious, to which of these three airlines — Continental, PSA, or Flying Tiger — should we grant an L/C? Do any of them really face exchange risk, and if so, why? Is there any crucial additional information that we need?

"Second, what do you think of Barkley's argument that he can always hedge his company's yen debt with futures?

"Finally, why are these American carriers so excited about yen financing? Is there some apparent market imperfection or arbitrage opportunity?"

Special Issues: Taxation, Control and Reporting

Ian H. Giddy and Christine Weisfelder

Case 34

Dallas Semiconductor Company
An Exercise in International Tax Planning

Don Mardick, Assistant Treasurer of the Dallas Semiconductor Company, was considering a discussion he had just had with his new assistant. This young fellow, newly graduated from business school, was brimming over with suggestions for the improvement of the international cash management function. He had no idea, Don thought, of how difficult it is to manipulate the accounting and transfer prices of some well-entrenched overseas subsidiaries. Nevertheless, he was intrigued by the suggestion that the company's international tax burden could be reduced by altering the legal structure or the intracompany pricing policies of the worldwide company.

Don decided he would have to undertake a systematic review of foreign-source earnings, foreign taxes paid, and U.S. taxes associated with each of the firm's foreign affiliates. This done, Don could assess his assistant's suggestion that the group's after-tax earnings could be increased by persuading the firm's Belgian subsidiary to lower prices on components shipped to the assembly plant in Taiwan. Tapping out some numbers on his calculator, Don figured that this strategy might increase the Taiwan unit's pre-tax earnings by $10 million (and reduce profits in the Belgian unit by the same amount). He decided to try to compute the effect of this transfer price change on his 1992 taxes and income after taxes, assuming nothing else had changed.

Don glanced at the Dallas Company's 1992 results for overseas operations. Forty-eight percent of the company's total pre-tax earnings, amounting to $245.76 million, had been earned abroad. By the end of 1991, Dallas had accumulated $25.5 million in excess foreign tax credits, of which $5 million could not be carried forward beyond the 1992 tax year.

In 1992, the wholly-owned German subsidiary had before-tax earnings of $80 million. Its policy had been to declare a dividend of 50 percent of before-tax earnings in order to take advantage of the lower German tax rate on distributed profits. The subsidiary reported that it also had paid $40 million in value-added taxes (VAT) to the German government in 1992. Don suspected that in the United States, the VAT could not be included in allowable taxes for the foreign tax credit to offset the U.S. tax on foreign earnings.

Dallas Semiconductor's biggest operation was its wholly-owned European headquarters and manufacturing plant, located outside Brussels. In 1992, the before-tax earnings of this subsidiary had been $260 million. It declared a dividend of 50 percent of after-tax earnings.

The company also had a minor (7 percent) interest in a French electronics company, which in 1992 had declared dividends of $90 million (from before-tax earnings of $150 million). Don had heard that Dallas Semiconductor was considering increasing its ownership to 10 percent, at a cost of $16 million, and he wondered what the tax effects would be.

In addition to its European operations, Dallas Semiconductor had two affiliates in the Far East. In Singapore, it owned 50 percent of a joint venture with a local company that manufactured standard electronic components for export to the United States. In 1992, the Singapore affiliate declared a $10 million dividend on pre-tax earnings of $14.49 million.

The other Far East affiliate was a wholly-owned assembly operation in Taiwan, an investment structured to meet the approval of the Investment Commission and thus qualify for government tax subsidization. In 1992, the Taiwanese affiliate reported before-tax earnings of $30 million. It was Dallas Semiconductor's policy that the affiliate should pay out 100 percent of its after-tax earnings as a dividend.

Don knew, of course, that shifting income from one subsidiary to another could reduce foreign taxes, but he wondered whether any savings in Belgium would not be offset by an increase in taxes owed to the United

States. He recalled that the U.S. foreign tax credit was limited to the amount of taxes that would have been paid, had the income been earned within the United States. He also recalled that in the United States, foreign-source income (and its associated taxes) had to be allocated into "baskets" for foreign tax credit purposes.

As he began his computations, Don also thought about some of his assistant's other suggestions. Would changing the legal form from wholly-owned subsidiary to branch benefit Dallas? What would be the drawbacks? And could he reduce worldwide taxes by creating a holding company for the German subsidiary, one incorporated in a low-tax jurisdiction such as the Bahamas, and then channeling the German income into the subsidiary? He wondered whether the low tax rates of the Bahamas would offset the 25 percent withholding tax rate on dividends from Germany to a nontreaty country. Before he sought approval from the U.S. tax authorities for any changes, he wanted to understand the potential benefits and obstacles.

Exhibit 1 Dallas Semiconductor Co.[1]

| Country | National Corporate Rate[2] | Tax Base | Dividend Withholding Tax to U.S. Recipient | |
			Rate	Ownership
U.S.	34%	All profits	—	—
Bahamas	0%	—	0%	—
Belgium	39%	All profits	15% 5%	under 10% 10% or more
France	42% 34%	Retained profits Distributed profits	15% 5%	under 10% 10% or more
Germany	51.875% 37.350%	Retained profits Distributed profits	15% 5%	under 25% 25% or more
Singapore	31%	All profits derived within Singapore	0%	any
Taiwan	25%	All profits	20%[3]	any

[1] Valid as of 1992. Source of tax information: *1992 International Tax Summaries,* Coopers & Lybrand International Tax Network.

[2] For simplicity, assume that *all* corporate income is taxed at the highest rates shown; in actuality, most countries apply a lower rate to profits under a given threshold. Without the "solidarity surcharge" applied for the costs of unification, the German tax rates would have been 50 percent and 36 percent, respectively, for retained and distributed profits. The surcharge was in effect from July 1, 1991, to June 30, 1992. Thus, the additional 7.5 percent concerns half the income of two tax years (or 3.75 percent for each year).

[3] The rate is increased to 35 percent when the investment is not approved by the Investment Commission.

Ian H. Giddy

Case 35

Limpopo Hydro

THE WHIZZES OF OZ

John Mbeki was preparing a presentation to senior financial executives of Overseas Zimbabwe, the newly privatized flag airline of the Republic of Zimbabwe. An ambitious young technocrat who had risen in the Republic's civil service, Mbeki was keen to make a good showing of his explanation of the specialized, lease-based financing structure that he had helped engineer as Director of Financing for Limpopo Hydro.

John had compiled a set of handouts illustrating the financing, but he anticipated the major question would be: Did the technique have general applicability beyond the hydroelectric plant financing for which it had been used? For example, could it be used to finance aircraft? What, in fact, were the key elements that made a financial structure like this work? And what might be the stumbling blocks to its application elsewhere?

XYZ COMPANY AND LIMPOPO HYDRO INC.

Limpopo Hydro, Inc. was an autonomous company 100 percent owned by the Xholi Ymuprbubul Zimbabwe (XYZ) Company, the state monopoly for energy production and distribution in the Republic. In the past the Republic had done all international financing directly or by XYZ with a government guarantee. In practice XYZ had not had to tap the international markets because it had sufficient internal resources to engage in new investments. Recently, however, expansion needs exceeded funds available internally; moreover the Government of Zimbabwe had pressured state companies to borrow on their own credit standing. This in turn led XYZ to seek targeted "project financing" for self-contained projects such as the Limpopo hydroelectric venture. Wherever possible, each project was set up as a separate subsidiary with revenues used to service its own debt.

THE LIMPOPO HYDRO PROJECT

As a developing African country, Zimbabwe had rapidly increasing energy requirements. The new hydroelectric facility on the Limpopo River was expected to provide clean, low-cost electric power not only for the country itself but also for export through a power grid that encompassed South Africa, Mozambique and Malawi. Thus the plant was expected to be an important source of foreign exchange as well as energy for Zimbabwe.

The project entailed a pioneering "non-dam hydro" technique that was regarded as less damaging environmentally than conventional methods. The specialized equipment required for the Limpopo River's erratic seasonal flows had to be imported from the United States and the United Kingdom. Total cost of the equipment and construction had been US$302 million, of which $287 million was from the United States and the remainder from the United Kingdom. The project construction was to be done

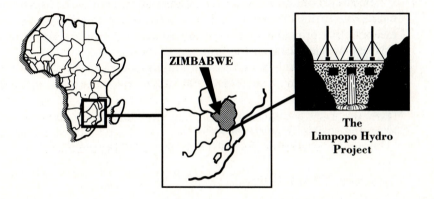

The
**Limpopo Hydro
Project**

and the equipment brought in by a U.S. contracting firm that would "build, operate and transfer" (BOT) so that after a decade the facility would be fully staffed by trained Zimbabweans. Payment was to take place in a series of installments over 11 years.

THE FINANCING

The equipment purchased from the United Kingdom was financed by British banks on market terms. The core of the U.S. financing, however, involved the Export-Import Bank of the United States. Eximbank typically provided support for U.S. exports by guaranteeing long term financing, particularly when the purpose of the funding enjoyed congressional support; in other words, when the financing fit U.S. foreign policy objectives. Such was the case with the Limpopo project.

As a result, XYZ was able to finance 85 percent (Eximbank's maximum) of the U.S. purchase with an Eximbank guarantee.[1] (See Exhibit 1.) The UK portion was too small to qualify for an ECGD (Britain's export credit agency) guarantee. The sterling amount was therefore borrowed from UK banks on market terms at a floating rate. The U.S. dollar financing was broken into two parts. The first was 11-year financing guaranteed by Eximbank: a syndicated bank loan at a floating rate of LIBOR + .30 percent which would be refinanced after 2½ years by a fixed rate loan from PEFCO, the Private Export Financing Company.[2] The PEFCO loan would be amortized over the 8½ years and had an average life of 7 years; the rate was Treasury plus 0.70 percent (the 7-year U.S. Treasury Bond yield plus 0.70 percent). The second was a 7-year fixed rate borrowing, with a 5.2-year average life, in the form of a private placement of notes with U.S. insurance companies at Treasury+400 basis points (the 5.2-year U.S. Treasury Bond yield plus 4.00 percent).[3] Eximbank agreed that the private placement would rank *parri pasu* (of equal rank) with Eximbank's claim.

Both portions carried an indirect guarantee from XYZ. As for repayment, the Eximbank-guaranteed debt had a grace period of 2½ years, meaning that principal repayments would start only in 2½ years, while the private placement had a 2-year grace period.

Each part of the U.S. dollar financing had some complexities that challenged the creativity of the finance staff at Limpopo Hydro. Eximbank had

---

[1] Eximbank, in turn, required that Limpopo Hydro's debt carry a full guarantee from its parent company, Xholi Ymurprbubul Zimbabwe.

[2] Eximbank's commitment fee of 1.8 percent and its country risk fee of 3.88 percent were included in the amount financed.

[3] As a comparison, it was estimated that the debt part of conventional project financing would cost about Treasury+350–450bp.

never been involved in a hydro project quite like this one so the U.S. agency took considerable persuading. That delayed the financing, so XYZ was forced to finance the project for the first seven months with only a verbal assurance from Eximbank that things would work out.[4] The bank portion was provided by a consortium of international banks with the Bank of New York as lead manager. The fixed-rate portion was also arranged by the Bank of New York and placed with a number of different insurance companies. Because of all the parties involved, as many as 41 separate contracts had to be drawn up!

However the most important feature of the U.S. dollar financing was that it was structured not as conventional debt, but as lease financing.

THE LEASE FINANCING STRUCTURE

Lease financing is a technique whereby the user of equipment has a contract to rent it from a leasing company and make periodic lease payments rather than owning it. The leasing company (lessor), not the user (lessee), owns the equipment. The lease payments received by the leasing company are used to pay interest and principal on monies borrowed to purchase the equipment; indeed it is typical for the lessee to guarantee that payments will be sufficient to service the lessor's debt. A significant advantage to the user is that lease payments are generally *fully* tax deductible, while principal payments made to amortize debt are not. (The few profitable state-owned companies in Zimbabwe were taxed at a high effective rate, estimated by some to be about 75 percent.) A condition for this is that the lease is regarded for tax purposes as a true lease, which normally requires that the lessor does not automatically take possession of the equipment at the expiration of the lease.

The deal was arranged as follows. (See Exhibit 2.) Limpopo Hydro set up a special leasing company, LH Leasing Co., in Zimbabwe. LH Leasing bought $287 million of equipment from another special purpose vehicle set up in the Bahama Islands, LH Bahamas Inc, and agreed to repay the debt in installment payments over 11 years. LH Bahamas borrowed the $287 million from the banks and insurance companies as described above, using the funds to purchase the equipment from suppliers. LH Bahamas also engaged in BOT contract concession agreements with the sellers of the equipment. The shares of LH Bahamas were held in a Trust (also in the Bahamas), and 85 percent of LH Bahamas' debt was guaranteed indirectly by the U.S. Eximbank. Because the debt was issued in the Bahamas

---

[4] Prior to this deal, Mbeki and his colleagues had no experience in dealing with export financing agencies. In fact they had no experience in international long-term financing or even in bank borrowing.

the interest was not subject to withholding tax, and a clause in the loan agreements stated that Limpopo Hydro would "gross up" the interest payments if ever such a tax were imposed by Zimbabwe, the Bahamas or any other applicable jurisdiction.

As a result LH Leasing owned the hydroelectric equipment and owed installment payments, in U.S. dollars, to LH Bahamas for 11 years. LH Leasing then leased the equipment to Limpopo Hydro. Lease payments would be made by Limpopo Hydro to LH Leasing in Zimbabwe dollars,[5] in amounts sufficient to cover the installment payments that LH Leasing had to make to LH Bahamas. These Z$ cash flows were guaranteed by XYZ. The arrangement had tax benefits of two kinds. First, as noted above, lease payments are fully tax deductible so Limpopo Hydro obtained a tax shelter on what were in effect its entire debt servicing payments. Second, a 5 percent withholding tax would normally be imposed on interest paid by a Zimbabwean company to foreigners; but the tax does not apply to installment payments, so LH Leasing avoided this tax.

In any leasing structure it is imperative that the leasing company has tax deductible costs equal to its revenues so that it pays no taxes. LH Leasing was able to ensure that it would not be liable for any taxes in Zimbabwe because accelerated depreciation over 8½ years would create deductible costs equal to revenues. An operating company such as Limpopo Hydro could only depreciate equipment over its useful life of 15½ years. Since the equipment was being installed during the first 2½ years, payments received in this period from Limpopo Hydro were regarded for tax purposes as advance payments. LH Leasing booked revenues over the remaining 8½ years, and depreciated the equipment over the same period. Exhibit 3 illustrates this.

THE INTEREST RATE OPTION

To add a final measure of complexity, the financing deal was arranged in such a way as to give Limpopo Hydro a measure of flexibility on the fixed interest rate to be paid to PEFCO upon refinancing of the bank debt. The fixed interest rate did not have to be set immediately: Limpopo Hydro had the right to pay a floating rate at first (at LIBOR+0.30 percent to the Bank of New York syndicate), and fix the rate at any time in the first 2½ years, at the market level at the time. When Limpopo Hydro decided to fix the rate, the bank debt would be replaced by fixed rate PEFCO debt. For this the company paid a 0.125 percent commitment fee up front, and a 0.375 per-

---

[5] The exchange rate at the time was US$1=Z$4.9.

cent commitment fee at the time of fixing for any undisbursed funds. At the time the deal was done, the 7-year U.S. Treasury bond rate was 5.9 percent and 6-month LIBOR was 3.75 percent. The 5.2 year Treasury rate was 5.1 percent.

Questions
1. Using the diagram in Exhibit 2, explain how the deal was structured.
2. The lease payments were to be made in Zimbabwe dollars, while the ultimate debt was denominated in U.S. dollars. Explain what would happen if the Zimbabwe dollar falls against the U.S. dollar.
3. Explain the tax benefits of the leasing structure.
4. What do you think happens to the equipment after 11 years?
5. Could this financing structure be applied to other projects such as aircraft purchases? What might be the obstacles to its application elsewhere?
6. How valuable do you think the interest rate protection is to Limpopo Hydro? How would the lenders protect themselves?

Exhibit 1 **Composition of financing of Limpopo Hydro Project**

Financing Source	Amount, US$ equiv.	Currency	Guarantees	Rate
UK bank	$15 million	£	XYZ	£LIBOR+2.65%
U.S. bank syndicate, then PEFCO	$244 million	US$	U.S. Eximbank and XYZ	$LIBOR+.30%, then T+0.75
Private placements with U.S. insurance companies	$34 million	US$	XYZ	$LIBOR+2%, then T+4.00%

Exhibit 2 *Structure of the lease financing*

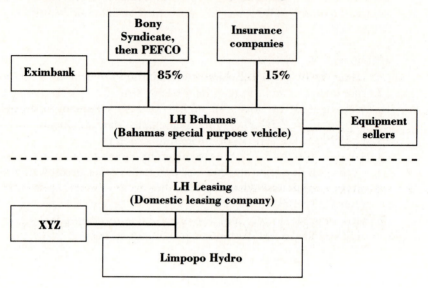

Exhibit 3 *Tax treatment of lease payments paid by Limpopo Hydro to LH Leasing*

CONSTRUCTION PERIOD	LEASE PERIOD
Advance payments: no taxable revenues	Taxable lease payments offset by depreciation of the equipment, so no taxes paid
$2\frac{1}{2}$ years	$8\frac{1}{2}$ years

M. Edgar Barrett

Case 36

Multiquimica do Brasil

"I'm really concerned about our position in Brazil. Our pharmaceutical products are being hurt by both local and foreign producers and our foreign exchange policies may well be to blame." So said Don Howard, controller of the foreign operations of the pharmaceutical group of Multichemical Industries, Inc. "Look at Levadol, for example, our sales are falling while those of Hoffman et Cie are up."[1]

This conversation took place in February 1983 as Don was reviewing the 1982 results of the foreign operations of the pharmaceutical group with the group's general manager, Paul McConnell. The men were in the company's corporate offices in Houston, Texas.

---

[1] Hoffman et Cie was a large, multinational firm based in Bern, Switzerland.

Exhibit 1 **Multiquimica do Brasil Financial Data:**
Consolidated Corporate Results (in millions of dollars)

	1982	1981
Income statement		
Sales		
Agricultural chemicals	$ 658	$ 600
Industrial chemicals	583	513
Petrochemicals	652	585
Pharmaceutical products	1,210	1,086
Subtotal	$3,103	$2,784
Cost of goods sold	1,300	1,169
Selling and administrative expense	884	793
Depreciation	296	262
Research expense	292	250
Subtotal	$2,772	$2,474
Operating income	$ 331	$ 310
Interest expense	45	42
Other income—net	41	30
Subtotal	$ 4	$ 12
Income before taxes	327	298
Income taxes	126	110
Net income	$ 201	$ 188
Balance sheet		
	1982	**1981**
Current assets	$1,016	$1,001
Net property, plant, and equipment	1,536	1,338
Other assets	241	139
Total assets	$2,793	$2,478
Current liabilities	363	297
Long-term debt	394	309
Deferred income taxes	140	124
Stockholders' equity	1,896	1,748
Total liabilities and stockholders' equity	$2,793	$2,478

Source: Multichemical Industries Inc. 1982 Annual Report.

BACKGROUND

Multichemical Industries Inc. sold seventy-five different products in over fifty countries during 1982. Sales for the year were $3.1 billion (see Exhibit 1 for financial data). The company's principal product groups were: pharmaceuticals; industrial chemicals; agricultural chemicals; and petrochemicals. Multichemical's overseas subsidiaries accounted for 35 percent of sales in 1982, with the majority of the activity taking place in Europe.

Multiquimica do Brasil (MB) was responsible for all sales and manufacturing that took place in Brazil. Thus, its managers had responsibility for products in several of the firm's product groups. Sales during the year were $65 million, 6 percent of foreign sales. This wholly owned subsidiary was formed in 1977 with the initial purpose of establishing manufacturing facilities for agricultural chemical, industrial chemical, and pharmaceutical products in Brazil. Prior to that time, Multichemical had been active in Brazil through export sales. In other words, products that were manufactured in the United States had been sold in Brazil through local, independent importers. Multichemical did not operate either manufacturing facilities or a division office in the country until 1977.

The new subsidiary began manufacturing and selling herbicides in 1977. MB did not show a profit until 1980. The losses that were incurred were primarily attributable to two factors: the large startup costs associated with a new business and a weak economic period in Brazil. As a result of the losses sustained during the 1977 to 1980 period, MB was entitled to a substantial amount of tax loss carryforwards on its Brazilian tax return.[2]

In late 1979, the company installed a manufacturing plant to process Levadol, an aspirin-free pain reliever. Such facilities were included in the original operating plans for MB. They were scheduled, however, for the early 1980s. They went onstream sooner than originally planned due to an increase in the amount of duty on imports.

The manufacture of this product involved shipping the raw materials in bulk form from the United States. The raw materials were formulated, converted into tablet form, and packaged in the Brazilian plant and then sold to distributors. MB sales of Levadol in 1982 were $6.8 million.

PRODUCT AND PRICING FLOW FOR LEVADOL

The raw materials for Levadol were shipped from a domestic subsidiary of Multichemical to MB. The invoiced price for transferred goods during

[2] The term "tax loss carryforward" refers to the fact that net operating losses, to the extent that they exceed taxable income of the preceding three years, can be carried forward, thus reducing future taxable income.

1982 averaged $60/case equivalent. The invoice was denominated in U.S. dollars.

The cost of goods sold on MB's books for Levadol averaged $131/case. This figure included the $60/case raw material costs, plus $31/case for import duty and $40/case to formulate, convert, and package it.

The product was sold to wholesalers serving both drug stores and chain stores, usually on ninety-day payment terms, for a price of approximately $218/case. The $87/case difference between the sales price and the cost of goods sold consisted of marketing costs (roughly 20 percent of sales), administration, distribution, and interest expenses and approximately a 5 percent profit margin before taxes. The distributors, in turn, usually added a 10 to 20 percent margin. This was designed to both cover their costs and provide a profit margin.

DOLLAR LINKAGE BILLING

On their tax and fiscal books, MB benefited from a system known as dollar linkage billing. A statement on the invoice that was sent from the domestic subsidiary to MB said, "payable at the exchange rate in effect on the date of the receipt of goods." (Management books, on the other hand, were kept on the assumption that the invoice was to be paid in dollars — thus, effectively, using the exchange rate in effect at the time of payment.)

Brazilian law, at the time, required 180-day payment terms on imports. Since the Brazilian cruzeiro lost value in relation to the dollar on a more or less continuous basis, a foreign exchange loss would normally show up on a Brazilian firm's cruzeiro-denominated books. Given the above-mentioned system, however, the foreign exchange loss showed up on the U.S. tax books.

DOMESTIC SALES WITHIN BRAZIL

Even within the context of the Brazilian domestic market, MB's reported profit in dollar terms was affected by the more or less continuous devaluation of the cruzeiro. The major problem here was tied to the fact that competition had forced MB to offer ninety-day payment terms to their customers. Given the fact that the cruzeiro was formally devalued approximately once every ten days, any domestic subsidiary with terms of ninety days was faced with a translation loss whenever its books were translated back into dollar terms.[3]

---

[3] This "translation loss" would be caused by the fact that the *dollar value* of the original *cruzeiro denominated* sale would exceed the *dollar value* of the actual *cruzeiro denominated* collection of the account receivable some 90 days later.

In an attempt to deal with the situation, MB put into place a method known as "forward pricing." Under the assumptions of this method, MB's management predicted the amount of cruzeiro devaluation that would occur during the forthcoming ninety days. This estimate then served as the basis for raising the then-current sales price. In other words, they passed along the expected loss due to the devaluation of the cruzeiro to the customer. As a result of this policy, product prices were revised at least monthly.

HEDGING POLICIES

From 1977 to 1979, the annual inflation rate in Brazil was in the general range of 30 to 50 percent. In 1979, however, Brazil — which imported the vast majority of its crude oil — began to feel the effects of the increasing price of crude oil. As a result, the domestic inflation rate took off *and* the cruzeiro was devalued by 30 percent during the year. MB reacted by pushing up its prices, a policy which it continued to adhere to throughout 1982.

Beginning in late 1979, the corporate treasurer's office of Multichemical began to "encourage" MB to borrow locally. Such a policy was designed to match assets and liabilities in cruzeiro terms and thus offset the translation loss on assets with a translation gain on liabilities. By having the subsidiaries borrow locally, the corporate treasurer was hoping to eliminate the risk of having to report large translation losses on the corporate income statement. Local borrowing, in essence, helped to smooth the corporation's reported income stream by substituting a periodic interest expense for less frequent, but presumably larger, losses due to translation. There was a cost, however. The nominal interest rate in Brazil in 1982 was approximately 160 percent. (See Exhibit 2 for foreign exchange and inflation rate data.)

PERFORMANCE MEASUREMENT POLICIES

Multichemical had recently changed its internal reporting system. Previous to the change, operating managers had been held responsible for the performance of their units as measured by the "operating income" figures. This meant that items such as other income, other expense, interest expense, and translation gains and losses were not focused upon in the quarterly business results review meetings. Over time, the senior management at the corporate level had come to feel that this system of performance measurement ignored the impact of some business decisions which could (or should) be taken by some of the operating managers in question.

Exhibit 2   Multiquimica do Brasil
Yearend foreign exchange rates (per U.S. dollar)

	Brazilian Cruzeiro	Swiss Franc
1976	12.34	2.45
1977	16.05	2.00
1978	20.92	1.62
1979	42.53	1.58
1980	65.50	1.76
1981	127.80	1.80
1982	252.67	1.99

Source: *International Financial Statistics,* International Monetary Fund.

Consumer price index numbers and yearly percentage changes

	Brazil		Switzerland		U.S.	
1976	254.3		147.3		146.6	
1977	357.3	.41	149.2	.01	156.1	.06
1978	494.2	.38	150.8	.01	167.9	.08
1979	742.5	.50	156.2	.04	187.2	.11
1980	1321.2	.78	162.5	.04	212.4	.13
1981	2584.9	.96	173.1	.07	234.1	.10
1982	6394.7*	1.47	182.8	.06	248.2	.06

* Estimated
Source: *Monthly Bulletin of Statistics,* United Nations, February 1983, p. 200.

After a thorough study of both the then-existing internal reporting system and a set of alternative systems, a new system was designed and introduced. "Full Responsibility Accounting," as the new system was called, was made effective with the 1983 data. Under the terms of this new system, both individual product managers and product group managers were to be held responsible for the relationship between their profit after tax figures and the net assets under their control on both a worldwide and a "major" country basis. The term "net assets" for a particular subunit of the overall corporation was defined as net property (gross property less accumulated depreciation) plus net working capital. Thus, both individual product managers and product group managers now bore some of the responsibility for such items as interest expense, translation gains and losses, and the amount and composition of both short- and long-term assets.

The new system was designed with the intention that it would, among other things, force top management to delegate expansion and curtailment decisions to lower levels. The individual product managers and their superiors (the product group managers), sometimes in conjunction with an (geographic) area manager, were to have total responsibility for the assets that they employed in the process of producing, distibuting, and selling their particular product. The firm's capital budgeting and operational budgeting systems were to be altered such that the full year's capital expenditures would be approved at once and there would be agreement reached during the operational budgeting cycle as to the appropriate levels for inventories and receivables for the budget year in question.

While the new system was very focused upon a return on assets figure, two other measures were to receive emphasis under the terms of the new program. Both net income and cash flow were to be measured and monitored. The former would be measured against a budgeted target and the latter would be assessed in respect to an understanding of the underlying strategy for the subunit. Thus a subunit with a growth strategy might be expected to generate little or no cash (or indeed, even use cash) over a short- to medium-term time period.

Of particular concern to product group managers, such as Paul McConnell, was the fact that he was now responsible for both translation gains and losses *and* interest expense, the latter of which could be very high in the case of local borrowing. Fortunately, the translation losses that were to be reported were to be highly specific in nature. That is, they were to be directly traced to specific items on the local subsidiary balance sheets and, thus, would be tied to items directly related to the pharmaceutical group's products. Interest expense and translation gains, on the other hand, were not easily identified with such specific items. This lack of easy identification was caused by the fact that the corporate treasurer would sum all of the Brazilian borrowings and then allocate both translation gains and interest expense to each product group based on a formula tied primarily to sales.

COMPETITION

MB had been able to successfully position Levadol such that a significant amount of the population asked for Levadol when they wanted an aspirin-free pain reliever. This had become an important issue as the product became more widely stocked by the various grocery chains and cooperatives (with their open, free-standing shelves). Every year MB sold a greater amount of Levadol through grocery stores than it had the year before. During 1982, it was estimated that 60 percent of the retail sales of all aspirin-free pain relievers in Brazil took place in grocery stores, while the remaining 40 percent were sold through some type of drug related outlet.

During 1982, MB lost both volume and market share on Levadol. Over

36,000 cases of Levadol were sold in 1980. Fewer than 32,000 were sold in 1982 (see Table 1 for volume and market share data). Although it was considered a premium product, an increasing number of distributors were reacting to the recession by substituting lower cost product.

MB's primary competition during 1982 was the Swiss firm Hoffman et Cie which sold a similar, but not identical, product. Hoffman's product was priced slightly lower than Levadol. The Swiss Franc (in relation to the cruzeiro) had not revalued as fast as the U.S. dollar over the most recent two-year period (see Exhibit 2). Thus, the apparent incentive for Hoffman to raise its price to cover a translation loss was not as great as MB's. Also, Hoffman had been known to be somewhat more concerned with market share than with short-term reported profit.

Other reasons for Hoffman's strength had to do with the company's size in Brazil. In addition to having a large percentage of the pharmaceutical market, it also had a very large share of the market in agricultural chemicals. Its field sales force was about three to four times the size of MB's. Also, Hoffman gave somewhat longer payment terms. Hoffman's management apparently felt that they could squeeze the profit margin in pharmaceuticals a bit because of their strong position and high profits with agricultural chemicals.

In addition to Hoffman and other foreign based firms, two local producers sold a generic substitute. The raw materials for the generic product were sourced in Brazil. The local patent covering this product had already expired. One result of this was that the industry was currently afflicted with an overcapacity of manufacturing facilities for products such as generic brand pain relievers. The price of the generic aspirin-free pain reliever had risen 16 percent in the past two years. On the other hand, the price of Levadol had risen 20 percent, making the price difference $18/case (see Table 2).

TABLE 1 Aspirin-free pain relievers (percentage of market share by major competitors)

	MB	Hoffman	Generic	All Other	Total Volume
					(thousands of cases)
1977	3%	7%	31%	59%	125
1978	8	12	25	55	152
1979	9	17	21	53	202
1980	15	25	17	43	240
1981	13	32	13	42	287
1982	10	32	15	43	320

TABLE 2 Average wholesale price of aspirin-free pain relievers (U.S. dollars per case)

	MB	Hoffman	Generic
1980	$182	$180	$172
1981	201	198	187
1982	218	212	200

CONCLUSION

"My greatest fear at this moment in Brazil is that we're being finessed by firms with a better knowledge of international business. Levadol should not be losing market share to Hoffman," said Paul McConnell. "I could understand some loss of market to the locals, but even there we should be able to sell the customer on our product superiority. Hoffman has a premium product. But it's not as good as ours."

Frederick D.S. Choi

Case 37

Continental A.G.

Dietrich Becker and Tom Opderbeck, tire analysts for a global investment fund located in Houston, are examining the 1990 earnings performance of two potential investment candidates. Reflecting the company's investment philosophy of picking the best stocks wherever they are located in the world, both junior analysts have adopted an approach of undertaking matched comparisons of leading firms in the tire industry. For starters, Dietrich and Tom have focussed on Goodyear Tire & Rubber Company (United States) and Continental A.G. (German) as their first screen.

> *Dietrich:* Well, what do you think Tom?
> *Tom:* Looking at the income trends (see Exhibit 1), I sort of like Continental.

Exhibit 1 *Goodyear ($ millions)*

	1986	1987	1988	1989	1990
Sales	9,040	9,905	10,810	10,869	11,273
Net income (loss)	124	771	350	207	(38)

Continental (DM millions)

	1986	1987	1988	1989	1990
Sales	4,969	5,098	7,906	8,382	8,551
Net income (loss)	115	139	195	228	93

Dietrich: Yeah, I agree. Goodyear's results are much more volatile.

Tom: I always look to see how a company has done in a bad year. Owing to the continued consolidation of the industry, excess capacity created by reduced demand for autos and trucks as well as reduced consumer spending for replacement tires in light of economic and political uncertainties, 1990 was a disaster for every major company in the industry. Given that environment, Continental's performance was stellar!

Dietrich: Maybe we'd better check with Masaki, our accountant, to see if we're reading the tea leaves correctly.

Tom: I'll give him a call.

(After a five minute conversation)

Dietrich: Well, what did he say?

Tom: He said, we're probably correct in our overall assessment (I think he's just being polite), but that we'd better check the companies' accounting policies. He says German accounting principles tend to impart a conservative bias to corporate earnings. He's faxing us a summary of some major GAAP differences between the United States and Germany right now.

The facsimile is reproduced as Exhibit 2.

Tom: (Having examined the facsimile) Looks like there are some major differences in reporting rules between the United States and Germany.

Dietrich: Do you think we should attempt to restate Continental's accounts to a U.S. GAAP basis?

Tom: Why don't we try.

Dietrich: Where should we start?

Exhibit 2 **Major accounting differences between Germany and the United States**

	Germany	United States
Goodwill	Written off against reserves or amortized, commerical law prescribes four years; most companies amortize over 15 years for tax purposes.	Capitalized and amortized to income over a period not to exceed 40 years.
Long-term leases	Generally no lease capitalizaiton.	Capitalization required when specific criteria met.
Depreciation	Highest rates allowable for tax.	Generally straight line over estimated useful lives.
Reserves	Contingency reserves provided when a loss or future expense is possible.	Contingency reserves prohibited.
Inventory	Costing must mirror physical flow of goods. Average costing is common.	LIFO costing method is common.
Pensions	Normally unfunded. Liability based on obligation at balance sheet date discounted at rates allowable for tax. Past service costs written off immediately or within three years.	Normally funded. Obligation based on estimated future benefits and discounted at market rates. Past service costs amortized over an extended period.

Tom: Let's examine the financial statements to see if there are any glaring differences in specific account balances in terms of their relative magnitude and see if accounting differences might help to explain those differences.

Dietrich: Maybe we should just attempt one or two adjustments, particulary those for which we have sufficient information. If these adjustments have a significant earnings impact, then let's press the right buttons and see if we can't get the company to give us some additional information so that we can do a more comprehensive analysis.

Tom: Sounds good. Let's get started.

Selected excerpts from the annual reports of both Goodyear and Continental are provided in Exhibit 3.

Exhibit 3

Continental Aktiengesellschaft
Consolidated Balance Sheet at December 31, 1990

Assets	See Note No.	DM 000	12/31/1990 DM 000	12/31/1989 DM 000
Fixed assets and investments				
Intangible assets	(1)	430,920		11,944
Property, plant and equipment	(2)	2,196,724		1,797,125
Investments	(3)	225,729	2,853,373	189,428
				1,998,497
Current assets				
Inventories	(4)	1,611,566		1,506,771
Receivables and other assets	(5)	1,475,557		1,386,212
Marketable securities	(6)	51,426		339,219
Liquid assets	(7)	144,625		134,079
			3,283,174	**3,366,281**
Prepaid expenses	(8)		31,070	41,092
			6,167,617	5,405,870

Shareholders' equity and liabilities	See Note No.	DM 000	12/31/1990 DM 000	12/31/1989 DM 000
Shareholders' equity				
Subscribed capital	(9)	439,097		435,022
Capital reserves	(10)	962,275		956,240
Retained earnings	(11)	137,788		133,770
Minority interests	(12)	94,286		46,692
Reserve for retirement benefits	(13)	2,861		3,691
Net income available for distribution		36,383		70,984
			1,672,690	1,646,399
Special Reserves	(14)		80,552	118,103
Provisions	(15)		1,733,440	1,386,799
Liabilities	(16)		2,680,935	2,254,569
			6,167,617	5,405,570

Exhibit 3 (Cont.)

Continental Aktiengesellschaft
Consolidated Statement of Income for the period from January 1 to December 31, 1990

	See Note No.	DM 000	1990 DM 000	1989 DM 000
Sales	(17)		8,551,015	8,381,880
Cost of sales	(18)	6,490,128		6,256,858
Gross profit on sales			2,060,887	2,125,002
Selling expenses	(19)	1,255,474		1,174,268
Administrative expenses	(20)	504,277		474,932
Other operating income	(21)	194,266		164,076
Other operating expenses	(22)	140,218		91,351
Net income from investments and financial activities	(23)	− 138,777		− 116,536
Net income from regular business activities			216,407	431,991
Taxes	(24)	122,972		204,153
Net income for the year			93,435	227,838
Balance brought forward from previous year			1,380	1,199
Minority interests in earnings	(25)	−	88	58
Withdrawal from the reserve for retirement benefits		+	830	+ 544
Change in reserves		−	59,174	− 158,539
Net income available for distribution			36,383	70,984

Based on an audit performed in accordance with our professional duties, the consolidated financial statements comply with the legal regulations. The consolidated financial statements present, in compliance with required accounting principles, a true and fair view of the net worth, financial position and results of the Corporation. The management report for the Corporation is in agreement with the consolidated financial statements.

Berlin/Hanover, April 8, 1991

KPMG Deutsche Treuhand-Gesellschaft
Aktiengesellschaft
Wirtschaftsprüfungsgesellschaft

Dr. Richter
Certified Public
Accountant

Kirste
Certified Public
Accountant

Exhibit 3 (Cont.)

Principles of Accounting and Valuation

Assets

Acquired intangible assets are carried at acquisition cost and amortized by the straight-line method over their anticipated useful life. Capitalized goodwill resulting from the acquisition of companies is deducted in instalments from retained earnings on the balance sheet, over periods estimated individually at from 10 to 20 years.

Property, plant and equipment is valued at acquisition or manufacturing cost, less scheduled depreciation.

Continental Aktiengesellschaft uses the declining balance method to depreciate movable fixed assets, while the straight-line method is used for all other fixed assets. We change over from the decling balance method to the straight-line method as soon as this leads to higher depreciation. In the financial statements of Continental Aktiengesellschaft, the special depreciation permitted by the tax laws is taken insofar as necessary in view of the fact that the commerical balance sheet is the basis for the balance sheet prepared in accordance with the tax regulations.

Since 1989, pursuant to internationally accepted accounting principles, additions have been depreciated exclusively by the straight-line method in the consolidated financial statements.

The following table shows the useful life taken as a basis for depreciating the major categories of property, plant and equipment:

Buildings up to 33 years;
additions from 1990 on, up to 25 years,
Technical facilities and machinery
10 years,

Plant and office equipment 4 to 7 years
Molds up to 4 years.

Additions to movable assets made during the first six months of the year are depreciated at the full annual rate, and those made during the last six months at half the annual rate. Minor fixed assets are written off completely in the year of acquisition.

These depreciation rules are applied by each of the domestic and foreign companies as of the date it became part of the Corporation.

Interests in affiliates and other companies held as investments are valued at acquisition cost, less the necessary writedowns.

Interest-bearing loans granted are shown at face value; loans which bear little or no interest are discounted to their cash value.

Inventories are carried at the lower of acquisition/manufacturing cost or market. Manufacturing cost includes direct costs, as well as a proportional part of material and production overhead and depreciation. Appropriate adjustments are made for declines in value due to reduced usability or prolonged storage.

In valuing receivables and miscellaneous assets, we make reasonable allowances to cover all perceivable risks, as well as lump-sum deductions to cover the general credit risk.

Marketable securities are valued at the lower of cost or market.

Insofar as permissible, we have continued to take all the extraordinary depreciation and writedowns, as well as the depreciation and write-downs for tax purposes, which were taken in previous years on fixed assets, investments, and current assets.

Discounts and issue costs of loans and bonds are shown as prepaid expenses and amortized over the term of the individual loans and bonds.

Shareholders' Equity and Liabilities

Provisions based on sound business judgment are set up for all perceivable risks, undetermined obligations and impending losses.

At our German companies, the provisions for pension plans and similar obligations are set up at a 6% interest rate, on the basis of actuarial computations in accordance with the statutory method.

Pension commitments and similar obligations of foreign companies are also computed according to actuarial principles, discounted to the present value at the interest rates prevailing in the respective countries, and covered by appropriate provisions for pension plans or by pension funds. Employee claims for severance benefits under national laws have also been taken into account.

The pension obligations of American companies are valued according to the stricter valuation rules that have been in force in the U.S.A. since 1987. The provision made for this purpose in the balance sheet is slightly higher than if the corresponding German method of computation had been applied.

The obligations of General Tire Inc., Akron, Ohio, for post-retirement medical benefits are fully covered by provisions computed according to actuarial principles. New U.S. regulations (FASB No. 106) require that by no later than 1993, a provision be established for not only the retirees and vested work force, but also

Exhibit 3 *(Cont.)*

for the non-vested employees. Although this regulation allows a build-up of the provision over a twenty year period, we have already transferred the full additional amount required (DM 270.7 million) to the provisions shown on the consolidated balance sheet. To balance this item, goodwill deducted from consolidated retained earnings at the time of the acquisition of General Tire has been capitalized in the same amount.

As a rule, provisions for repairs that have been postponed to the subsequent year are established in the amount of the probable cost. When there are temporary differences between the values of the individual companies' assets and liabilities as determined according to the tax laws and those appearing in their balance sheets, which are prepared according to valuation principles that are uniform throughout the Corporation, deferred taxes may result. We show the latter only when they are reflected in provisions for future tax expenses. Liabilities are stated at the redemption amount.

Selected Notes

(10) Capital Reserves

This item includes amounts received upon the issuance of shares in excess of their par value totaling DM 724.9 million, as well as the premium of DM 237.4 million paid upon the exercise of warrants attached to the bonds issued in 1984, 1986 and 1987 and to the 1988 convertible debentures. Capital reserves increased by DM6.0 million due to the exercise of the conversion and option rights in 1990.

(11) Retained Earnings

DM 000	Continental AG	Consolidated
As of 12/31/1989	141,699	133,770
Differences from currency translation	–	– 55,009
Other	–	147
Allocation from net income	8,000	59,174
As of 12/31/1990	149,699	137,788

(12) Minority Interests

This item shows the interest of outsiders in capital and earnings. The increase was due primarily to the scheduled capital contribution made by the Japanese partners to our joint venture GTY Tire Company, Akron, Ohio, U.S.A.

(13) Reserve for Retirement Benefits

The parent company's reserve for retirement benefits was established to compensate for shortfalls in the provision for pension plans, which cannot yet be made up for tax purposes. This reserve was reduced, according to schedule, by DM 0.8 million to DM 2.9 million.

(14) Special Reserves

DM 000	12/31/1990		12/31/1989	
	Continental AG	Consolidated	Continental AG	Consolidated
Reserve under § 3. Foreign Investment Act	59,766	15,000	84,312	38,265
Reserve under § 6b, Income Tax Act	–	448	–	289

Exhibit 3 (Cont.)

	12/31/1990		12/31/1989	
	Continental AG	Consolidated	Continental AG	Consolidated
Reserve under § 52 Par. 8, Income Tax Act	705	1,069	940	1,425
Governmental capital investment subsidies	–	57,664	–	60,988
Other	2,533	6,371	4,137	17,136
	63,004	80,552	89,389	118,103

The decrease in special reserves is due, in particular, to the elimination of the special reserve pursuant to § 3 Foreign Investment Act, following the write-down made in connection with Semperit (Ireland) Ltd., Dublin, Ireland.

The special reserves are divided into an equity portion of DM 69.5 million and a debt portion of DM 11.1 million, representing deferred taxes, which will be paid in due course when the reserves are eliminated. Including the shareholders' equity of DM 1,672.7 million shown on the balance sheet, the actual shareholders' equity amounts to DM 1,742.2 million and the equity ratio to 28.2%.

(15) Provisions

DM 000	12/31/1990		12/31/1989	
	Continental AG	Consolidated	Continental AG	Consolidated
Provisions for pensions and similar obligations	220,977	972,173	206,374	636,626
Provisions for taxes	31,937	72,210	53,144	92,265
Miscellaneous provisions	191,465	689,057	188,817	657,908
	444,379	1,733,440	448,335	1,386,799

The Corporation's provisions for pensions and similar obligations rose considerably. Apart from normal allocations, this increase was due, in particular, to an addition to cover claims for medical benefits which may be made by employees of General Tire Inc., Akron, Ohio, U.S.A., after their retirement.

At two of our retirement benefit organizations, there is a shortfall of DM 22.0 million in the coverage of pension obligations. The provisions at four other German companies have been funded only to the maximum amount permitted for tax purposes.

Lower tax liabilities permitted a reduction in provisions for taxes, which include amounts relating both to the current fiscal year and to previous years.

Provisions for deferred taxes in the individual financial statements, after deduction of the net prepaid taxes arising from consolidation procedures, amounted to DM 7.4 million.

Miscellaneous provisions cover all perceivable risks and other undetermined obligations. In addition to provisions for warranties, bonuses and miscellaneous risks, they consist mainly of provisions for personnel and social welfare payments, deferred repairs and service anniversaries.

(16) Liabilities

Continental AG

DM 000		Due in			Due in	
	As of 12/31/1990	less than 1 year	more than 5 years	As of 12/31/1989	less than 1 year	more than 5 years
Bonds, convertible*	72,479	242	2,237	71,508	230	1,278
Bank borrowings	444,361	436,398	–	60,828	49,306	–
Advances from customers	–	–	–	849	849	–
Trade accounts payable	132,067	132,067	–	147,887	147,502	–

* total amount secured by mortages: DM 78.0 million

Exhibit 3 (Cont.)

Payables to affiliated companies	286,465	271,638	14,827	137,288	123,489	13,799
Payables to companies in which participations are held	9,290	9,290	–	5,823	5,823	–
Other liabilities*	90,182	84,166	–	89,904	81,879	–
tax liabilities	(23,751)			(17,821)		
liabilities relating to social security and similar obligations	(20,268)			(21,577)		
	1,034,844	933,801	17,064	514,087	409,078	15,077

*total amount secured by mortgages: DM 78.0 million

(20) Administrative Expenses

This item consists primarily of personnel and other expenses which cannot be directly allocated to production or sales.

(21) Other Operating Income

	1990		1989	
	Continental AG	Consolidated	Continental AG	Consolidated
DM 000				
Gains on the disposal of fixed assets and investments	6,179	33,423	2,435	10,753
Credit to income from the reversal of provisions	1,418	17,312	7,400	33,559
Credit to income from the reduction of the general bad debt reserve	—	1,101	—	2,014
Credit to income from the reverse of special reserves	26,385	38,824	12,645	32,456
Miscellaneous income	120,143	103,606	106,843	85,294
	154,125	194,266	129,323	164,076

In addition to current income from rentals, leasing and miscellaneous sideline operations, other operating income includes indemnification paid by insurance companies and income attributable to other fiscal years.

For the parent company, this item consists mainly of cost apportionments received from other companies belonging to the Corporation.

(22) Other Operating Expenses

	1990		1989	
	Continental AG	Consolidated	Continental AG	Consolidated
DM 000				
Losses on the disposal of fixed assets and investments	2,015	6,694	306	4,315
Losses on the disposal of current assets (except inventories)	1,414	19,197	257	22,818

Exhibit 3 *(Cont.)*

(22) Other Operating Expenses

	1990		1989	
	Continental AG	Consolidated	Continental AG	Consolidated
DM 000				
Allocation to special reserves	—	168	46,995	1,278
Miscellaneous expenses	111,504	114,161	89,374	62,940
	114,933	140,218	136,932	91,351

The miscellaneous expenses relate primarily to sideline operations and the establishment of necessary provisions; at the parent company, they include cost apportionments paid to other companies belonging to the Corporation.

(24) Taxes

	1990		1989	
	Continental AG	Consolidated	Continental AG	Consolidated
DM 000				
On income	45,747	59,884	75,612	141,476
Other taxes	14,186	63,088	17,527	62,877
	59,993	122,972	93,139	204,153

(25) Minority Interests in Earnings

This item shows the profits and losses relating to minority shareholders in Germany and abroad.

Miscellaneous Data

Costs of Materials

	1990		1989	
	Continental AG	Consolidated	Continental AG	Consolidated
DM 000				
Cost of raw materials and supplies and merchandise	1,364,120	3,200,096	1,347,077	3,035,180
Cost of outside services	215,246	330,159	195,168	263,868
	1,579,366	3,530,255	1,542,245	3,298,838

Personnel Expense

	1990		1989	
	Continental AG	Consolidated	Continental AG	Consolidated
DM 000				
Wages and salaries	849,519	2,403,812	796,484	2,185,244
Social welfare contributions and expenses related to pensions and other employee benefits	174,137	624,696	164,100	539,536
expenses for pensions	26,861	77,658	25,122	66,690
	1,023,656	3,028,508	960,584	2,724,780

Number of employees (quarterly average)	Continental AG	Consolidated
Salaried employees	4,544	11,217
Wage earners	11,244	36,986
	15,788	48,203

Exhibit 3 *(Cont.)*

CONSOLIDATED STATEMENT OF INCOME
The Goodyear Tire & Rubber Company and Subsidiaries

(Dollars in millions, except per share)

	Year Ended December 31,		
	1990	1989	1988
Net sales	$11,272.5	$10,869.3	$10,810.4
Other Income	180.6	216.1	217.6
	11,453.1	11,085.4	11,028.0
Cost and Expenses:			
Cost of goods sold	8,805.1	8,234.7	8,291.0
Selling, administrative and general expense	1,999.6	1,863.7	1,745.1
Interest expense	328.2	255.3	231.8
Unusual items	103.6	109.7	78.8
Other expenses	74.5	44.6	37.0
Foreign currency exchange	72.1	87.9	87.6
Minority interest in net income of subsidiaries	14.1	18.6	19.2
	11,397.2	10,614.5	10,490.5
Income before Income Taxes and Extraordinary Item	55.9	470.9	537.5
United States and Foreign Taxes on Income	94.2	281.5	187.4
Income (loss) before Extraordinary Item	(38.3)	189.4	350.1
Extraordinary Item — Tax Benefit of Loss Carryovers	—	17.4	—
Net Income (loss)	$ (38.3)	$ 206.8	$ 350.1
Per Share of Common Stock:			
Income (loss) before extraordinary item	$ (.66)	$ 3.28	$ 6.11
Extraordinary item — tax benefit of loss carryovers	—	.30	—
Net Income (loss)	$ (.66)	$ 3.58	$ 6.11
Average Shares Outstanding	58,215,897	57,727,577	57,322,165

The accompanying accounting policies and notes are an integral part of this financial statement.

Exhibit 3 (Cont.)

CONSOLIDATED STATMENT OF INCOME
The Goodyear Tire & Rubber Company and Subsidiaries

(*Dollars in millions*)	1990	1989
Assets		
Current Assets:		
Cash and cash equivalents	$ 220.3	$ 122.5
Short term securities	56.4	92.1
Accounts and notes receivable	1,495.2	1,244.6
Inventories	1,346.0	1,642.0
Prepaid expenses	206.3	170.7
Total Current Assets	3,324.2	3,271.9
Other Assets:		
Investments in affiliates, at equity	127.6	125.9
Long term accounts and notes receivable	292.5	189.2
Deferred charges and other miscellaneous assets	410.9	258.0
	831.0	573.1
Properties and Plants	4,808.4	4,615.3
	$8,963.6	$8,460.3
Liabilities and Shareholders' Equity		
Current Liabilities:		
Accounts payable — trade	$ 986.8	$ 924.0
Accrued payroll and other compensation	442.7	395.6
Other current liabilities	282.5	278.9
United States and foreign taxes	248.6	219.3
Notes payable to banks and overdrafts	247.6	316.0
Long term debt due within one year	85.4	66.4
Total Current Liabilities	2,293.6	2,200.2

Exhibit 3 (Cont.)

(Dollars in millions)	December 31,	
	1990	1989
Long Term Debt and Capital Leases	$3,286.4	$2,963.4
Other Long Term Liabilities	550.0	364.7
Deferred Income Taxes	622.9	681.8
Minority Equity in Subsidiaries	112.8	106.4
Shareholders' Equity:		
Preferred stock, no par value:		
Authorized, 50,000,000 shares, unissued	—	—
Common stock, no par value:		
Authorized, 150,000,000 shares		
Outstanding shares, 58,477,890 (57,806,869 in 1989)	58.5	57.8
Capital surplus	65.1	46.5
Retained earnings	2,135.4	2,278.4
	2,259.0	2,382.7
Foreign currency translation adjustment	(161.1)	(238.9)
Total Shareholders' Equity	2,097.9	2,143.8
	$8,963.6	$8,460.3

The accompanying accounting policies and notes are an integral part of this financial statement.

ACCOUNTING POLICIES
The Goodyear Tire & Rubber Company and Subsidiaries

A summary of the significant accounting policies used in the preparation of the accompanying financial statements follows:

PRINCIPLES OF CONSOLIDATION
The consolidated financial statements include the accounts of all majority-owned subsidiaries. All significant intercompany transactions have been eliminated.

The Company's investments in 20% to 50% owned companies in which it has the ability to exercise significant influence over operating and financial policies are accounted for on the equity method.

Accordingly, the Company's share of the earnings of these companies is included in consolidated net income. Investments in other companies are carried at cost.

Exhibit 3 (Cont.)

CONSOLIDATED STATEMENT OF CASH FLOWS

Cash and cash equivalents include cash on hand and in the bank as well as all short term securities held for the primary purpose of general liquidity. Such securities normally mature within three months from the date of acquisition. Cash flows associated with items intended as hedges of identifiable transactions or events are classified in the same category as the cash flows from the items being hedged.

INVENTORY PRICING

Inventories are stated at the lower of cost or market. Cost is determined using the last-in, first-out (LIFO) method for a significant portion of domestic inventories and the first-in, first-out (FIFO) method or average cost method for other inventories.

ACCOUNTS AND NOTES RECEIVABLE

PROPERTIES AND PLANTS

Properties and plants are stated at cost. Depreciation is computed on the straight line method. Accelerated depreciation is used for income tax purposes, where permitted.

INCOME TAXES

Income taxes are recognized during the year in which transactions enter into the determination of financial statement income with deferred taxes being provided for timing differences.

PER SHARE OF COMMON STOCK

Per share amounts have been computed based on the average of common shares outstanding, including for this purpose only, those treasury shares allocated for distribution under the incentive profit sharing plan.

RECLASSIFICATION

Certain items previously reported in specific financial statement captions have been reclassified to conform with the 1990 presentation.

OTHER INCOME

Other income includes income of $86.8 million, $132.4 million and $130.8 million for 1990, 1989 and 1988, respectively, on deposits. The primary source of interest income was funds invested in time deposits in Latin America, pending remittance or reinvestment in the region. The lower interest income was due to lower interest rates on deposits.

At December 31, 1990 approximately $128.4 million, or 46.4 percent of the Company's cash, cash equivalents and short term securities were concentrated in Latin America, primarily Brazil.

(In millions)	1990	1989
Accounts and notes receivable	$1,534.1	$1,283.2
Less allowance for doubtful accounts	38.9	38.6
	$1,495.2	$1,244.6

Throughout the year, the Company sold certain domestic accounts receivable under continuous sale programs. The Company increased the level of net proceeds from sales under these programs to $600.0 million in December, 1989, from $350.0 million. Under these agreements, undivided interests in designated receivable pools are sold to purchasers with recourse limited to the receivables purchased. Fees paid by the Company under these agreements are based on certain variable market rate indices and are recorded as Other expenses.

The Company sold accounts and notes receivable under these and other agreements, the net proceeds of which totaled $3,911.6 million, $3,118.8 million and $2,451.6 million during 1990, 1989 and 1988, respectively.

Exhibit 3 *(Cont.)*

INVENTORIES

(In millions)	1990	1989
Raw materials and supplies	$ 234.5	$ 330.5
Work in process	67.5	90.1
Finished product	1,044.0	1,221.4
	$1,346.0	$1,642.0

The cost of inventories using the last-in, first-out (LIFO) method (approximately 38.4% of consolidated inventories in 1990 and 44.7% in 1989) was less than the approximate current cost of inventories by $335.4 million at December 31, 1990 and $330.6 million at December 31, 1989.

PROPERTIES AND PLANTS

(In millions)	1990			1989		
	Owned	Capital Leases	Total	Owned	Capital Leases	Total
Land and improvements	$ 297.2	$ 8.1	$ 305.3	$ 279.8	$ 9.4	$ 289.2
Buildings	1,137.6	71.5	1,209.1	1,032.3	76.2	1,108.5
Machinery and equipment	5,049.5	125.4	5,174.9	4,611.8	124.1	4,735.9
Pipeline	1,393.3	—	1,393.3	1,351.2	—	1,351.2
Construction in progress	535.4	—	535.4	565.2	—	565.2
Properties and plants, at cost	8,413.0	205.0	8,618.0	7,840.3	209.7	8,050.0
Less accumulated depreciation	3,669.9	139.7	3,809.6	3,299.8	134.9	3,434.7
	$4,743.1	$ 65.3	$4,808.4	$4,540.5	$ 74.8	$4,615.3

The amortization for capital leases included in the depreciation provision for 1990, 1989 and 1988 was $11.1 million, $10.1 million and $11.2 million, respectively.

International Banking

Ian H. Giddy

Case 38

Passing the Buck at Banco

"Do I deserve this?" mused Bertram, leaning against the frame of his office window overlooking the Praca de Republica. He heard his secretary leave for the day but made no move, continuing to stare blankly at the overflow of desk paper on his window ledge.

Bertram L. T. Worthington was the general manager of the Sao Paulo branch of Banco Internacional de North America (BINA) Corporation, a subsidiary of a major U.S. bank holding company. Two days earlier a director of one of his bank's biggest clients, Uniao Fabril S.A., had threatened to withdraw his family's deposits, and perhaps his company's business, unless he received written clarification from BINA on the status of his U.S. dollar deposits. It appeared that the fellow got concerned about what would happen to his money if the Brazilian authorities walked in one day and froze all dollar deposits.

Bertram had been told of this by his deputy, recently transferred from the Lisbon branch, Luis Filipe David da Gloria Nunes e Oliveira. The client, it seemed, had argued that since his money was in U.S. dollars, he assumed that he would be able to collect it from the New York office of BINA. This was obvious, he said, since dollar funds were always paid out of New York correspondent balances anyway.

Bertram Worthington was not so sure.

"Ollie, old man," he had said, "what if we had already loaned the dollars to a Brazilian company? Then they wouldn't be in New York." Or would they? he wondered silently to himself. "Also, how can a branch in one country be responsible for all branches that accept dollar deposits in other countries?"

"You forget I have a law degree," replied Dr. Luis Filipe etc. Oliveira. "We are a branch, not a subsidiary. In accordance with corporate law and with general principles of corporate responsibility, a bank may be held liable at its home office for deposits placed in its foreign branches, U.S. v. First National City Bank, 321 F.2d 14, 19–20, Cir. 1963."

"Listen, Ollie, I agree, but according to the separate entity doctrine, a branch is treated for some purposes like a distinct business entity. Deposits placed at a branch are normally payable only at the branch, which means that the law of the jurisdiction where it is located controls the bank's liability on deposits in the branch."

"Oh? Are you going to tell our depositors, in writing, that neither BINA nor the parent bank will repay deposits seized in an offshore branch? What do you think that will do to our image as a global bank?"

Bertram had later obtained some legal advice. He had been informed that a British or American court might well consider sympathetically a claim by a depositor in a foreign branch, even where acts of the host state had resulted in a loss of the depositor's rights or the loss of assets by the foreign branch. Two precedents were highlighted. First, Section 138 of New York State's Banking Law implies that head offices of New York banks have liability for deposits seized in a foreign branch except in proportion to the book value of assets also seized.

Second, in a recent decision, the U.S. Court of Appeals upheld the claims of a group of Vietnamese who had had funds deposited in Chase Manhattan's Saigon branch when that city was overrun by the North Vietnamese in 1975. The claims were upheld despite the fact that the deposits were in local currency, piasters, and that the new government had seized all remaining assets of the branch.

It was no help to Bertram Worthington that virtually all his branch's assets, in both dollars and cruzeiros, were invested in Brazil. If there were an official seizure of Brazilians' deposits, there was little the Sao Paulo branch could do legally. If the head office in London paid out such funds, the bank could find itself subjected to double liability. He thought of advising his client to transfer the funds to BINA's Cayman Islands branch, but his counsel had heard of a case where a New York court had placed an attachment on funds deposited in the Cayman branch of a Brazilian bank, on the grounds that the branch was just a "nameplate" entity, with its funds held and managed by the bank's New York branch.

"I don't want to lose those deposits," thought Bertram. "Next thing, the client will be telling his swimming-pool set, I wonder what Citibank would do? In his shoes I'd put my money in the U.S. of A., where the sheriff is in charge. Let's see what the rates are." He glanced at his rate sheet. "Gees, look what we're paying him! He deserves to take some extra risk. The only question is, how can I put it to him?"

Three-month deposits, One million minimum

New York (Parent) US$	14.125%
London (BINA) US$	14.5%
Cayman Is. (BINA) US$	14.5%
Singapore (Parent's branch) US$	14.625%
Sao Paulo (BINA) US$	14.875%
Sao Paulo (BINA) Cr$	37%

Bertram's stomach rumbled. He turned on his heels and strode over to his desk. B. L. T. Worthington had reached a decision. "This is a job for New York, quoth he, here comes one grande Telexo; Boy will New York be surprised to get one from old Bertie that does not concern the latest round of musical ministers; and if I make this look good, maybe I get promoted to the San Francisco Edge; here goes . . ."

Can you help Bertie get his promotion? Consider what the bank's written statement on its worldwide obligations to depositors should be:

(1) What is the status of deposits in U.S. dollars, compared to those in local currencies?

(2) If in local currencies, should deposits be repayable, at the customer's option, in dollars (or sterling)? At what exchange rate?

(3) Under what circumstances should the bank refuse to repay at the head office or a different branch? If the branch fails? If Brazil freezes all deposits? If there is an illegal insurrection that forces the branch to cease business?

(4) Does it matter whether the deposit is undocumented, or is evidenced by a certificate of deposit?

(5) Does the interest premium over domestic deposits make a difference?

(6) What if the U.S. authorities try to freeze Eurodollar deposits, as happened in the Iranian case?

(7) Should the parent bank provide explicit guarantees on offshore deposits?

Ian H. Giddy

Case 39

Funding the Teledyne Loan

MEMO TO: James Jones, Treasury Department, Piggibank London
FROM: Aristide Phitides, Loan Funding Manager

SUBJECT: Funding the Teledyne Loan

The bank has the opportunity to provide a profitable loan to the UK subsidiary of Teledyne Corporation. However we must be able to obtain £50 million of three-month funds immediately. Could you let me know what our cheapest cost of funds would be for three-month money? (I have attached some data but I don't know what to do with them!)

You should consider the following alternatives:

- Borrow three-month money in the Eurocurrency market in pounds sterling
- Borrow one-month money in the Eurocurrency market in pounds sterling
- Borrow three-month Eurolire, change them into sterling at the spot exchange rate, and hedge the repayment by purchasing Italian lire in the forward exchange market.

What are the relative costs and merits of these three funding methods for our three-month loan to Teledyne?

Eurocurrency Interest Rates

Dec 10	Short term	Seven days notice	One month	Three months	Six months	One year
Sterling	$9\frac{5}{8}$–$9\frac{1}{2}$	$9\frac{3}{4}$–$9\frac{5}{8}$	$10\frac{5}{32}$–$10\frac{3}{32}$	$10\frac{3}{8}$–$10\frac{1}{4}$	$10\frac{1}{2}$–$10\frac{3}{8}$	$10\frac{1}{2}$–$10\frac{3}{8}$
U.S. Dollar	$3\frac{3}{8}$–$3\frac{1}{4}$	$3\frac{3}{8}$–$3\frac{1}{4}$	$3\frac{7}{8}$–$3\frac{5}{16}$	$3\frac{7}{16}$–$3\frac{5}{16}$	$3\frac{9}{16}$–$3\frac{7}{16}$	$3\frac{13}{16}$–$3\frac{11}{16}$
Ital. Lira	15–13	$14\frac{1}{4}$–$13\frac{1}{4}$	$14\frac{1}{4}$–$13\frac{3}{4}$	$14\frac{1}{4}$–$13\frac{3}{4}$	$14\frac{1}{4}$–$13\frac{3}{4}$	$14\frac{1}{2}$–14

Foreign Exchange — Sterling Spot and Forward

Dec 10	Day's spread	Close	One month	% pa	Three months	% pa
U.S.	1.9000–1.9105	1.9075–1.9085	1.09–1.07cpm	6.79	3.23–3.20pm	6.74
Italy	2134.3–2139.7	2137–2138	7–9 lire dis	–4.49	20–22 dis	–3.93
Ecu	1.3865–1.4000	1.3870–1.3880	0.08–0.13 dis	–0.91	0.17–0.24 dis	–0.59

Ian H. Giddy

Case 40

Continental vs Saudi

Marc de Troit had just joined the syndication group at Banque Paribas, the big French bank. He had been asked to summarize his view on whether the bank should respond to invitational telexes concerning two forthcoming syndicated loan deals. The first, from JP Morgan in London, was an invitation to participate in a three-year, $3.5 billion financing for the government of Saudi Arabia. The second was from Frankfurt, where Deutsche Bank was seeking participation in a five-year, DM500 million revolving credit for Continental, the German tire group.

Marc decided he should begin with the relative pricing of the two deals. The Saudi loan, for which there were no front-end fees, paid 50 basis points over the London interbank rate. In the Continental deal the return was made up of a facility fee — paid whether or not the loan was drawn down — of ³⁄₁₆ percent and an interest margin of the same level. Returns were supplemented by front-end fees, which ranged down from ⅛ percent for a DM35 million commitment, and utilization fees. If more than one third was drawn, an extra five basis points was payable; if more than two thirds, an extra 10 basis points.

As for risk, both issuers were very well known. Deutsche Bank deals usually were well accepted although Continental was not considered in the top rank of European credits. A more serious problem, perhaps, was the 100 percent risk weighting applied to corporate borrowers under the Basle rules, the standards set by the Bank for International Settlements' committee on bank supervision. According to the rules, banks had to set aside capital equivalent to 8 percent of the amount lent, and 4 percent on amounts committed but not lent. By contrast, the government of Saudi Arabia was the only one outside the Organization for Economic Cooperation and Development treated as an OECD government for bank capital purposes. As a result, banks were not required to set aside any capital for their loans to it.

Weighing these factors, which deal do you think would be most attractive to Paribas?

Ian H. Giddy

Case 41

Trading in Spain

J. F. O'Reilly was the Director of the International Division of the Royal Bank of Ireland. Two years ago the RBI had acquired a small bank in Spain as part of its effort to become a pan-European financial services institution. In late 1987 O'Reilly received a request from the manager of the sub in Madrid. The treasury unit of the Spanish subsidiary wished to expand its trading activities in the Spanish bond market. So far, profitability had been good in this market, and after consideration, the parent bank was considering an injection of an additional $2.5 million into the subsidiary.

O'Reilly's concern was to ensure that the bank was not exposing itself to excessive risk in this operation. He wanted to establish a system that limited the risk assumed by the traders to a reasonable level, while giving them sufficient flexibility to be able to undertake active, profitable trading.

At his request a consultant had drafted a proposal to institute a risk management system for the Spanish unit. The principle was that a system of "risk points" would be necessary to ensure comparability of positions in different kinds of instruments. The system was tentatively called the RBI scoring system.

O'Reilly wondered whether this system was the right approach. Would it be sufficient to limit the important risks? Based on the risks and rewards, was $2.5 million too much, too little, or just about the right amount of capital at this stage? Was the method sufficiently flexible to be adapted to different instruments and techniques in the future, such as shorting securities, swaps, and options as they became available in Spain?

ROYAL BANK OF IRELAND

MEMORANDUM

To: J. F. O'Reilly   Date: January 8, 1988
From: Finbarr Bradley   Re: Trading Risk Limits

Introduction: This memo looks at a trading position risk measurement system. The purpose of a measure of position risk is to know how exposed the trading desk is and to set reasonable limits on that exposure relative to capital allocated to the unit.

What follows is based on the "Interim Risk Management System for Spain." It is a *Risk Point* system, for price risk, supplemented by *dollar limits,* for counterparty risk.

Objectives: Reduce the probablity of wiping out capital to an acceptably low level.

Provide incentives for risk-taking and risk control

Approach: 1. Estimate the time-to-close. How many days would it take, on average, to close out or liquidate your positions? (suggestion: one day).

2. Estimate the variability (technically, the probability distribution) of prices of the securities and instruments traded, during the time-to-close.

3. Assign a tolerable loss of capital (e.g., 10 percent of total capital).

Then: Limit the trading exposure to a position whose *aggregate* variability (based on the variability of individual bond/instrument positions) during the time to close has an acceptably low probability (say, 1 percent) of wiping out the assigned capital.

Measuring Price Variability

1. Historical variability based on daily price changes for (say) the past six months, or
2. Estimated variability based on
   a. interest rate volatility
   b. the instrument's price sensitivity to rate changes
   c. an additional variability factor to reflect credit risk changes
   d. an additional variability factor to reflect the instrument's liquidity

Because we do not have reliable data to compute historical price volatility, we use the second approach.

Measuring Maximum Loss for Each Instrument

The table that follows provides estimates of the relative riskiness of 16 classes of Spanish bonds. *The result measures the dollar loss that could occur for a $1 million position if interest rates moved by a very large amount* (more than they have historically done) 99 percent of the time or approximately three standard deviations.

This maximum dollar loss figure is shown in column 6 of Table 1. Example: $1 million equivalent in a six-month T-bill (Letras del Tesoro) has a maximum daily close-out loss of $1,950 calculated as follows:

$1 Million		[Daily Volatility of Interest [Rates		Sensitivity Factor		Credit Risk Factor		Liquidity] Factor		Maximum Dollar Loss on $1 Million
	x		x		+		+		] =	
$1 Million	x	[0.39%	x	0.50	+	0%	+	0%]	=	$1,950

Notes:

DAILY VOLATILITY	From the recent history of daily yield movements in each sector, we estimate a yield change considered maximum: three standard deviations, which should occur only about 1 percent of the time.
SENSITIVITY FACTOR	Is simply an estimate of the percentage price change that would correspond to a 100 basis points change in yield, as measured by the modified duration.
CREDIT RISK FACTOR	A factor that measures the maximum potential additional price drop in percentage terms, that could result from a downgrading of the market's credit perceptions of the instrument. If there is no credit risk, this factor is 0 percent. If a downgrading could produce a 0.10 percent price drop, the factor is 0.10 percent.
LIQUIDITY FACTOR	A factor that represents the percent loss that could be taken from trying to close a position in a market where there may be few bids for offers. For example, if the bid could drop by 20 basis points in a time of illiquidity, the liquidity factor would be 0.20 percent.

Definition of Risk Points

For convenience, each bond is assigned a certain number of risk points. The instrument's risk points are simply an index of how much could be lost in a day from a position in that instrument.

Arbitrarily I have assigned the one-year Treasury bill a risk point index of 1. The greater the potential one-day loss, the greater the number of risk points, as a multiple of the one-year T-bill potential loss.

Example: Based on its duration, credit risk and liquidity risk, the maximum loss on a $1 million two-year corporate bond position is $8,130. This is 2.1 times as great as the $3,900 risk exposure of the benchmark one-year T-bill, so two-year corporate bonds are assigned 2.1 risk points.

Trading Risk Limits

a. Assuming a tolerable loss of 10 percent of capital, i.e. 10 percent of 2.5 million or $250,000, the trading desk could have an *overall maximum of 64 risk points at any one time* (250,00/3,900 = 64.1).

b. To avoid getting squeezed in any one sector, a sub-limit of 32 risk points (half of the total) is set for each category of instruments (Treasury bills, Treasury bonds, corporate bonds and commercial paper).

c. We may want to set a third limit on total exposures in any one *maturity* sector.

Suggestion:

0–1 year	32 Risk Points
1–3 years	32 Risk Points
3–5 years	32 Risk Points
5+ years	32 Risk Points

Counterparty Risk Limits

To limit the risk of nondelivery as a result of counterparty default or other events, we may want to set another two limits:

a. Overall dollar value of position. (For Spain, this has been set at $15 million.)

b. Limit on delivery exposure to any single counterparty (Example: $5 million per counterparty).

Caveat

1. The limits designed here depend on our empirical estimates of rate volatility, based on five months' data from 1987. They also depend on the validity of the Credit Risk and Liquidity Risk factors assigned to each instrument.

2. This system takes no account of short positions, or of any hedging instruments. The reason is the absence of any such instrument in Spain. A good risk management system will take account of these, and a supplementary memo on that topic will follow.

CONCLUSIONS

We suggest *five* risk limits

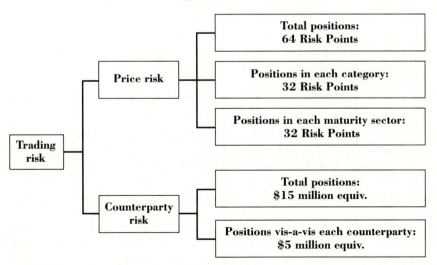

SUGGESTED SIMPLE RISK POINT SYSTEM FOR SPANISH TRADING ACCOUNT

ASSUMPTIONS:
TOTAL CAPITAL $2.5 MILLION
RISK LOSS EXPOSURE LIMIT 10.00% OF CAPITAL
HENCE MAXIMUM POSITION LOSS IS $250,000
WHICH IS EQUIVALENT TO 64 RISK POINTS

ABSOLUTE DOLLAR POSITION LIMIT $15 MILLION

MATURITY	DAILY VOLATILITY OF INTEREST RATES (*)	SENSITIVITY FACTOR (**)	CREDIT RISK FACTOR	LIQUIDITY FACTOR	MAX DOLLAR LOSS ON $1MIL IN 1 DAY (99% PROB)	RISK POINT INDEX	POSITION LIMIT IN $MIL	CATEGORY LIMITS
1	**2**	**3**	**4**	**5**	**6**	**7**	**8**	**9**
T-BILL: 6 month	0.39%	0.50	0.00%	0.00%	$1,950	0.5	$15.00 –	
12 month	0.39%	1.00	0.00%	0.00%	$3,900	1.0	$15.00 –	–$15 MIL, 32 RP
18 month	0.39%	1.50	0.00%	0.10%	$6,850	1.8	$15.00 –	
T-BOND: 2 year	0.39%	1.70	0.00%	0.00%	$6,630	1.7	$15.00 –	
3 year	0.39%	2.50	0.00%	0.00%	$9,750	2.5	$12.80 –	–$15 MIL, 32 RP
6 year	0.37%	4.15	0.00%	0.10%	$16,355	4.2	$7.63 –	
7 year	0.37%	4.85	0.00%	0.10%	$18,945	4.9	$6.59 –	
CORPORATE: BONDS 1 year	0.39%	0.90	0.05%	0.05%	$4,510	1.2	$15.00 –	
2 year	0.39%	1.70	0.05%	0.10%	$8,130	2.1	$15.00 –	–$15 MIL, 32 RP
3 year	0.37%	2.50	0.10%	0.10%	$11,250	2.9	$11.09 –	
6 year	0.37%	4.10	0.40%	0.20%	$21,170	5.4	$5.40 –	
COMMERCIAL: PAPER 3 month	0.39%	0.25	0.05%	0.00%	$1,475	0.4	$15.00 –	
6 month	0.39%	0.50	0.05%	0.00%	$2,450	0.6	$15.00 –	–$15 MIL, 32 RP
12 month	0.39%	1.00	0.10%	0.05%	$5,400	1.4	$15.00 –	
18 month	0.39%	1.50	0.20%	0.05%	$8,350	2.1	$14.95 –	
24 month	0.39%	2.00	0.20%	0.05%	$10,300	2.6	$12.12 –	

(*) THREE STANDARD DEVIATIONS IN ABSOLUTE DAILY INTEREST RATE CHANGES
(**) PERCENT CHANGE IN PRICE FOR 100 BASIS POINT CHANGE IN YIELD

Roy C. Smith and Ingo Walter

Case 42

The Privatization of Bancomer

In the summer of 1991, Antonio (Tony) Mendez de la Valera was called in to join a meeting with senior executives of the VISA Group, a large Mexican industrial holding company involved in beverages, packaging, and various other industries. The group of executives was meeting to consider whether or not to bid — and if so, how much to bid — for one of the large Mexican banks the government had announced it would "privatize" later in the year.

As a corporate finance specialist, Tony knew that he was being asked to participate in the discussion because a number of viable alternatives for becoming involved in the privatization of banks would have to be analyzed. Assuming VISA decided to proceed, one of these would have to be selected. Tony understood that the Group was especially interested in Bancomer, Mexico's largest and most emphatically retail-oriented banking company.

BACKGROUND

On September 1, 1982 — following a balance of payments crisis, imposition of exchange controls, and a substantial devaluation of the peso — President José Lopez Portillo nationalized Mexico's commercial banks.

During the following six years, the government exercised its control over Mexican depositary institutions in channelling their resources to finance the national fiscal deficit. Throughout this period, the management teams of banks under government control were given limited discretion over investment and personnel decisions, and there was little scope for strategic planning. Instead, management's focus was on making financial resources available to the government through deposit gathering, in return for the right to levy fees and other charges on the banks' depositors. As a result, the Mexican banking system effectively ceased to be the primary provider of market-oriented financial products and services to the Mexican public.

On June 28, 1990, the Mexican Constitution was amended to permit individuals and companies to once again own controlling interests in commercial banks. Subsequently, the Ley de Instituciones de Crédito (the Mexican Banking Law) was enacted to regulate the ownership and operation of commercial banks. The Comité de Desincorporación Bancaria (the Bank Privatization Committee) was created in 1990 to oversee the sale of Mexico's banks to private investors.

During most of the decade of nationalization, Mexico's banking sector had shown a high level of overall stability, sustained growth and profitability. The banks had been well capitalized and had maintained good asset quality. During 1986–90 the Mexican banking sector had also undergone significant consolidation and, most recently, substantial deregulation.

Mexican banks had not experienced the type of system-wide asset quality problems that had occurred in other Latin American countries, such as Argentina, Chile, Brazil and Colombia, where a combination of factors — including high concentrations of loans to a small number of borrowers, extension of credits to affiliated companies, and lack of proper auditing systems and supervision by the banking authorities — had contributed to such problems. Indeed, Mexico's financial institutions had experienced fewer problems than those of the United States.

With the enactment of the Financial Groups Law in 1990, the Mexican government adopted "universal banking" as a model to permit diverse financial services to be conducted under a common financial services holding company. This model was intended to make Mexico's financial system more efficient and competitive, as financial institutions were permitted to try to realize potential economies of scale and scope, enter new markets, exploit synergies, and explore new growth and cross-marketing opportunities. See Appendix A for background information on the Mexican banking system.

OVERVIEW OF BANCOMER

Bancomer had undergone a significant evolution since 1988. As a result, management believed Bancomer was profitable, well-capitalized and well-positioned to take advantage of the emerging opportunities in the Mexican market.

In December 1988, several senior executives joined Bancomer and began to redirect operation of the bank, primarily by giving managers greater responsibility over business operations and adopting, as a strategic goal, the regaining of market leadership in Bancomer's traditional niches — consumer and middle market lending. The new management also emphasized investment in technology and development of the already extensive branch network.

In 1989 and 1990, Bancomer further improved its asset quality, absorbing a series of non-recurring charges. In 1990, to strengthen Bancomer's financial condition still more, management created reserves for loan losses which subsequently exceeded all required regulatory levels. A similar move was planned for 1991.

Bancomer's profitability during 1989–90 reflected these charges and reserves, as well as the costs of refocusing the business and the impact of recent declines in the Mexican rate of inflation. By early 1991, the results of these strategies had already begun to appear. During that year, Bancomer's net income was forecasted to grow to about $400 million, an increase of over 50 percent in real terms over 1990, representing a return on average assets of 1.7 percent and a return on average equity of 24 percent.

Especially noteworthy was the expected increase in net interest margin from 7.22 percent in 1990 to about 7.4 percent in 1991, despite declining inflation. This was due to several favorable factors: (a) A shift in the composition of the balance sheet from lower-yielding government securities to higher-yielding private-sector loans; (b) Growth of higher-yielding consumer loans as a percentage of the total loan portfolio; and (c) Lower-cost peso-denominated deposits comprising a larger portion of Bancomer's funding base.

Approaching privatization, Bancomer thus had a growing, high-quality asset base. At June 30, 1991, Bancomer's assets totalled $24 billion. Asset growth during 1991 reflected, among other things, impressive growth in the Mexican economy, strong demand for credit in both pesos and dollars, and Bancomer's increased market share in lending.

At June 30, 1991, higher-quality credits comprised 95 percent of Bancomer's classified portfolio. Past-due, lower-quality credits made up 1.78 percent of the classified portfolio, compared to 2.79 percent at year-end 1990.

Reserve coverage for lower-quality credits improved during the year. At June 30, 1991, the allowance for loan losses was 88 percent of past-due, lower-quality credits compared to 54.56 percent at year-end 1990. Moreover, a pre-privatization credit review conducted by independent auditors concluded that Bancomer's credit portfolio was appropriately classified in all material respects.

Bancomer was well capitalized. At June 30, 1991, the bank's ratio of net capital to risk-weighted assets was 7.4 percent, exceeding both the 6 percent minimum requirement during 1991 and the 7 percent minimum requirement for 1992.

Bancomer's net worth was projected to be about $2 billion as of the end of 1991. The Mexican government was expected to be an aggressive seller, and would invite as many potential bidders as it could. Tony knew it expected a substantial premium over book value. Some earlier bank privatizations had already been completed at significant premiums over book value.

A detailed description of Bancomer's business, including the relevant financials, is contained in Appendix B.

THE VISA GROUP

The VISA Group was a complex of public and private industrial holdings, mainly in the beverages business, operating through a structure designed to insure an optimum balance between leverage and control. Through a 60 percent subsidiary (FEMSA), VISA controlled industrial properties with annual revenues of $1.8 billion. The balance of FEMSA was owned 15 percent by Citibank, 14 percent by the Mexican public, and 11 percent by the IFC and other banks.

VISA itself was 86 percent owned by a holding company, PROA, controlled by the family of Eugenio Garza Lagüera, with 11 percent of the remainder owned by allied investors and 3 percent by the Mexican public. PROA also controlled 59 percent of Valores de Monterrey, S.A. (VAMSA), a publicly traded financial services holding company whose principal subsidiary was Seguros

Monterrey, a major insurance company. The PROA group had extensive experience in banking, and prior to the 1982 nationalizations had controlled Banca Serfin, S.A., Mexico's third-largest bank. In the view of the VISA management group, ties between VAMSA and the Bancomer group could produce substantial synergies and new opportunities, both of which could be realized in the coming years.

Among VAMSA's other financial subsidiaries were several engaged in the financial leasing, factoring, warehouse bonding and brokerage businesses.

Combined, Arrendadora Bancomer and VAMSA's Arrendadora Monterrey would constitute Mexico's market leader in the lease financing business, with a combined 23.9 percent market share. Management believed that there was significant growth potential in the Mexican leasing business, particularly in the middle-market sector, which historically did not have ready access to this type of financing. As of year-end 1988, total lease financings were equal to 2.49 percent of total commercial bank loans in Mexico. By June 30, 1991, total lease financings had risen to 16.8 percent of total commercial bank loans in Mexico.

ABSA, another VAMSA subsidiary, was Mexico's eighth largest brokerage house in terms of trading volume. Management expected securities brokerage to benefit directly from ABSA's affiliation with Bancomer. Management believed, for example, that many of Bancomer's regional directors would use ABSA for their brokerage services, and the bank intended to use ABSA for its own investment and brokerage needs.

VAMSA's Factor de Capitales would be combined with Factoraje Bancomer. By mid 1991, Factoraje Bancomer and Factor de Capitales together represented the second-largest factoring company in Mexico, with total assets of $379.4 million and a market share of approximately 11 percent.

VAMSA's other principal non-bank subsidiary was Almacenadora Monterrey, Mexico's largest warehouse bonding company, with 23 percent of the market. Almacenadora Monterrey issued negotiable warehouse bills of lading and certificates of deposit representing warehoused goods. These could be used as collateral to obtain financing. Management believed that Almacenadora Monterrey would be able to strengthen its business and increase its market share as a result of cross-selling opportunities with Bancomer's client base.

STRUCTURING A BID

Tony's assignment was to coordinate the structuring of a bid for Bancomer and its subsidiaries. The bid would have to include a viable financing plan, and would have to meet the stated and hidden objectives of the Mexican government in putting such an important part of the Mexican financial system up for sale.

Among these objectives, Tony knew, was price, a concern for transparency, the preservation of benefits to be obtained by free-market competition in the financial sector, and an optimal degree for foreign participation. Tony assumed that optimal meant the minimum foreign participation needed to satisfy all of the other considerations.

From what Tony had seen so far, foreign banks would not be aggressive bidders. Many were severely strapped for capital. The maximum foreign ownership percentage was strictly limited by government rules. On the other hand, the Mexican securities market — reflecting strong confidence in the economic policies of the government — had been extremely buoyant lately and had attracted considerable buying interest from outside Mexico.

He also had to consider what sort of price range VISA would have to face in bidding for Bancomer, and how to put together a financial package that could win in competition with other bidders. These were expected to include several important Mexican industrial and financial groups, possibly allied in some cases with foreign banks. He wondered whether it was really worthwhile to pay the two to three times book value that some other groups had paid for Mexican banks that had been privatized in recent months (see Exhibit 1). This multiple represented franchise value, the booming economy, rising stock prices and the protection from foreign bank entry (until 1996) that the government was seeking to negotiate as part of the NAFTA agreement.

Tony wondered whom VISA should pick as a financial advisor for the task. Should it be a Mexican bank that knew the local situation well, or a foreign bank with extensive experience in valuation? The American commercial and investment banks had been the most impressive players in privatization discussions to date. VISA was close to J.P. Morgan, which had often acted as banker to the Mexican government, and in addition it had done business with, or knew well, Shearson Lehman Brothers, First Boston, Morgan Stanley and Goldman Sachs. In picking an advisor, Tony knew VISA would have to rely not only on their financial engineering ability, but also on their ability to judge markets and distribute any securities issues associated with the transaction.

Exhibit 1 Multiples Resulting from the Privatizations of Mexican Banks as of end-August, 1991

Bank	Date of Auction	Price of Sale	% Sold	Book Value	P/Book Value	Earnings, LTM	P/Earnings, LTM	Forecasted Earnings	P/Forecasted Earnings
MERCANTIL	Jun-07-91	$ 611.20	77.19%	$ 297.6 (a)	2.66 x	$ 62.2 (a)	12.73 x	$ 69.3	11.43 x
BANPAIS	Jun-14-91	544.99	100.00%	180.1 (a)	3.03 x	30.7	17.73 x	24.6	22.15 x
CREMI	Jun-21-91	748.29	66.70%	329.9 (a)	3.40 x	51.3 (a)	21.87 x	41.7	26.90 x
CONFIA	Aug-02-91	892.26	78.68%	304.0 (b)	3.73 x	83.9	13.52 x	108.6	10.44 x
BANORIE	Aug-09-91	223.22	66.00%	83.7 (b)	4.04 x	14.3 (b)	23.65 x	18.4	18.38 x
BANCRESER	Aug-16-91	425.13	100.00%	163.5 (b)	2.60 x	8.4 (b)	50.48 x	48.6	8.75 x
BANAMEX	Aug-23-91	$9,744.98	70.72%	$5,242.1 (c)	2.62 x	$1,233.0 (c)	11.18 x	$1,264.1	10.90 x

$ = billions of Mexican Pesos
(a) As of April 1991
(b) As of June 1991
(c) As of July 1991

Appendix A

The Mexican Banking System
Stability and Growth

The Mexican financial services sector, which includes, in addition to banks, insurance companies, brokerage houses and other financial intermediaries, has historically been less volatile than the overall Mexican economy and has exhibited positive growth even during periods of protracted recession such as during the 1980s (see chart below).

Real Growth in Mexican GDP and Financial Services Sector
1961–1990

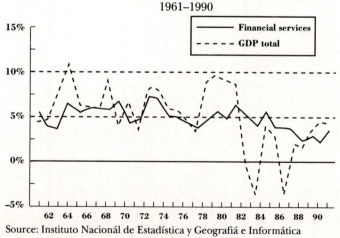

Source: Instituto Nacionál de Estadística y Geografiá e Informática

From 1987 to the summer of 1991 the combined assets of the three largest Mexican banks, Bancomer, Banamex and Serfin, commonly referred to in Mexico as Tier 1 banks (the Tier 1 Banks), were forecast to grow by more than 70 percent in real terms and their combined equity increased 93 percent in real terms. (See tables below):

Summary Financial Data for Bancomer, S.A., Banco Nacional de Mexico, S.A., and Banca Serfin, S.A. 1987–1991

Net Income (millions of nominal dollars)

	1987	1988	1989	1990	Forecast 1991
	For the years ended December 31,				
Bancomer.........	$220	$232	$245	$223	$ 400
Banamex...........	246	263	163	353	500
Serfin	73	93	105	123	120
Total	$540	$589	$514	$699	$1,020

Assets (millions of nominal dollars)

	1987	1988	1989	1990	Forecast 1991
Bancomer	$ 9,038	$13,059	$15,701	$18,297	$30,000
Banamex...........	10,427	14,240	18,138	22,155	31,000
Serfin	4,658	6,576	8,466	15,746	22,000
Total........	$24,123	$33,875	$42,304	$56,198	$83,000

Total Stockholders' Equity (millions of nominal dollars)

	1987	1988	1989	1990	Forecast 1991
Bancomer	$ 463	$ 920	$1,164	$1,477	$1,900
Banamex...........	612	1,169	1,126	1,622	2,100
Serfin	132	285	399	595	700
Total........	$1,207	$2,373	$2,689	$3,694	$4,700

Source: Comisión Nacional Bancaria

CONSOLIDATION

The Mexican banking industry has undergone significant consolidation and concentration. Starting in 1974, the Mexican government adopted a policy favoring rationalization and consolidation of the banking industry, primarily by encouraging the formation of multiple-banking institutions (*bancos multiples*) through mergers of smaller institutions. As a result, the number of depositary institutions in Mexico was reduced from 109 in 1974 to 45 as of December 31, 1982, and was further reduced to 18 between 1982 and 1988.

During the period of government ownership of banks, the Mexican government divested the banks of many of their non-bank financial and industrial holdings. As a consequence, during this period many of Mexico's former bankers reinvested their capital in the brokerage, insurance and leasing industries, in many cases by purchasing from the Mexican government the non-bank financial affiliates of the nationalized banks. These businesses rapidly became the primary (although not adequate) providers of financial products and services to the Mexican public because of the government's reliance on the banking sector to meet its funding needs.

Today, Mexican banks are generally grouped into three categories consisting of six national banks, seven multi-regional banks and five regional banks. As of the summer of 1991, Mexico's six national banks held approximately 77 percent of all global peso deposits *(captación global)* in the Mexican banking system. The seven multi-regional banks held approximately 18 percent of such deposits, with the remaining 5 percent held by the regional banks. In Mexico, global deposits are defined as demand deposits, savings deposits, time deposits, open-end funds, trusts and money market funds, but exclude interbank lines.

Summary Information for Mexican Banks

Bank	Branches	Assets ($ millions)	Global Deposits ($ millions)[1]
National Banks			
Bancomer[2]	738	$ 30,260	$19,050
Banamex[2,3]	716	30,893	17,890
Serfin[2]	603	20,106	12,090
Comermex	345	8,099	5,952
Internacional	365	7,296	4,169
Somex	306	4,440	3,428
Multi-Regional Banks			
Bancreser[3]	70	4,146	3,065
BCH	118	2,765	1,716
Atlantico	203	3,512	2,632
Mercantil de Mexico[3]	98	3,650	2,634
Confia[3]	123	2,642	1,795
Cremi[3]	115	3,389	1,910
Banpais[3]	101	1,228	913
Regional Banks			
Banorte	127	1,713	1,262
Promex	153	1,328	940
Bancen	105	1,079	484
Bánoro	73	1,143	845
Banorie[3]	38	418	458
Total	4,397	$128,107	$81,233
Percent of Total			
National Banks	69.9%	78.9%	77.0%
Multi-regional Banks	18.8%	16.7%	18.1%
Regional Banks	11.3%	4.4%	4.9%

Source: Comisión Nacional Bancaria

[1]Global deposits is a measure of total deposits in pesos and includes off-balance sheet deposits in the form of funds and trusts.

[2]Tier 1 Banks.

[3]Controlling stakes have been sold to private sector investors.

The concentration of banking business and the market dominance of the Tier 1 Banks are significant. As of 1991, the Tier 1 Banks accounted for approximately 63 percent of the total assets ($128 billion) held in the Mexican banking system, approximately 60 percent of the total peso deposits ($81 billion) and approximately 78 percent of sector-wide reported profits.

DEREGULATION

Starting in 1988, the Mexican government initiated a series of measures to deregulate important aspects of the Mexican financial system when it significantly reduced reserve requirements on bank deposits through the introduction of a new liquidity coefficient, replacing several earlier mechanisms requiring Mexican banks to invest funds in government-designated debt obligations and below-market loans. The new liquidity coefficient lowered the percentage of bank funds required to be invested in such instruments to 30 percent, thereby reducing the burden on the banks of financing the fiscal deficit. This change was made possible because of the strengthening of public finances. In 1991, a further liberalization of these compulsory investment regulations was implemented. See "Supervision and Regulation — The Banking Sector — Liquidity and Reserve Coefficients." In October of 1988, the Mexican government liberalized its restrictions on the interest rates payable by banks on savings deposits and similar liabilities; and it also began to grant more flexibility to the banks' management teams by allowing them to establish independent budgets, investment programs, organization structures and employee benefit packages.

In general, liberalization and deregulation have had a positive effect on the banking sector. Products and services that were discontinued or not developed during the period of nationalization of the Mexican banks, such as consumer lending, capital markets transactions and promotion of bank credit cards, were quickly reintroduced or developed, as banks once again sought to compete for customers and funding sources. GFB's management expects the process of deregulation to continue and anticipates that new products developed in response to regulatory changes will provide additional opportunities for growth and profitability.

ADOPTION OF THE UNIVERSAL BANKING MODEL

With the enactment of the Financial Groups Law in 1990, the Mexican government adopted the universal banking model adhered to in one form or another in numerous European Common Market countries, including Germany, Spain and the United Kingdom. Under the Financial Groups Law, commercial banking, stock brokerage, investment banking, leasing, factoring, foreign exchange and insurance activities may be conducted under a common financial services holding company. This model is intended to make Mexico's financial system more efficient and competitive, as financial institutions are permitted to seek economies of scale and scope, enter new markets, exploit synergies and explore new growth opportunities. Cross-marketing among subsidiary financial institutions (*e.g.*, by sharing customer lists and offering combined services) is encouraged under the Financial Groups Law.

Management believes that adoption of the universal banking model may contribute to the trend toward consolidation and concentration within the Mexican banking system as financial groups realize the economies of scale permitted under the model.

PROFITABILITY

As indicated in the following table, during each of the last five years, annual returns on average equity (measured in nominal peso amounts) for the Tier 1 Banks exceeded 20 percent. During that period, average annual returns on average assets for these banks exceeded 1.41 percent.

Return on Average Assets[1] (in percent)

	1987	1988	1989	1990	Year-End Forecast 1991
Bancomer	2.22%	2.12%	1.69%	1.31%	1.64%
Banamex	2.13	2.16	1.00	1.75	1.75
Serfin	1.45	1.67	1.38	1.00	0.65
Weighted average	2.03%	2.05%	1.33%	1.42%	1.41%

Return on Average Equity[1] (in percent)

	1987	1988	1989	1990	Year-End Forecast 1991
Bancomer	44.76%	33.79%	23.24%	16.86%	23.24%
Banamex	40.34	29.78	14.21	25.59	24.77
Serfin	51.29	45.06	30.29	24.62	19.58
Weighted average	43.34%	33.11%	20.13%	21.83%	23.37%

Source: Comisión Nacional Bancaria

[1] Average is two point average of beginning and end of period totals. Returns are calculated in nominal pesos.

CAPITALIZATION

Despite the fact that the combined assets of the Tier 1 Banks were expected to have tripled from year-end 1987 to year-end 1991, their combined ratio of total shareholders' equity to total assets was forecast to grow from 5.0 percent to 5.7 percent over the same period. The following table presents summary data for the Tier 1 Banks.

Capitalization Period-End Total Stockholders' Equity/Assets[1] 1987–1991 (in percent)

	1987	1988	1989	1990	Forecast 1991
Bancomer	5.13%	7.04%	7.42%	8.07%	6.43%
Banamex	5.87	8.21	6.21	7.32	6.90
Serfin	2.83	4.33	4.71	3.78	3.02
Weighted average	5.00%	7.01%	6.36%	6.57%	5.69%

Source: Comisión Nacional Bancaria

[1] These ratios do not correspond to the two regulatory measures of capital adequacy in Mexico: net capital/risk-weighted assets and *capital basico*/risk-weighted assets.

The strong capitalization of the Tier 1 Banks can be attributed primarily to two factors. In 1987, the Mexican government sold non-voting equity in the banks in the form of Certificados de Aportación Patrimonial (CAPs).The CAPs allowed limited public ownership of the banks and diluted government ownership, in some cases to 66 percent. Second, a strong growth in retained earnings occurred as a result of high profitability, low dividend payout rates and the revaluation of fixed assets and non-monetary investments to reflect the impact of inflation. See Appendix C. The decline in the total stockholders' equity-to-assets ratio during 1991 is largely a result of rapid asset growth. The combined assets of the Tier 1 Banks were forecast to grow 28.2 percent in real terms between year-end 1990 and year-end 1991.

ASSET QUALITY

Reported domestic asset quality for the Tier 1 Banks remained high during the 1987 to 1990 period, with past due loans as a percentage of the total portfolio averaging 3.1 percent. In 1991, past due loans as a percentage of the total loan portfolio (including rediscounted loans) was expected to grow to 4.3 percent, in large part as a result of changes in government regulations and stricter loan review by the banks.

Asset Quality Gross Past Due Loans/Total Gross Loans[1] 1987–1991 (in percent)

	1987	1988	1989	1990	Forecast 1991
Bancomer	1.24%	1.20%	1.76%	3.63%	3.42%
Banamex	2.08	2.30	2.05	3.33	5.47
Serfin	1.44	1.66	1.90	2.29	4.11
Weighted average	1.62%	1.75%	1.91%	3.13%	4.35%

Source: Bancomer; Banamex; Serfin.

[1] Total gross loans includes rediscounted loans.

Appendix B

Bancomer Business Description Overview

Since its inception, Bancomer has been a bank with strong ties to local communities throughout Mexico. Bancomer's origins can be traced to the Banco de Comercio, S.A., which was founded in 1932 in Mexico City. Over the next 25 years, Banco de Comercio acquired or founded 34 regional banks throughout Mexico and established a network of affiliated banks known as the Banco de Comercio system. Banco de Comercio also established a mortgage bank and a finance company, which were merged in 1957 to solidify the bank's position in the industrial and mortgage market. In 1977, management decided to consolidate the various depositary institutions comprising the Banco de Comercio system into a multi-purpose bank under the name of Bancomer. The merger allowed Bancomer to maintain its strong ties with local communities and simultaneously to realize the benefits of a single operational network.

Throughout its 60-year history, Bancomer's owners and management have pursued a business strategy focusing primarily on growth in the retail and middle market sectors, with a strong marketing orientation. Until nationalization of the banks in 1982, this strategy enabled Bancomer to sustain its position as Mexico's leading retail bank. Prior to nationalization, Bancomer operated with a decentralized management structure, allowing it to be highly responsive to community needs. As a nationalized bank, however, management decisionmaking was centralized in a government-appointed general manager, and Bancomer's officers and directors exercised only limited discretion with respect to strategic planning, personnel decisions and investment decisions. As a nationalized bank, Bancomer did not continue to add new branches, but rather focused on gathering deposits for investment primarily in Mexican government securities.

As a result of these government policies, Bancomer's management operated under a system of incentives inconsistent with profit maximization. Bancomer developed the reputation of being bureaucratic, overstaffed and non-aggressive — particularly when viewed in contrast to its pre-nationalization record of growth and community-based service. Nevertheless, throughout this period, Bancomer remained profitable.

Following a management reorganization that resulted in several new management appointments in 1989, Bancomer adopted as its strategic objective regaining the market position it had lost since nationalization. In the ensuing years, Bancomer has succeeded in this objective. By year-end 1991, Bancomer ranked first among Mexican banks in deposit-taking, with a 23.5 percent market share, and first in extension of credit, with a 23.8 percent market share. Bancomer is the second largest Mexican bank, measured by total assets, and has the largest branch network of any commercial bank in Mexico. Since 1986, Bancomer has averaged a return on equity of 30.80 percent.

Bancomer's management has pursued the following operating strategies since the December 1988 management reorganization:

■ Maintaining a leading market position in retail banking through a strong retail (consumer and middle market) orientation, introduction of new financial products and distribution of those products through an extensive branch network;

■ Spreading financial risk through size, industry and geographic diversification of Bancomer's customers and services;

■ Re-investing in Bancomer's business, particularly in technology, branch expansion and personnel training;

■ Maintaining conservative credit standards and diversifying risks so that no single credit can materially affect earnings; and

■ Maintaining a strong capital base.

Management believes that Bancomer's adoption of these operating strategies accounts in large measure for Bancomer's sustained profitability since 1988. Management believes that the continuation of these strategies will allow Bancomer to maximize its overall profitability, particularly with respect to the consumer and middle-market sectors. Management further believes that opportunities for profitable growth continue to exist in these sectors, not only because of an expected expansion of the Mexican economy, but also because Mexico's financial services sector is substantially underdeveloped.

MARKET POSITION

DEPOSIT GATHERING

By year-end 1991, Bancomer's global deposit base (*captación global*) which includes certain off-balance sheet deposits and money desk funds was forecast to reach $20 billion, representing an increase of approximately 13 percent in real terms over year-end 1990 figures. Moreover, by year-end 1991, Bancomer was expected to rank first among Mexican banks in global deposit gathering, with a market share exceeding 23 percent. As of year-end, Banamex and Serfin, Bancomer's principal competitors would rank second and third, respectively, in global deposit gathering. Bancomer's market position in peso deposit gathering has improved steadily from 1988, when Banamex led Bancomer by three percentage points, to 1990, when Bancomer captured the leading market share. These three banks have consistently captured approximately 60 percent of the Mexican global deposit market.

Market Shares in Mexican Global Deposit Gathering
(*"Captación Global"*)[1]
(in percent)

	For the Month Ending				
	December 31,				Forecast November 30,
	1987	1988	1989	1990	1991
Bancomer..................................	25.2%	24.3%	21.0%	22.9%	23.5%
Banamex..................................	25.4	27.5	22.7	23.0	22.0
Serfin...	13.8	12.6	12.3	15.3	14.9
Total of Tier 1 Banks................	64.4%	64.4%	56.0%	61.2%	60.4%

Source: Mexican Banking Association

[1] Amounts for 1987 figures include only traditional deposits (*captación traditional*)

CONSUMER AND COMMERCIAL LENDING

In the three years since the Mexican government reinstalled market-oriented management at Bancomer, the bank has been able to recapture much of the ground it had lost between 1982 and 1987 in consumer and commercial lending. Management attributes this success to, among other things, Bancomer's return to a decentralized management approach, its renewed service orientation, its willingness and flexibility to hire qualified managers and consultants, its ability to respond quickly to customer needs for new products and services and its reliance on and reinvestment in its extensive branch network. See Overview above.

By year-end 1991, Bancomer's gross loan portfolio, including rediscounted loans, was forecast to reach $19.8 billion. During 1991, a year in which credit grew approximately 32 percent in real terms in Mexico, Bancomer's loan portfolio was forecast to increase 43 percent in real terms.

Market Shares in Mexican Credit Market
(in percent)

		For the Month Ending			
	1987	December 31,			Forecast November 30, 1991
		1988	1989	1990	
Bancomer..................................	24.9%	25.5%	21.4%	21.8%	23.8%
Banamex	24.6	24.6	27.8	24.2	23.2
Serfin..	14.8	16.1	15.1	16.6	14.8
Total of Tier 1 Banks................	64.3%	66.2%	64.3%	62.6%	61.8%

Source: Mexican Banking Association

REGIONAL MARKET SHARE

By November 1991, the most recent date for which data is available, Bancomer was expected to capture 25.3 percent of the deposit market and 22.9 percent of the credit extension market outside of Mexico City. Management believes that Bancomer commands larger market shares in areas outside of metropolitan Mexico City due to its branch coverage and its regional boards structure. Management expects higher growth in the interior region than in the Mexico City metropolitan area, where funding is generally less expensive (see table below):

Bancomer's Position by Region in Deposit Gathering and Credit Markets
November 1991 (Forecast)

| Mexican region | Regional Deposit Gathering | | | Regional Credit Markets | | |
	Deposits ($ millions)	Market Share (%)	Market Position	Credit Extension ($ millions)	Market Share (%)	Market Position
Mexico City (D.F.)	$ 9,471	21.8%	2	$ 5,700	25.0%	2
Interior regions:						
Northwest..................	1,219	22.5	1	1,538	23.6	1
Northeast...................	1,940	21.7	2	1,357	17.3	2
West	1,522	21.3	1	1,184	18.7	2
Central........................	1,341	33.0	1	897	27.9	1
South	1,328	28.8	1	928	28.4	1
East	1,221	28.1	1	873	25.4	1
Southeast....................	1,008	30.9	1	920	30.9	1
Total interior..................	9,579	25.3	1	7,697	22.9	1
Total country..................	$19,050	23.5%	1	$13,396	23.8%	1

Source: Mexican Banking Association

BRANCH NETWORK AND TECHNOLOGY

At December 31, 1990, Bancomer had a network of 750 branches, of which approximately 115 were in the Mexico City metropolitan area and approximately 627 were in the country's other regions. By the end of 1991, Bancomer was expected to have more branches than any other commercial bank in Mexico, or about 17 percent of all bank branches in the country. Bancomer also continues to lead the Mexican ATM market; as of year-end 1991, it owned and operated 1,298 ATMs, or 42 percent of the total ATMs in operation in Mexico. Its closest competitor, Banamex, had 908 ATMs or 29 percent of the total ATMs.

Management is committed to expanding and remodeling Bancomer's branch network because it believes this is the focal point of economic activity in the local communities it serves, and is therefore fundamental to expanding and maintaining Bancomer's customer base, selling more of its existing financial products and introducing new products and services throughout all regions of Mexico.

In an effort to serve its clients better, in 1989 Bancomer developed a program to redesign its branches to provide higher-quality service to specific market segments at each branch. Initiated after an extensive marketing study, the *Nueva Sucursal Bancomer* (New Bancomer Branch) project calls for the segmentation of the banking floor of branches into four distinct service areas: VIP banking, targeted to high net worth individuals; personal banking, targeted to affluent individuals who do not qualify for VIP banking; retail banking, targeted to less affluent customers, expected to constitute approximately 90 percent of Bancomer's customer base; and middle market corporate banking. In New Bancomer Branches the floor space and personnel allocated to each area are tailored to meet the specific needs of the customer base at that location, thereby allowing the branch to deliver services and products more efficiently to its clients base.

In the first two years of the program, over 300 branches were restructured according to the New Bancomer Branch concept, resulting in increased customer use of the branch and the attraction of new customers. More conversions are scheduled through 1993, with the goal of strengthening Bancomer's market position (see the following table):

The New Bancomer Branch
Program Schedule and Status

December 31,	Total number of branches	Number of branches remodeled during the year	Total number of branches remodeled
1990................................	750	172	172
1991[1]................................	742	134	306
1992[1]................................	790	206	512
1993[1]................................	850	182	694

[1]As currently planned.

Bancomer, through Immobiliaria Bancomer, S.A., its real estate subsidiary, owns substantially all of its branch premises. This ownership has resulted in lower fixed costs than if the premises were leased.

A principal investment related to the development of the New Bancomer Branches is investment in technology for these branches, which, in management's view, will better position the bank to take advantage of market opportunities and more efficiently and effectively monitor and control its growing business. An example is Bancomer's communications network that relies on fiber optic linkages among all its regional centers and substantially all its branches. Bancomer has centralized its data processing operations in one large facility in Mexico City and is building a back-up facility. By year-end 1991 approximately 85 percent of Bancomer's branches were expected to be capable of on-line operations through its centralized computer network. Bancomer spent $118.6 and $99.3 (hardware, software and self-service automation equipment) in 1989 and 1990, respectively. In addition, during the period 1991 to 1995, Bancomer plans to spend an additional $434 million on technology.

LENDING ACTIVITIES

Bancomer's lending activities are concentrated in the areas of middle market and retail lending, which includes consumer, credit card and mortgage loans. The following chart shows the composition of Bancomer's interest earning assets, all of which are credit-related (except cash and government securities which are largely liquidity-related investments). Also shown below is an estimate of the composition of Bancomer's 1991 interest income by source. Of particular note is the relatively high contribution of middle market and retail lending. Middle market lending, which was forecast to comprise 25 percent of interest earning assets by December 31, 1991, was estimated to account for approximately 31 percent of interest income in 1991. Bancomer defines middle-market companies as those whose annual sales are between $0.7 million and $39.7 million. Retail-related assets, which were forecast to comprise 23 percent of interest earning assets by year-end 1991, were estimated to account for approximately 32 percent of interest income in 1991.

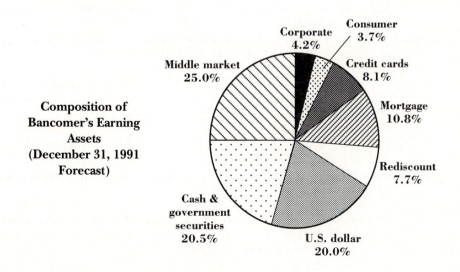

Composition of Bancomer's Earning Assets (December 31, 1991 Forecast)

- Corporate 4.2%
- Consumer 3.7%
- Middle market 25.0%
- Credit cards 8.1%
- Mortgage 10.8%
- Rediscount 7.7%
- Cash & government securities 20.5%
- U.S. dollar 20.0%

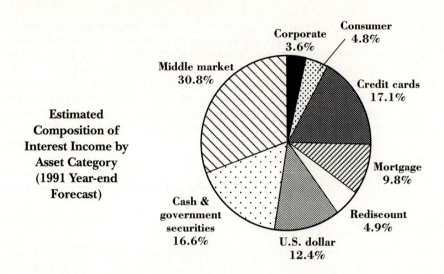

Estimated
Composition of
Interest Income by
Asset Category
(1991 Year-end
Forecast)

By year-end 1991, Bancomer's net interest margin (*margen financiero*) of its average interest earning peso-denominated assets, including rediscounted loans, was forecast to reach 10.82 percent. Bancomer uses two methodologies to price its loans. With respect to consumer, credit card and mortgage loans, which are generally longer term, Bancomer generally charges a variable interest rate computed as a multiple of its benchmark rate (the greater of CETES or *Costo Pocentual Promedio* [CPP], the bank funding rate in Mexico), subject to a floor expressed as a fixed spread over the benchmark rate. With respect to traditional loans (including corporate and middle market loans), which generally have a stated maturity of 28 days, Bancomer charges a fixed spread over CETES, and with respect to dollar-denominated loans, including trade-finance loans, working capital loans to Mexican companies and loans to the Mexican government, Bancomer charges a fixed spread over the London Interbank Offered Rate (LIBOR). (Bancomer defines the corporate market as consisting of companies with annual sales in excess of $39.7 million.) In addition, Bancomer charges upfront commissions on consumer, credit card and mortgage loans.

RETAIL BANKING

Since 1990, consumer lending in Mexico has experienced considerable growth due to a general decline in interest rates, improved economic conditions and the renewed availability of credit. Bancomer has experienced substantial increases in loan originations in its three principal retail business lines — consumer loans, credit cards and mortgage loans.

Bancomer offers a full range of retail services, including checking and savings accounts, fixed and floating rate loans, mortgages, automobile financing, traveller's checks, credit cards and related services, and trust and custodial services. Bancomer also offers asset management through its investment funds and money market accounts. During 1991, the average yield of Bancomer's retail credit portfolio fluctuated between 150 and 200 percent of the prevailing CETES rate.

Management believes that the asset quality of Bancomer's retail loans is high because Bancomer maintains conservative lending criteria and its customers, in the aggregate, are not overleveraged. In fact, because of the general unavailability of consumer credit and high levels of inflation in Mexico during the last decade, the Mexican population in general has a relatively low level of personal indebtedness (see table below):

Characteristics of Consumer Debt in Mexico
(billions of dollars, except as indicated)

Year	Mortgage Loans	Other Consumer Loans[1]	Total Consumer Loans	Ratio of Consumer Debt to GDP(%)	Consumer Debt Per Capita[2]
1989	$ 3.0	$2.2	$ 5.2	2.48%	$ 65.53
1990	5.7	4.2	9.9	4.15	122.07
1991 (Forecast)	10.1	7.5	17.6	6.34	212.42

Source: Bancomer; Banamex; Serfin; Institut Nacional de Estadística y Geografia e Informática.

[1] Includes credits for automobiles, credit cards and others.

[2] Not in billions. Consumer debt per capita in Mexico was computed by extrapolation from consumer credits extended by the Tier 1 Banks on the assumption that these banks account for 85 percent, 70 percent and 75 percent of Mexican credit card loans, mortgage loans and other consumer loans, respectively.

CONSUMER LOANS

Historically, Bancomer's consumer loan portfolio consisted largely of loans for the purchase of a wide range of consumer durables. In 1989, Bancomer introduced *Planauto,* an automobile financing program which was to help boost Bancomer's automobile loan volume to 76.2 percent of all consumer loans and 3.7 percent of total loans made by Bancomer by year-end 1991. Under *Planauto,* Bancomer provides pre-approved financing for up to 80 percent of the purchase price for an automobile, accessible by the client through its Bancomer credit card. When Bancomer introduced *Planauto,* it had approximately 23,250 car loans outstanding, for a total of $139.5 million. By year-end 1991, Bancomer was forecast to have approximately three times as many car loans outstanding (69,200), for a total of $654.6 million. By December 1991, it was estimated that 17.5 percent of all cars sold in Mexico would be financed by Bancomer, making it Mexico's largest originator of automobile loans for that month. Management believes that in addition to the success of *Planauto,* Bancomer's close ties with car distributors throughout Mexico have contributed to Bancomer's performance in this sector. Bancomer has maintained a high degree of credit quality in the car loan segment.

Bancomer has continued to introduce new consumer loan products. Recent programs include *plan crédito,* a program of personal credit lines targeted at purchases of consumer durable goods; *plan mejoras de vivienda,* a program of home improvement loans; and *plan micro,* aimed at financing purchases of personal computers by consumers.

CREDIT CARDS

Management believes that Bancomer's extensive retail network favorably positions Bancomer in the credit card market, since Bancomer is able to reach more consumers through its branches than its competitors. Currently, approximately 220,000 retail outlets accept Bancomer credit cards. By year-end 1991, Bancomer was expected to have the highest market share (in terms of monthly and annual billings) in the peso-based credit card market. By December 31, 1991, credit card balances were expected to comprise 11.3 percent of Bancomer's outstanding loans and constitute the most profitable segment of Bancomer's credit portfolio.

The interest-bearing peso credit card market in Mexico consists of Bancomer, Banamex and Carnet (a consortium of 11 banks, including Serfin). The following table sets forth summary market share data for the interest-bearing peso-based credit card market in Mexico. The table excludes billings on American Express cards, which are non-interest bearing.

Share of Annual Peso Based Credit Card Billings in Mexico

	Annual Billings ($ billions)		Market Share (%)	
	1990	1991 (Forecast)	1990	1991 (Forecast)
Bancomer	$2.9	$ 4.5	31.4%	36.9%
Banamex	3.7	3.8	39.7	31.2
Carnet	2.7	3.9	28.9	31.9
Total	$9.3	$12.3	100.0%	100.0%

Source: Bancomer, Banamex and Carnet

In 1990, management introduced more stringent credit standards which reduced credit card losses. This adoption of more stringent credit standards caused Bancomer to experience a significant reduction of market share during 1990. However, in 1991 following the introduction of a new marketing program, Bancomer's market share of monthly billings was expected to increase. Bancomer took the market lead in monthly credit card billings in February 1991. Its relative position was forecast to rise to a 4.3 percentage point advantage over its nearest competitor by year-end 1991. By December 1991, 37.1 percent of peso credit card billings, totalling $1.3 billion, were forecast to be Bancomer credit cards.

RESIDENTIAL MORTGAGE LOANS

Management expects the residential mortgage loan sector to grow significantly due to an unmet demand for housing in Mexico, currently estimated at six million units according to *Programa Nacional de Solidaridad* and the *Departamento del Distrito Federal*. By December 31, 1991, Bancomer's mortgage portfolio total was forecast to be $2.7 billion, representing 15.1 percent of Bancomer's total loan portfolio. By year-end 1991, Bancomer was expected to have over 60,000 home mortgages outstanding which would reflect a 364 percent real increase in market rate residential mortgages.

By November 30, 1991, Bancomer was expected to be a leader in this growing segment of the mortgage loan business, with a 35 percent market share. Management believed that the forecast ranking is due in large part to the innovative mortgage products Bancomer has created, allowing consumers to choose from a wide range of maturities, interest rates and amortization schedules.

Despite its rapid growth in this product segment, Bancomer has maintained its conservative credit standards. Virtually all of Bancomer's residential mortgage loans are for single family homes with sole mortgages. Families and extended families that acquire homes in Mexico have historically had a very low default rate, primarily because of the special importance of the home to the Mexican family and rising property values in an inflationary environment. Bancomer's general policy is to extend mortgage credit only if the initial loan-to-value ratio does not exceed 80 percent in the case of inexpensive homes, or 50 percent in the case of more expensive homes. Given Mexico's current moderate rate of inflation, loan-to-value ratios on outstanding mortgage loans are expected to decrease over the life of these loans. Moreover, in light of the current acute housing shortage in Mexico, mortgage lenders generally do not find it difficult to locate acceptable alternative buyers in the market if they are required to foreclose.

During the 1980s, only a small number of residential mortgage loans were made in Mexico. The home mortgage loans that banks offered were available primarily because of a government program that promoted loans for low-income housing. As required by law, Bancomer participated in this market to lend certain amounts to qualifying customers. Loans extended under this program, known as VIS *(Vivienda de Interés Social)*, carried below-market interest rates and fixed margins established by the Mexican government. Under the VIS program, participating banks bear the credit risk of default prior to maturity of VIS mortgage loans, but the government is obligated to pay the bank any outstanding principal remaining at maturity. Bancomer regards the risk of default prior to maturity of VIS loans (and therefore its credit exposure) to be relatively low in light of the subsidized interest rates, favorable repayment terms mandated under the program and the fact that the government purchases these loans from the lending bank and forgives the remaining balance at maturity if the borrower is current as of that date. In April 1989, the Mexican government terminated mandatory participation in the VIS program by banks. Since April 1989, Bancomer has made new VIS loans which earn a fixed spread and are funded by *Fondo de Fomento de la Vivienda* (FOVI), the Mexican housing development agency. The returns on this business are supplemented by the related business done with the developers of these projects.

MIDDLE MARKET BANKING

The middle market (consisting of companies with annual sales between $0.7 million and $39.7 million) is a rapidly growing segment that was constrained by limited access to credit during the 1980s. In 1991, Bancomer's middle market loan portfolio was growing at a rate of 21 percent in real terms.

Management believes that Bancomer is well positioned in this segment because of its strong historical ties to the middle market client base, especially in the regions outside the Mexico City metropolitan area, and its access to middle market clients through its network of regional board members. Bancomer continues to target the middle market because of its potential for further growth and because this market offers direct cross-selling opportunities for non-bank services (e.g., leasing, factoring and brokerage) which can be provided by GFB's other subsidiaries. Bancomer's middle market banking activities include traditional lending, commercial lending, mortgage loans, trade financing, foreign exchange and fiduciary and custodial services. Rediscounted loans are another product actively used by middle market companies. Rediscounted loans are below market rate loans which are made to encourage investment in high priority projects designated as such by the Mexican development agencies. Funding for these loans is provided to Bancomer by government development agencies such as Fomex and *Nafinsa*. The terms and rates of the funding ensure that Bancomer earns a positive spread on these loans.

INSTITUTIONAL BANKING

As part of the early 1991 general reorganization of Bancomer, senior management decided to create an Institutional Banking Division and integrate under it areas such as international banking, corporate banking, corporate finance and public finance. The division was created to establish a presence in each of these market segments by delivering products and services through specialized channels. By December 1991 it was expected that 147 corporations would be serviced in this division, classified under 18 sectors of economic activity. The industries include: motor vehicles, communications, electrical products and electronics, financial groups, tourism, rubber, mining, cement, food and beverage, chemical, retailing, pharmaceuticals, brokerage houses and insurance companies. By year-end 1991, the Institutional Banking Division was expected to account for approximately $33.6 million of Bancomer's profits.

INTERNATIONAL

In 1982, in order to increase its international presence, Bancomer acquired Grossmont Bank, which operates in San Diego, California. In June 1986, Bancomer formed Mercury Bank and Trust, Ltd., located in Grand Cayman, Cayman Islands, currently the only Mexican-owned bank in the Cayman Islands. According to a year-end 1991 forecast, Grossmont Bank would have assets of $363 million and a book value of $38.0 million. Mercury Bank and Trust, Ltd. would have year-end 1991 assets of $337 million and a book value of $21.1 million. GFB has filed applications with the Federal Reserve Board and the California Banking Department for approval to acquire indirect control of Grossmont (by virtue of its acquisition of control of Bancomer). Pending such approval, shares of the immediate holding company for Grossmont Bank have been placed in a trust, whose trustee has been instructed to sell such stock to one or more investors acceptable to the Federal Reserve Board and the California Banking Department in the event either application is denied.

Bancomer has had its own offices abroad since 1945, and today has branches in London and the Cayman Islands, agencies in New York and Los Angeles, and representative offices in Madrid, São Paulo, Buenos Aires, Santiago, Tokyo and Hong Kong. In addition, Bancomer has correspondent relationships with approximately 1,000 banks located in the world's financial centers. Bancomer has had established correspondent relationships with foreign banks since 1933.

SPECIALIZED FINANCIAL SERVICES

Specialized financial services at Bancomer include tourism investment and lending and other equity investments. In addition, Bancomer's Trust Division manages assets for clients seeking to take advantage of the Mexican fixed-income and equity markets.

LENDING AND INVESTMENT IN TOURISM

In 1984, Bancomer began to build a group specializing in tourism investment and lending in order to participate in Mexico's growing tourism market. This division performs credit analysis for Bancomer's tourism industry loans and analyzes and manages Bancomer's equity investments in tourism and hotel developments. Bancomer recognizes that any tourism loan or equity investment must be conservatively analyzed because of the substantial risks involved, including dependence on favorable economic conditions (in Mexico and in other countries) and exchange rates. The division's project analysts are tourism experts and are dedicated solely to the field.

Bancomer is one of the leading Mexican lenders to the tourism sector, with outstanding loans of $266 million to 126 projects forecast for year-end 1991. Past-due loans were expected to represent 0.03 percent of the tourism portfolio by year-end 1991.

Most of Bancomer's equity investments relating to tourism are conducted through Desarrollos Turísticos Bancomer, S.A., Bancomer's tourism holding company with 28 subsidiaries. Bancomer holds equity stakes in three prominent hotel developments in Mexico. First, Bancomer holds a 21 percent equity interest in the Presidente Stouffer chain, which consists of seven five-star luxury hotels and has been in operation since 1985. Second, Bancomer has a 29 percent interest in Club Med Huatulco, which opened in 1988. Its partners in the venture are Club Med, with a 34 percent equity stake; American Express with a 15 percent stake; and Fonatur, a Mexican government development company, with a 22 percent stake.

Bancomer's largest tourism investment is the Conrad Hotel project. Bancomer holds a 100 percent stake in the development of the Conrad chain in Mexico, a new group of luxury hotels and time-sharing condominiums, consisting of three projects, one each in Cancún, Puerto Vallarta, and Los Cabos (Baja California). Bancomer is committed to investing $317 million in these projects, of which $165 million has already been invested. This investment is expected to be recouped through time share sales, with the remainder financed through long-term loans. The Conrad Hotel in Cancún has been open since March 1991 and the Puerto Vallarta hotel is almost complete and was scheduled to open in June 1992. The Los Cabos project is still under construction and is scheduled for completion in the winter of 1992. Marketing for the hotels and the sale of time-sharing units is being handled by an affiliated company, Americas Resort Group in Los Angeles, California, and Corporación Mexitur in Mexico. Approximately 13 percent of the time-sharing units were expected to be sold by year-end 1991.

OTHER EQUITY INVESTMENTS

Bancomer maintains a diverse portfolio of equity investments in addition to its tourism investments. By December 31, 1991, this portfolio was expected to consist of 20 projects with capital contributions amounting to $23.5 million. Bancomer's average participation in the registered capital of non-tourism companies was 21 percent. These investments are minority positions acquired with a view to being sold in the medium-term. They involve active participation in directing and managing the projects. During 1991, Bancomer approved new equity investments totalling $9.6 million.

FUND MANAGEMENT

Bancomer manages several open- and closed-end funds and trusts, including money market equity and fixed-income funds and trusts. Many of these investment vehicles were originally created to serve as funding conduits for the bank at a time when regulatory reserve requirements favored such arrangements. Today Bancomer manages Ficomer F, a fixed-income fund targeted at the retail market. This fund pays investors competitive market rates and was designed to fill a market need for investments offering higher returns than traditional savings accounts. It has also been used to diversify Bancomer's funding source. In addition, Bancomer manages VALMER I and VALMER II which are Mexican equity funds; Figober, a fixed-income Mexican government securities fund; and Protec, a fund which invests in dollar-denominated securities.

Appendix C
Bancomer — Selected Financial Information
Bancomer — Unconsolidated Summary Financial Data[1]
(billions of nominal pesos, except per share data)

	Year Ended December 31,				
	1987	1988	1989	1990	1991 Forecast
Summary of Operations					
Interest income	Ps.7,245.0	Ps.9,524.4	Ps.8,326.1	Ps.11,115.1	Ps.13,805
Interest expense	6,476.4	8,017.9	6,769.8	8,166.4	9,232
Net interest income	768.6	1,506.5	1,556.3	2,948.7	4,573
Provision for loan losses	89.9	33.1	120.7	517.8	751
Net interest income after provision for loan losses	678.7	1,473.4	1,435.6	2,430.9	3,822
Non-interest income	350.7	470.0	1,070.8	1,567.0	2,071
Non-interest expense	524.6	991.6	1,491.1	2,994.7	3,872
Earnings before income taxes	504.8	951.8	1,015.3	1,003.2	2,021
Income taxes	195.5	421.0	407.6	369.3	819
Net income	Ps.309.3	Ps.530.8	Ps.607.7	Ps.633.9	Ps.1,201
Shares outstanding[2] (millions)	1,098.6	1,233.2	4,951.5	4,639.8	4,639
Per Share Data[3]					
Net income	Ps.381.4	Ps.456.7	Ps.196.8	Ps.132.2	Ps.259
Cash dividends[4]	0.0	0.0	8.1	24.2	27
Book value	942.1	1,714.6	630.8	948.4	1,280
Cash Dividends Paid on Common Stock	Ps.0.0	Ps.0.0	Ps.25.2	Ps.116.0	Ps.127
Balance Sheet Items — Period-End					
Assets	Ps.20,110.5	Ps.29,970.1	Ps.42,070.2	Ps.54,526.2	Ps.92,334
Gross loans[5]	13,521.8	16,236.8	24,503.9	36,103.2	60,740
Peso-denominated deposits	11,057.2	12,918.8	15,895.8	23,527.5	43,153
Total stockholders' equity	1,030.6	2,110.5	3,119.9	4,400.6	5,939

1 As required by Mexican accounting practices for banks, the reported assets of Bancomer do not include the assets of Bancomer's subsidiaries, but do include Bancomer's share of the equity of such subsidiaries. Bancomer's reported net income does not include the net income of its subsidiaries, except to the extent such subsidiaries distribute such income as dividends.

2 The number of shares outstanding at year end 1987 were adjusted for a 100:1 stock split in 1988. The figures for number of shares outstanding at year-end 1987, 1988 and 1989 have been adjusted to give effect to the conversion of the convertible subordinated debt. Per share data for 1987, 1988 and 1989 reflect these adjustments.

3 Based on two-point average of shares outstanding at beginning and end of period.

4 Dividends paid during each year.

5 Includes on-balance sheet loans and rediscounted off-balance sheet loans.

Bancomer
Unconsolidated Summary Financial Data (Cont.)
(billions of nominal pesos, except per share data)

	Year Ended December 31,				
	1987	1988	1989	1990	1991 Forecast
Convenience Translations (millions of dollars)[6]					
Net income	$ 220.2	$232.1	$245.0	$222.9	$398
Assets	9,038.4	13,058.9	15,700.8	18,297.4	30,026
Gross loans[5]	6,077.2	7,074.8	9,144.9	12,115.2	19,752
Peso-denominated deposits	4,969.5	5,629.1	5,932.4	7,895.1	14,033
Total stockholders' equity	$ 463.2	$919.6	$1,164.4	$1,476.7	$1,931
	(in percent)				
Selected Ratios					
Return on average total assets[7]	2.22%	2.12%	1.69%	1.31%	1.64%
Return on average sthareholders' equity[7]	44.76	33.79	23.24	16.86	23.24
Shareholders' equity to total assets — period-end	5.12	7.04	7.42	8.07	6.43
Total risk-based capital to risk-adjusted assets[8]	8.50	8.19	8.13	7.81	7.49[9]
Dividend payout[13]	8.15	0.00	19.07	20.13	NA
Net interest margin — pesos only[10]	8.16	8.45	8.52	11.58	10.82
Net interest margin[7]	6.59	6.91	5.15	7.22	7.37
Non-interest income to average total assets[7]	2.51	1.88	2.97	3.24	2.82
Non-interest expense to average total assets[7]	3.76	3.96	4.14	6.20	5.27

[5] Includes on-balance sheet loans and rediscounted off-balance sheet loans.

[6] See "Exchange Rates and Inflation" for the applicable exchange rate and Appendix A for a full set of constant peso coverted into dollar and nominal dollar financial statements.

[7] Based on average of beginning and end of period.

[8] See "Supervision and Regulation — The Banking Sector — Capital Adequacy."

[9] Capital adequacy requirements were modified in May 1991.

[10] Net interest margin (margen financiero) is defined as net interest income divided by the average interest earning peso-denominated assets, including rediscounted loans.

Bancomer
Unconsolidated Summary Financial Data (Cont.)
(in percent)

	Year Ended December 31,				1991 Forecast
	1987	1988	1989	1990	
Credit Quality Ratios					
Past-due loans to period-end gross loans[11]	1.23%	1.20%	1.76%	3.63%	3.42%
As a percentage of period-end classified portfolios[12]					
C, D and E credits	NA	NA	NA	4.67	3.87
Past-due C, D and E credits	NA	NA	NA	2.79	1.81
As a percentage of average gross loans[11]					
Net charge-offs	−0.25	0.53	−0.19	0.30	1.10
Allowance for credit losses	2.13	0.70	0.91	1.90	1.78
Allowance for credit losses as a percentage of period-end:					
Gross loans[11]	1.45	0.64	0.76	1.59	1.42
Past-due loans	117.64	53.33	43.06	43.81	41.49
C, D and E credits	NA	NA	NA	32.64	41.13
Past-due C, D and E credits	NA	NA	NA	54.56%	87.97%

[11] Includes rediscounted loans.

[12] The ratio for 1991 is based on the June 30, 1991 classification, the most recent available.

[13] Distributions out of 1991 net income are subject to approval at Bancomer's annual general shareholders meeting.

REVIEW AND DISCUSSION OF HISTORICAL FINANCIAL PERFORMANCE

The following summary discussion should be read in conjunction with the audited financial statements for 1990 appended hereto and the summary of significant differences between Mexican GAAP, Mexican accounting practices for banks and United States GAAP included in Appendix D. The following discussion addresses the financial condition and performance of Bancomer, the principal subsidiary of GFB. As required by Mexican accounting practices for banks, Bancomer does not consolidate the financial results of its subsidiaries. Accordingly, the income and expense numbers capture only the results of activities conducted at Bancomer and exclude the results of

its subsidiaries. Discussion of the non-bank subsidiaries of GFB and Bancomer is included below under "— Non-bank Subsidiaries."

Although Bancomer's business is principally peso-denominated and its books and records are kept in pesos, to facilitate analysis, peso amounts have been converted into nominal dollars, and nominal dollar amounts will appear hereafter. Summary financial statements in nominal dollars are shown below. Dollar amounts have been derived by translating peso amounts on Bancomer's historical balance sheets and income statements into nominal dollars at the year-end and average exchange rates, respectively, for each year.

Bancomer
Summary Income Statement
(For years ended December 31, 1987–1991 Forecast)
(millions of nominal dollars)

	1987	1988	1989	1990	1991 Forecast
Net interest income	$547.2	$658.7	$627.5	$1,036.8	$1,515
Provision for loan losses	64.0	14.5	48.7	182.1	248
Net interest income after provision for loan losses	483.2	644.2	578.8	854.8	1,266
Non-interest income	249.7	205.5	431.7	551.0	686
Non-interest expense	373.5	433.6	601.2	1,053.0	1,282
Earnings before taxes and non-recurring charges[1]	$359.4	$416.2	$438.4	$ 475.0	$ 669
Earnings before taxes	359.4	416.2	409.4	352.8	669
Provision for taxes	139.2	184.1	164.3	129.9	271
Net income	$220.2	$232.1	$245.0	$ 222.9	$ 398

[1] See below" — Net Income — Non-interest Expense."

REVIEW AND DISCUSSION OF HISTORICAL FINANCIAL PERFORMANCE (Cont.)

Bancomer
Summary Balance Sheet
(December 31, 1987–1991 Forecast)
(millions of nominal dollars)

	1987	1988	1989	1990	1991 Forecast
Cash and due from banks	$ 438	$ 805	$ 695	$ 644	$ 807
Government securities	1,412	3,423	3,028	3,250	4,287
Net loans[1]	5,704	6,505	8,269	10,945	17,644
Other assets	1,485	2,326	3,709	3,459	7,289
Total assets	$9,038	$13,059	$15,701	$18,297	$30,027
Local-currency deposits	4,970	5,629	5,932	7,895	14,033
Other interest-bearing funds	2,048	4,500	6,278	5,636	8,040
Other liabilities	1,558	2,011	2,326	3,289	6,022
Total liabilities	8,575	12,139	14,536	16,821	28,095
Total stockholders' equity	463	920	1,164	1,477	1,932
Total liabilities and stockholders' equity	$9,038	$13,059	$15,701	$18,297	$30,027

[1]Gross loans less specific reserves.

TO FACILITATE ANALYSIS OF CHANGES IN REAL TERMS, *I.E.*, INFLATION-ADJUSTED TRENDS, SUMMARY FINANCIAL STATEMENTS IN CONSTANT CURRENCY UNITS EXPRESSED AS AN INDEX ARE SHOWN BELOW.

Bancomer
Summary Income Statement
(constant currency units expressed as an index)
(1987 = 100)

	1987	1988	1989	1990	1991 Forecast
Net interest income	100.0	91.5	78.8	117.9	149
Provision for loan losses	100.0	17.2	52.2	176.9	209
Net interest income after provision for loan losses	100.0	101.4	82.3	110.0	141
Non-interest income	100.0	62.6	118.8	137.3	147
Non-interst expense	100.0	88.3	110.6	175.4	184

REVIEW AND DISCUSSION OF HISTORICAL FINANCIAL PERFORMANCE (Cont.)

Bancomer

Summary Income Statement (Cont.)

(constant currency units expressed as an index)

(1987 = 100)

	1987	1988	1989	1990	1991 Forecast
Earnings before taxes	100.0	88.0	78.3	61.1	100
Provision for taxes	100.0	100.6	81.1	58.0	105
Net income	100.0	80.1	76.4	63.0	97

Bancomer

Summary Balance Sheet

(constant currency units expressed as an index)

(December 31, 1987 = 100)

	1987	1988	1989	1990	1991 Forecast
Cash and due from banks	100.0	125.1	105.4	83.6	90
Government securities	100.0	164.9	142.3	130.7	149
Net loans	100.0	77.6	96.2	109.0	152
Other assets	100.0	106.5	165.7	132.2	242
Total assets	100.0	98.3	115.2	115.0	163
Local-currency deposits	100.0	77.0	79.2	90.2	139
Other interest-bearing funds	100.0	149.4	203.4	156.3	193
Other liabilities	100.0	87.8	99.0	119.9	190
Total liabilities	100.0	96.3	112.5	111.4	161
Total stockholders' equity	100.0	135.0	166.8	181.0	205
Total liabilities and stockholders' equity	100.0	98.3	115.2	115.0	163

VIII

Integrated Financing and Organization Decisions

Raymond Vernon

Case 43

Sola Chemical Company

ORGANIZING THE INTERNATIONAL FINANCE FUNCTION

The year was 1970. The subject before Sola Chemical's board of directors was a set of proposals by Multinational Consultants, Inc., recommending a drastic overhaul in the organization of Sola's overseas business. The board had already agreed, albeit a bit uncertainly, that the International Division would have to be abolished and that its responsibilities for overseas production and overseas marketing would have to be distributed among some new regional divisions. Now the question was: What to do about the finance and control functions for which the International Division had been responsible?

ORIGINS

Ever since World War II, Sola had been doing what came naturally in the expansion of its foreign business. In the years just after the war, Sola thought of itself as one of five or six companies that made up the leadership in the industrial and agricultural chemicals industry in the United States. At that time, a company with annual sales of $150 million could claim a leadership position. Besides, sales of the company at that time were reasonably well concentrated in only four main product groups. From the perspective of 1970, after nearly twenty-five years of growth and of diversification into new products and new markets, operations in the immediate postwar period seemed extraordinarily neat and tidy.

In the first years after the war, the foreign business of Sola was a limited affair. Mainly it consisted of the sales that a small export department could drum up in Western Europe and Latin America, relying largely on commission merchants, wholesalers, and industrial buyers in those areas. From time to time, Sola would discover that one of its newer products had taken hold in some country, generally at a time five or six years after it had found a market in the United States. After a few years of expansion in any foreign market, however, the attractiveness of the particular line in the area would generally fall away as quietly as it had appeared.

Apart from the seemingly episodic and sporadic lines of business of this sort, Sola's main "foreign" commitment in the years up to World War II was a manufacturing subsidiary in Canada, a subsidiary that Sola had set up in the late 1920s in response to a sharp increase in Canada's industrial tariffs. Except for a few shares nominally held by Canadian directors, this subsidiary was wholly owned by Sola. When the Imperial Preference tariff system was established in 1932, the Sola management had congratulated itself on its foresight in establishing a subsidiary inside the Commonwealth so that it could meet British competitors such as Imperial Chemical Industries on equal terms. From Sola management's viewpoint, however, the Canadian subsidiary could hardly be called "foreign." Situated not far from Windsor, Ontario, it was close enough to Sola's midwest headquarters to be run like any other branch plant. The product policies and marketing policies of Sola seemed to apply about as well to the Canadian plant as any other. True, there were some occasional crises of an unfamiliar sort, as when the Canadians tinkered with the value of their currency in relation to the U.S. dollar, or when they set up unfamiliar provisions in relation to the taxation of profits. But an occasional consultation with the company's bankers and tax attorneys was generally sufficient to deal with crises of this sort.

Quite different from Sola's relationship to its Canadian subsidiary in the years immediately after World War II were its ties to a French subsidiary that had been set up at about the same time. Unlike the Canadian subsidiary, only 53 percent of the equity of this company was owned by Sola, the rest being in the hands of Cie. Chimie Tricolor, a leading French manufacturer whose product lines fell largely within two of Sola's four product groups. Nobody at Sola could quite recall how this particular liaison had first developed. But there was an impression that Sola had been confronted with an ultimatum by the French chemical industry at one point in the 1920s: either she must invite a French business interest to join her in the creation of a French manufacturing subsidiary or she must risk losing a lucrative market that was being supplied by exports from the United States. There was some recollection among Sola's oldtimers that the ultimatum had been backed up by hints from the French ministry of industry that the threats might not prove hollow. In any event, whatever the origins of the French partnership might be, the subsidiary had grown away from Sola over the years. By the late 1940s it was thought of as almost an independent entity, operating under the stewardship of the French partner and negotiating with Sola for product information and technology very much on an arm's-length basis.

So much for the situation at the beginning of the postwar era.

Between that time and 1970, the foreign business of Sola had expanded at an astonishing rate, considerably faster than the United States. And as the foreign business grew, not only the policies and strategies but even the very structure of Sola was greatly affected. Step by step, additional locations had been selected for the establishment of new manufacturing subsidiaries: the United Kingdom in 1952; Germany in 1955; Mexico in 1956; Brazil in 1960; Italy in 1962; Australia in 1965; and so on, until Sola's manufacturing facilities covered fifteen different countries. At the same time, operations in Canada had been considerably expanded, covering more of Sola's product lines. In each of these cases, Sola had preferred to go it alone, without local partners. And after a nasty confrontation or two with the French partners over the management of the French facility, a friendly divorce had been arranged, leaving Sola with a wholly owned manufacturing facility in France in lieu of the old partnership.

Although Sola had not set up more than a portion of the U.S. product line in any one country, the total number of products manufactured overseas was widening every year. In fact, there were even three or four cases in which the U.S. plants had suspended operations on an old staple item, assigning what was left of the business to one of the foreign facilities where the product still seemed to command a market. When that happened, the foreign facility took over Sola's third country markets as well.

While the manufacturing subsidiaries were spreading over the globe, Sola was setting up other units to facilitate the handling of its foreign business. Sola had discovered very early the tax advantages of a western hemisphere trade corporation and had set up a company in Delaware to qualify under the U.S. tax code. A corporation could qualify if it derived practically all its income from trade or business (as distinguished from investment), and confined its business to the western hemisphere outside the United States. The profits of such a corporation were taxed at a rate 14 percentage points less than the standard U.S. rate. To exploit this advantage, U.S. Sola billed its exports to western hemisphere countries from the United States through its western hemisphere trade corporation. As a rule, such exports were billed out by U.S. Sola to the trade corporation at the lowest possible appropriate figure, which Sola calculated in accordance with a formula that included an 8 percent mark-up over cost. This formula had the effect of placing most of the profit on such sales in the trade corporation.

Other arrangements to minimize taxes had been made as well. Back in 1958, before the Revenue Act of 1962 had restricted the use of foreign-based holding companies as "tax havens" — that is, as vehicles for postponing the payment of U.S. taxes on foreign income — Sola's treasurer and tax attorney had pushed through the establishment of a Swiss holding company. U.S. Sola owned Sola-Switzerland, which in turn held nominal ownership over Sola's subsidiaries outside the United States. In those days, Sola-Switzerland could perform all kinds of useful services for U.S. Sola. For one thing, like the western hemisphere trade corporation, it could act as an intermediary in export sales from the United States. When Sola-Switzerland was used as an intermediary, the tax benefits to U.S. Sola were rather different than those associated with the use of the western hemisphere company. Sola-Switzerland's profits were subject to normal tax rates once they got into the U.S. tax jurisdiction. But that did not occur until the profits were declared to U.S. Sola in the form of dividends. Meanwhile, Sola-Switzerland could shuttle the cash generated by export profits to any point in the Sola system that required it.

Sola-Switzerland's cash flow could be built up not only by exports but also by the dividends, royalties, interest and fees generated in the Sola subsidiaries that Sola-Switzerland nominally owned. As long as Swiss law did not tax the income of the Swiss holding company and as long as a U.S. law did not classify the funds as taxable in the United States, Sola-Switzerland was a highly useful mechanism.

That particular arrangement had deferred quite a lot of tax payments for a few years. Subsidiaries could declare dividends and could pay interest, agency fees, administrative charges, and royalties to the holding company without subjecting the income to U.S. taxation; the U.S. tax bite would come only when the income moved upstream as dividends to the U.S. parent. Though the U.S. system of tax credits on foreign-earned income ensured that the income would not be taxed twice when it finally appeared on the U.S. parent's books, still there was something to be gained at times from deferring the U.S. tax. The tax advantage was especially important when the subsidiary's payments to its parent had not been taxed locally because they represented expenses to the subsidiary, or when the subsidiary's income had been taxed at rates well below those in the United States. In those situations, when the payments finally were received as dividends in the United States, some U.S. taxes would be due.

When the Internal Revenue Code was amended in 1962 to restrict the use of tax haven companies, many of the tax advantages involved in the maintenance of such a company disappeared. The provisions that expose the income of such tax haven companies to U.S. taxation are exceedingly complex. But Sola's Swiss holding company clearly fell within its terms. It was controlled by U.S. Sola, and it derived more than 70 percent of its income from the dividends, interest, royalties and other fees received from Sola's operating subsidiaries located in third countries. Accordingly, the income of Sola-Switzerland was fully taxable under U.S. law just as if it had been paid directly to U.S. Sola itself.

One tax advantage associated with foreign holding companies still remained, however. Loath to discourage exports from the U.S. in any way, Congress had exempted from the new provisions such income as the tax haven companies were garnering from their role in the handling of U.S. exports. As long as a spread could exist between the price at which U.S. Sola invoiced its goods for export and the price at which the goods were invoiced for import in the foreign country of destination, there were still tax advantages in assigning the spread to an intermediate company located in a tax-free area.

Despite the fact that Sola-Switzerland had lost much of its original purpose, there was some hesitation about liquidating the Swiss company. It would entail the transfer of the equity of many underlying operating subsidiaries, the transfer of the Swiss company's claims to the long-term and short-term debt of some of the operating subsidiaries, and the shift of the Swiss company's title in patents and trade names abroad that were being licensed to the subsidiaries.

Numerous contractual ties between the Swiss company and the subsidiaries also would have to be dissolved, such as the right of the Swiss company to receive payment for administrative and technical services and for sales agency services. All these rearrangements were bound to generate administrative and legal problems in a number of different countries, where the increasing curiosity and sophistication of the regulatory authorities could be counted on to stir up difficulties.

Accordingly, Sola decided to leave the Swiss holding company in existence and to create several other intermediate companies besides. One would be a Luxembourg company, set up to capture some of the profits on U.S. exports, which still were entitled to tax deferral treatment. Another enterprise would be set up to segregate the income generated by subsidiaries in advanced countries. Under the 1962 law, income originating in subsidiaries in the less-developed areas, unlike income from the advanced countries, could still be kept beyond the reach of U.S. tax collectors to the extent that it was reinvested in less-developed areas. Accordingly, a holding company was set up in Curaçao to own Sola's subsidiaries in less-developed areas and to receive the income of such subsidiaries for routing to destinations where the income was needed. Curaçao's virtue as a holding company headquarters consisted *inter alia* of its willingness to leave such income virtually untaxed as it passed through the holding company on its way to a new destination.

As if this complex cluster of intermediate companies was not enough, Sola decided in 1966 that another intermediate structure would be useful, namely, a holding company created under the laws of Delaware to act as Sola's alter ego in floating bond issues in the European market.

Well before 1966, it was clear to U.S. Sola that its European subsidiaries' voracious appetite would have to be fed by more borrowing from abroad. Sola itself was under a handicap when raising money in Europe, because U.S. internal revenue requirements obliged it to withhold 30 percent of interest or dividend payments to non-resident recipients. That provision placed a heavy handicap on the securities of U.S. issuers in Europe. Sola's Swiss holding company had been used two or three times before as the nominal borrower of dollar-denominated funds from European sources. Operating under the umbrella of a guarantee from U.S. Sola, the Swiss holding company had been able to borrow medium-term money at reasonable rates from private European sources. Though the interest costs had run a little higher than they would have in the United States, these flotations had saved the bother of registration with the Securities and Exchange Commission, the problem of qualification under the "blue sky" laws of the state regulatory agencies, and so on; the difference in costs, therefore, was not as great as the interest rates indicated. At the same time, Sola had developed some excellent European banking ties that might be in a position to help out in the event that the U.S. government really clamped down on the export of capital from the United States. As early as 1958 or 1959, that contingency had become something to worry about, as U.S. officials began to express their misgivings over the condition of the U.S. balance of payments.

By 1965, contingency had turned to reality. "Voluntary" controls had been imposed over the outflow of funds from the United States to subsidiaries in Europe. Although the controls were very loose and left many different ways in which Sola could arrange for the generation of cash flows in its overseas subsidiaries, Sola tried to respond to the spirit of the regulations by raising a larger proportion of its needed funds outside the United States.

One possible step to that end was to continue using the Swiss holding company, as it had been used in the past, to borrow from European sources. But Sola was not eager to expand the use of the Swiss holding company, now that it had lost most of its usefulness as a tax haven. True, such a holding company still had some advantages that U.S. Sola did not share, such as the fact that its payments of dividend and interest to non-U.S. recipients were not subject to the reporting and withholding requirements of U.S. tax law. But the use of such a company also had some disadvantages, when compared with a Delaware company, such as the fact that losses if any could not be consolidated in U.S. Sola's income tax return in the United States.

The upshot was that Sola decided in 1966 to create a second Delaware holding company, with functions carefully designed to retain the advantages of a Swiss holding company as a financing intermediary while avoiding some of its disabilities. The main purpose of the second Delaware holding company was to borrow funds outside the United States with the guarantee of U.S. Sola and to lend those funds to Sola's foreign subsidiaries. As long as the new holding company confined itself to this sort of operation, its only significant income — namely, interest payments from the subsidiaries — was regarded as of foreign origin. Since 80 percent or more of its income was of foreign origin, the Delaware company, like the Swiss company, was not required to withhold any sums in connection with interest payments to non-U.S. recipients. Such profits as the Delaware company might have were within the reach of the U.S. and Delaware tax jurisdiction. But profits were likely to be trivial, given the purpose of the company. Besides, Delaware tax provisions were traditionally benign in such matters, and U.S. tax provisions, ever since the adoption of the 1962 amendments, made only small distinctions between the profits of domestic holding companies and those of foreign holding companies of U.S. taxpayers.

The creation of the Delaware finance company proved to be a very wise step indeed. On January 1, 1968, the so-called voluntary program of capital export controls became mandatory. At the same time, the program was tightened up so that the various alternative means of transferring funds abroad became more restricted. Under the new program, Sola's right to transfer funds abroad was tied to its historical record of investment in the years just prior to 1968. Investment for that base period was defined as capital transfers in cash or in kind made to foreign subsidiaries plus profits retained in the subsidiaries during the period. Once that base figure was calculated, its application was differently defined for different groups of countries. Subsidiaries in the less-developed countries, the "Schedule A" countries, were allowed to continue receiving investment from U.S. Sola at their old levels, even a little higher. Then there was a "Schedule B" group, which the U.S. regulators thought of as being especially dependent on U.S. capital flows — the oil countries, the United Kingdom, Japan, and a few other areas. Added investments from the United States in these areas were cut down but not eliminated; capital flows to these areas were restricted to 65 percent of the base period. Canada, originally in this group, was exempted from the regulations altogether.

The real problem for Sola, therefore, was the European subsidiaries, that is, the subsidiaries located in "Schedule C" countries. These were cut back drastically. At first, added investment from U.S. Sola could only take place through retained earnings. And even the retained earnings could not be used under the rules if this meant a retention rate higher than base period rates or if it meant an investment rate higher than 35 percent of the base period.

If it had not been for the fact that borrowings outside the United States were exempted from the restrictions, Sola would have been in real trouble at first. That exemption carried the company through 1968. And in 1969 and 1970, the restrictions came to be somewhat eased. But the experience impressed on the minds of Sola's management more than ever the need to have an intimate knowledge of the world's sources of capital and to have the flexibility in organization to use the sources as needed. This heightened recognition centered attention on just how decisions were taken on such matters inside the organization.

THE FINANCIAL ORGANIZATION

As Sola expanded its overseas operations, the legal instrumentalities and national environments that concerned it increased rapidly in number. From World War II until 1970, therefore, there was a constant need to restructure the internal organization and procedures that were responsible for formulating and executing financial policies and for controlling financial operations. That restructuring was tied in intimately, of course, with other changes in Sola's organization, including changes in the marketing and production systems associated with a growing overseas operation.

In the early 1960s, the foreign business had grown to such proportions that it was thought advisable to create an international division. The first executive in charge of that division, an aggressive and ambitious manager, decided that one of his major needs was to pull together the haphazard structure that up to that time had been formulating financial policy for the foreign areas. With the approval of Sola's top management, therefore, a new structure was created. Some of the essential elements of the organization tying together the financial function at that stage are suggested by the diagram in Exhibit 1.

A word or two of elaboration is needed in order to relate Sola's structure in the early 1960s, portrayed in Exhibit 1, to financial decisions as taken at that time.

Major investment decisions, such as decisions to create a new foreign subsidiary or substantially to increase its capitalization, were generally recommended in the first instance by the international manager to Sola's president; he, in turn, usually sought the advice of his board of directors, as well as the advice of many other sources.

Major policies aimed at reducing taxes on overseas operations were usually initiated by the international treasurer, discussed with U.S. Sola's treasurer and tax attorney, then cleared with the finance committee.

Policies with regard to borrowing by foreign subsidiaries were no problem. Apart from accounts payable and accrued liabilities and except for a rare local loan initiated by the international treasurer, such transactions did not arise. Subsidiaries were not authorized to borrow; indeed they were not thought of as managing their own cash flow. Funds were channelled to the subsidiaries by the international treasurer as needed. Before 1965 these funds had come mainly from the parent or the Swiss holding company, in the form of short-term dollar debt. Later on, after the Delaware company was formed and had begun to raise dollars through the sale of Eurobonds, it became the principal creditor for Sola's foreign subsidiaries.

Apart from decisions on whether and how to provide the subsidiaries with their working capital needs, the other major area of financial operating policy was how to withdraw funds from a subsidiary that held surplus cash. In this case, the main problem was viewed as minimizing the tax burden associated with withdrawal, and the main policy variable was the choice between dividends, royalties, interest, and management fees. That choice was made by the tax attorney, on the basis of data provided by the international treasurer.

The international controller, as Exhibit 1 suggests, bore a somewhat

Exhibit 1 *Sola Chemical Company. Financial offices in the structure of Sola Company, 1962*

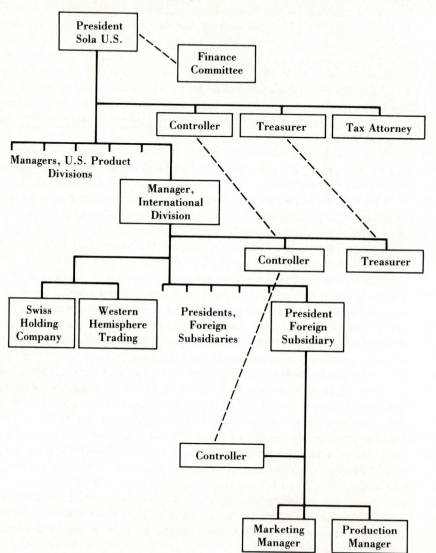

different relation to the organization than the treasurer. Unlike the treasurer, the controller had representatives in each of the subsidiaries. This difference reflected the fact that the treasurer saw his function as that of managing the money flows of the system, whereas the controller saw his function as that of monitoring the performance of its various parts. The first function, so it seemed, could be performed well enough from the bridge of the enterprise, whereas the second function required getting down into the various holds below.

PROPOSALS FOR REORGANIZATION

As a rule, the international treasurer's problems were not the sort of subject that got discussed very much among Sola's directors. When a major investment abroad was involved, that of course was fairly well explored. But the discussion mostly involved questions of strategy, rather than financing and cash flow problems. These were left pretty much for the finance committee and the treasurer's office to worry about. As far as the finance committee was concerned, that group was free to admit that its ability to second-guess the treasurer's office on overseas' financing was quite limited. The subject was just too specialized, it appeared. So the international treasurer proved to be performing a vital function.

Fortunately for Sola Chemical, it had filled that post very well indeed. Milray Thaler had been international treasurer ever since 1958 when the post was first created. He had come out of the old export department, seasoned by years of selling in a world of inconvertible currencies. He had learned all about the ways in which blocked currencies could be turned into usable cash, and ways in which avoidable taxes could be avoided. As international treasurer, he ran a tight organization. He kept close touch with the problems of every subsidiary, especially their problems of cash flow. As far as he could see, the foreign subsidiaries had been well provided for, without having to worry about money and credit questions for which they were hardly equipped. And as far as taxes were concerned, the foreign side of Sola had done marvelously well in avoiding the avoidable.

Despite that fact, by 1970, the financial organization was showing certain signs of strain. By that time, Thaler's unflagging efforts to hold down taxes and to generate money where it was most needed had made a shambles of the periodic profit and loss statements of the subsidiaries. The U.S. system of controls over the export of funds to subsidiaries had increased the complexities of financing. The objective of holding down the total tax bill was now constrained by restrictions on the outflow of capital from the United States. The importance of distinguishing between the treatment of subsidiaries in different countries also was increasing. The differences between less-developed countries and advanced countries, and between countries in Schedules A, B, and C, were important. Added wrinkles, such as Canada's special status under the U.S. capital export control program, had to be kept in mind. The difficulties were heightened further by the fact that some countries, especially the United States and Germany, were beginning to take seriously their various fiscal provisions relating to the international pricing of goods and services. Provisions such as Section 482 of the U.S. Internal Revenue Code, authorizing the tax authorities to use arm's-length prices in interaffiliate transactions, were beginning to be applied seriously. Thaler's consultations with the tax people and his demands on Sola's treasurer were constantly rising in number and urgency.

In addition, Thaler's difficulties with the controller's area seemed on the increase. The more strenuous the efforts of the treasurer, the more difficult the problem of the controller. If the reported profit and loss statements of the manufacturing subsidiaries could be taken at face value, most of them were operating at practically no profit; the only exception was the subsidiary in Canada. What actually was happening depends on what the word "actually" meant. Profits were appearing in the western hemisphere trading company, in the Swiss holding company, in the Swiss holding company in Luxembourg, and in Curaçao. Whether these profits were "actual" or not depended on what one thought of the validity of the prices charged for products traded among the affiliates, as well as the royalty charges and administrative fees. Sometimes there was a basis for testing these prices and fees against analogous arm's-length transactions. But more often, the goods or services involved were sufficiently distinctive so that no independent arm's-length standard could readily be found, assuming an effort were made to find one.

On top of this problem was the fact that Sola's subsidiaries in Europe, facing the elimination of trade barriers in the EEC and EFTA, found themselves competing in one another's territory with similar product lines. Here and there, the problem had been reduced by the timely intervention of the international manager. Once or twice, where specialty items were involved, the subsidiaries had agreed to allocate production tasks between them without bothering to involve the international office. In situations of that sort, the transfer price was fixed according to the bargaining strength of the subsidiaries and the transaction was recorded as if it were undertaken with an outside vendor. But as the number of subsidiaries and the number of product lines kept rising, this *ad hoc* approach was beginning to prove inadequate.

For the controllers in the local subsidiaries, all these problems presented growing headaches. The performance reports were beginning to make less and less sense, unless adjusted in various ways. Adjustments, however, required the refereeing role of the international controller when it involved a decision affecting the relative performance of two foreign subsidiaries, and it required the involvement of U.S. Sola's controller when the decision affected the U.S. company's reported performance. As a result of the accumulation of decision rules arising out of these adjudications, controllers' reports were beginning to bear less and less relation to the financial statements.

With these considerations and others in mind, Multinational Consultants, Inc., a prominent international consulting firm, was called in to advise on the reorganization of Sola's foreign business. After studying the operations of the company for a number of months, Multinational Consultants produced a voluminous report covering the problems of the foreign side of Sola's business. Among other things, it had a number of observations regarding the operation of the financial function, observations that boiled down to three propositions:

1. The treasurer's function had become much too complex and diffuse to be managed effectively from the center. Opportunities were being missed and errors committed. Among the errors cited, for instance, was the failure of the international treasurer to develop a systematic policy toward the threat of currency fluctuations. The opportunities missed as a result of the absence of such a policy were not the sort that were necessarily visible in Sola's financial statements. But once in a while, missed opportunities could be detected. One of these was the failure to hedge against a sterling devaluation in 1967, when the likelihood of the devaluation seemed extraordinarily high; this alleged oversight was said to have cost the company $350,000 in translation losses. Other opportunities overlooked, according to MCI, were those inherent in the possibilities for borrowing in local markets.

   The tight cash flow controls from headquarters, MCI guessed, reduced the likelihood that such opportunities were being recognized and exploited.

2. The treasurer was much too preoccupied with tax savings and too little concerned with reducing the cost of funds.

3. The financial data essential for the use of the treasurer's office was markedly different from the data needed for the performance of the controller's function, more so than in the case of complex operations within the United States proper. This difference was due to the fact that the units of Sola were in so many different jurisdictions with different rules covering taxation, access to capital, and so on. Essentially, the controller would be obliged to develop a separate score card, gauging the performance of profit centers on the basis of data that were compiled primarily for controls purposes.

As a first step toward achieving the needed shifts in direction, Multinational Consultants, Inc., proposed a number of major organizational changes. It was proposed that the international division should be broken up into several foreign area divisions, each of which would have status on a par with a U.S. product division. The international treasurer and the international controller would be moved upstairs into the offices of Sola's treasurer and controller respectively. A new layer of treasurers, controllers, and tax attorneys would be created at the area division level.

Under the new system, the lowest control center on the foreign side would be a given product line in a given area. Where more than one subsidiary in an area was involved in the product, the control center would combine the activities in the product of all such subsidiaries. Presumably, the treasurer could not ignore the performance of the subsidiary, since that performance would affect its tax liability. But for the controller's needs, an area-product approach to performance would be taken. Exhibit 2 indicates how the financial offices would sit in the revised Sola structure after reorganization.

Practically everyone on the foreign side of the Sola organization reacted to the proposals with some degree of hostility or reserve. The international manager saw himself as risking a major demotion: Either he would be moved upstairs into the staff of the Sola's president, or would be placed at the head of the "Europe and Africa" area. In either case, his status would be a notch lower. Of all the officers reacting to the change, however, it was Milray Thaler, the international treasurer, who felt most threatened.

Thaler was furious at the report of Multinational Consultants. A few days after it had been circulated in Sola, Thaler produced a 26-page reply, refuting the report point by point. Some of the extracts from his rebuttal were especially provocative.

2. Of course, the international side of the treasurer's function is growing more complicated. Governments get smarter every day. Regulations get more complicated. With Section 482 on one side and OFDI on the other, it is not easy to do business abroad. But what kind of an answer is MCI offering us? To set up a treasurer in every area, so one area doesn't know what the other is doing? Who will tell German-Sola to stop trying to make a record for itself by gouging Argentine-Sola with its high invoice prices for petrochemicals? And who will stop the subsidiaries from always trying to build up their equity, instead of building up accounts payable? Much better to give me a few more high-level assistants who have had a little experience with such complicated matters so that we can stay on top of such problems.

3. Maybe production and marketing need some decentralizing at the regional level. After all, the users of industrial chemicals in Nairobi are not exactly the same types you find in Hamburg or Rio. But the management of money is another matter; that should be centralized. Money is money once you get it out of the clutches of a country and make it convertible. A dollar out of Peru is a dollar out of Turkey, and it ought to be managed that way.

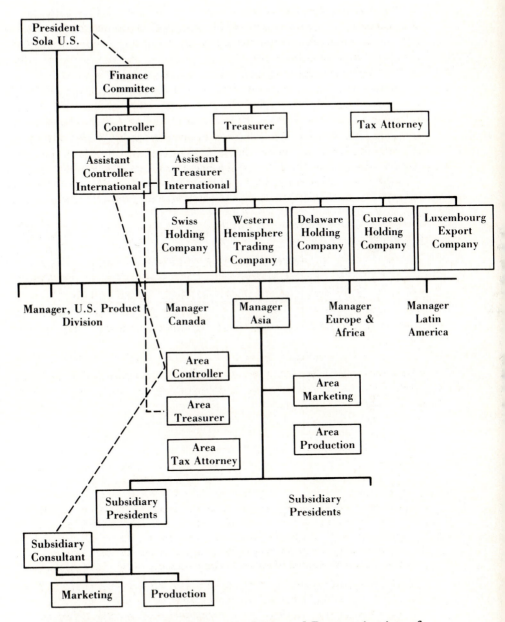

Exhibit 2 *Financial Offices in Proposed Reorganization of Sola Company, 1970*

5. How would a regional treasurer know how to use the Curaçao or Luxembourg companies, or why? Today, if Sola-Switzerland needs to pay a dividend to U.S. Sola, I can easily drum up the money by way of Curaçao and I know how to compare it with Berne's cash flow prospects.

14. That famous $350,000 translation loss from the devaluation of sterling is getting a little ridiculous. Translation losses are not money, they are bookkeeping. They mean nothing to Sola's cash flow. Tax payments are a different matter. There is where real money can be saved. If I were to worry about every currency that might devalue tomorrow, I would eat up the time of the company and the office chasing paper butterflies.

15. Once the controller starts making up his own score card and the treasurer makes up a separate one, it will be impossible to know where we stand. The controller has everything he needs, without the headaches of a special set of books, if he gets copies of the treasurer's instructions to the subsidiaries. If he wants to adjust his records because of these instructions, so that the effect of tax transactions and cash flow transactions are cancelled out, it is easy enough for him to do it.

16. Above all, once you start putting the profit centers in the regional offices, you are a dead duck. Europe is not yet a country. Neither is Latin America. The authorities in the central banks and in the national tax administrations are not about to give up their powers and go away. These are the offices you have to keep your eye on if you are going to survive in the international business.

Ian H. Giddy

Case 44

Nokia Comes Out of the Forest

Bent over against the first chill of autumn, Paula Perttunen hurried up Helsinki's esplanade toward her office in the Nokia Oy headquarters building. She tried to keep her mind clear so that she could properly evaluate the various financing proposals that had been discussed during the previous weeks with various bankers who had visited Helsinki. As Assistant Treasurer (International) for Nokia, the largest private industrial firm in Finland, Paula was responsible for the initial assessment and presentation of financing proposals for Nokia's international investments.

Once the central Finance Committee had approved the underlying concept, the actual implementation was divided between Nokia's International Finance office in Geneva and Corporate Treasury in Helsinki, depending on the regulatory constraints and tax considerations.

In the mid-1980s, the Nokia Group's products encompassed forest industries, cables, metal products and electronics, among others, with a recent emphasis on international production and sales of industrial and consumer electronics. A major corporate objective was to reduce its dependency on forest products. Sixty percent of its estimated US$3.6 billion sales in 1987 were outside Finland (Exhibit 1), although 85 percent of the Group's $2.37 billion assets remained within the country (Exhibit 2). Nokia was presently considering an investment of approximately $410 million in the United States, and Paula Perttunen was digging up ways to finance it. Her immediate task upon reaching her desk was to come up

Exhibit 1 *Nokia's international sales (in millions of Finnmarks)*

Sales in	1987 Estimate	1986
Finland	5,574	4,856
Exports from Finland	4,710	4,187
Foreign subsidiaries	3,714	2,951
Total	13,998	11,994

Profile of Foreign Sales by Market Area

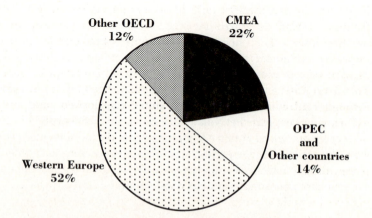

Nokia Group exports and turnover of foreign subsidiaries by market area

Exhibit 2 *Nokia group balance sheet — projected (in millions of Finnmarks) as at December 31, 1987*

Assets		
Cash and receivables	6,491	
Inventories	2,854	
Fixed assets	5,764	
Goodwill	718	
		15,827
Liabilities		
Current liabilities	4,028	
Long Term liabilities	5,396	
Minority interests in group companies	629	
Shareholders capital[1]	5,774	
		15,827

Notes
[1]Including net profit for the past year of FIM 187 million.

with a financing package for presentation to the Finance Committee that met regularly at the end of the month. The bankers had proposed a private placement with a U.S. insurance company or a Eurobond issue or, alternatively, issuing commercial paper that would be coupled with an interest rate swap to give Nokia fixed-rate money. In addition to these, Paula had some other ideas up her sleeve. But first, she thought, I had better make sure of how much and what kind of financing we need.

WHAT FINANCING WAS REALLY NEEDED?

Nokia was no newcomer to the international capital market. It had borrowed over $200 million in various currencies from international banks, and had issued a $40 million, seven-year Swiss franc bond in 1978. Its shares were even traded on the Stockholm stock exchange. Already well known in the area of modems for data transfer, Nokia had earlier in the year successfully launched a new product, a mobile hand-held radio-telephone, through a subsidiary called Mobira. Initial sales looked good and Nokia's top management was keen to get a jump on the U.S. consumer electronics market by producing a hand-held, remote computer terminal. This device would combine the modem and radio-telephone technology with a flat-screen display device developed by another Finnish firm, Lohja Oy. Even the Japanese had not quite caught up with that technology, although Nokia expected that they would be formidable competitors in the long run. Nokia had already set up a new subsidiary, Mobiterm, that had developed a prototype model that was reportedly reliable and cost efficient.

Knut Wikstedt, Nokia's electronics chief honcho and director of finance, was keeping an eye open for a U.S. assembler and distributor when he learned in early 1987 that Mattel, the U.S. consumer electronics firm, was seeking a buyer for its troubled Intellivision unit. The Board agreed with his view that such an acquisition could give Nokia a firm footing in the U.S. consumer electronics industry and serve as a base from which to launch the Mobiterm product.

The Bank of Finland and the Ministry of Finance had been informed of Nokia's interest — the authorities maintained discretionary control over all capital movements, especially outward investments (Exhibit 3) — and Nokia was seeking an export credit guarantee for the $25 million of equipment they expected to supply to any new U.S. subsidiary. Preliminary discussions with Mattel were underway, although the purchase price was by no means set in stone. Mattel refused to accept Nokia's Free Preferred Shares, but had agreed that part of the purchase price could be in the form of a $75 million five-year note at 12¾ percent; the rest would have to be cash. Nokia was being advised in the acquisition negotiations by the American investment banking firm, Goldman Brothers. Wikstedt's intention was to assemble the hand-held terminals at Mattel's plant in Dallas and initially sell them in the United States. After two years, if they were a success in the United States, the terminals would be sold in Europe as well; the aim was to achieve an 80 percent North America, 10 percent Europe sales mix, with the remainder going to the rest of the world.

Exhibit 3 **Summary of Finnish Government's role in Finnish companies' international borrowing**

Three authorities of the Finnish Government can be involved in a Finnish firm's international financing plans. The first and most important of these is the central bank, the Bank of Finland. The Bank administers Finland's rather strict capital controls, both on capital inflows and on capital outflows. Since Finland has a small capital market, the Bank wants to be sure that it is not depleted by borrowing for foreign investments. Capital outflows would also deplete Finland's rather limited foreign exchange reserves. Thus, only a very limited amount of domestic, Finnmark funds could be used to finance foreign investments. The Bank of Finland also influences all major funding abroad by Finnish, private or government-owned. The goals are to ensure that Finnish firms abroad displace neither one another nor the Government itself in tapping the international capital market, and to prevent excessive capital flows that could lead to monetary expansion. Any firm planning to issue equity, long-term debt or commercial paper abroad must therefore seek the Bank's approval.

A Bank of Finland official described the procedure for gaining such approval as follows. First, the Bank limits the number of potential issuers to major Finnish companies. Each year the Bank conducts a survey of such companies' prospective demand for foreign credits. The firms are assigned "quotas" of foreign funds that they may be permitted to raise. These quotas are based on the Bank's judgment of Finland's total access to the international capital market, and its internal analysis of the credit standing of each company — its profitability, indebtedness, and so forth. Such an evaluation, which can be done on an ad hoc basis for companies planning major borrowing, can take up to two weeks to complete. The Board of Management of the Bank of Finland must approve all amounts above FIM 50 million.

When the firm passes muster, it gets approval "in principle." Although the company may now in principle plan to do its financing any way it likes, in practice it must get a second approval each time it does a specific issue. This approval, which only takes a day or two, is designed to prevent bunching of Finnish issues abroad and to make sure that the proposed terms and conditions are fair and competitive.

The second Finnish government agency with an interest in capital flows is the Ministry of Finance. Its role is an informal one. Because the MOF borrows in the name of the Republic of Finland in the Eurobond and commercial paper markets, it will give the thumbs down to any issue that it feels might damage Finland's AAA rating.

Finally, the Ministry of Trade and Industry can also get involved in international capital movements involving equity financing, as for example in a bond issue carrying warrants or a convertible bond. The reason is that the Ministry administers the corporation law, including the severe restraints on property ownership imposed on any Finish company whose voting stock is more than 20 percent owned by foreigners.

Wikstedt had told Paula that Nokia or its new subsidiary, Mobiterm, would have to raise from outside sources all but $30 million of the purchase price. The $30 million had been generated from the European sales of Nokia's Swedish electronics subsidiary, Luxor. On the other hand, it was rumored that Nokia's soft-tissue unit located in Sweden, Nordic tissues, might be sold. This sale would reap at least FIM 700 million, or US$163 million at today's exchange rate of 4.3 Finnmarks to the dollar. Paula knew that Nokia's board was indeed considering such a move, but the outcome was quite uncertain as the Board was split right down the middle on this issue. "If they could only make up their bloody minds," she thought, "life would be so much easier!"

Wikstedt felt that funding should be such that repayment was deferred for at least seven years. Since Nokia had been burned during the last rise in short-term rates, it was generally understood that management's goal was to increase the proportion of fixed-rate debt to about 60 percent. At present, 53 percent of the company's total debt of FIM 9.4 billion was short-term or variable-rate debt. The currency mix of the company's debt at the end of 1987 was: FIM 56 percent, US$ 16 percent, DM 6 percent, SK 3 percent, GBP 4 percent, FRF 4 percent, CHF 7 percent, and other 4 percent.

SOURCES OF FUNDS

Paula began by writing down the likely mix of funds sources for the acquisition:

Purchase price	$410 million
Five-year note to Mattel	($75 million)
Cash on hand	($30 million)
New debt required:	$305 million

The obvious source of financing, she mused, is a syndicated revolving credit facility — a bank loan. Banque Francaise had been pestering Nokia's treasury people about this, saying that the bank could put together a $250–300 million syndicated credit at a cost of ⅝ percent above LIBOR, the London Interbank Offered Rate, plus the usual front-end fees. Such credits ranged up to 12 years' maturity and could be drawn down when needed. It was a "no-brainer" (a slang word Paula had picked up during her last visit in New York). The only problem was that Finland's two biggest banks together owned 21.4 percent of Nokia's stock and had board representation who resisted Francaise's lead management of any loan because they had been excluded from the management group of recent Scandinavian issues led by Francaise. In any case, in a recent telephone conversation Paula sensed that the French had back-pedalled a bit from the syndicated loan idea due to new capital adequacy standards that might curb even the appetite of government-owned banks from increasing their balance sheets. "What Nokia needs," the French bankers said, is "a MOF," a Multiple Option Facility, an offspring of a RUF, or revolving underwriting facility.

An alternative source of short-term funds would be for Nokia to issue commercial paper, either in Europe or preferably in the United States. To do the latter, the company would have to get a rating and pay about ½ percent for a back-up line from a decent bank. Metrobank alone was willing to provide a line for up to $100 million and to assist in placing the commercial paper, and had argued that this would be a good way for Nokia to become better-known in the United States. Despite their recent rapid expansion into the United States, Finnish companies still had a very low profile in North America. To assist Nokia in ensuring its paper's acceptability to U.S. institutional investors, Metrobank had offered letter of credit support for a fee of ¼ percent. This would give it an A1/P1 rating. The A1/P1 commercial paper rate yields were currently about 90 basis points below LIBOR.

Alternatively, someone who knew the private placement market could place medium-term Nokia notes directly with U.S. institutional investors, at a cost of a few extra basis points and fairly restrictive indentures.

Two other possibilities that Paula had discussed with the Metrobank people at a business lunch involved taking advantage of the short-term assets that the Intellivision unit had on its balance sheet. Mattel, who had provided an unaudited statement of accounts to Nokia (see Exhibit 4), estimated that about two-thirds of Intellivision's inventory consisted of silver for use in microchip circuitry. This silver inventory represented approximately six months' supply and served primarily to insulate the company's margin from any unexpected rise in silver prices; six months was the time it took to get higher silver prices reflected in the industry's wholesale prices for electronic consumer products.

Exhibit 4 **Mattel Inc. — *Intellivision Division unaudited balance sheet (millions of dollars)***

As at December 31, 1987 — Projected		
Assets		
Cash and marketable securities	11	
Accounts receivable	45	
Inventories	57	
Fixed Assets	208	
Goodwill	13	334
Liabilities		
Short-term bank debt	0	
Accounts payable	33	
Long-term debt	110	
Net worth	191	334

Metrobank would purchase the silver from Mobiterm for, say, three or six months at a time, meanwhile allowing Mobiterm to use the metal in its finished products. At the end of six months Metrobank would sell the silver back to Mobiterm at the going market price. And Metrobank was incredibly willing to do this for only 3½ percent per annum, "because of the value of the collateral"! When Paula voiced concern about the risk of exposing the company's cost to the volatile silver market, Metrobank had suggested that their precious metals group could assist in covering the position by purchasing silver futures at the London Metal Exchange (see Exhibit 5) "Futures are not expensive," one of the bankers remarked, "we know a discount broker who charges only £15 per contract." The bank would handle the margin requirement with an L/C and their cash management group might, for a small fee, take care of the daily settlement problems.

Exhibit 5 *Silver prices*

SILVER (CMX) — 5,000 TROY OZ.; CENTS PER TROY OZ.

	Open	High	Low	Settle	Change	Lifetime High	Lifetime Low	Open Interest
Aug	..	..	..	524.6	+6.0	536.0	509.5	205
Sept	519.0	529.5	517.0	526.5	+5.8	861.0	510.0	37,919
Dec	532.0	542.0	529.0	539.2	+5.9	886.0	525.0	28,141
Mr88	542.0	555.0	542.0	551.1	+6.0	910.0	534.0	9,988
May	..	..	..	559.1	+6.1	910.0	543.0	5,641
July	..	..	..	567.5	+6.2	761.5	550.0	3,611
Sept	576.0	579.0	576.0	575.9	+6.3	760.0	565.0	2,171
Dec	..	..	..	587.9	+6.3	742.0	568.0	827
Mr89	..	..	..	600.0	+6.3	665.0	583.0	509
May	..	..	..	608.4	+6.3	608.0	593.0	367

Est vol 20,000; vol Wed 12,509; open int 89,413, + 1,892

SILVER (CBT) — 1,000 TROY OZ., CENTS PER TROY OZ.

	Open	High	Low	Settle	Change	Lifetime High	Lifetime Low	Open Interest
Aug	525.0	522.0	515.0	522.0	+3.0	700.0	505.0	14
Oct	523.0	532.0	522.0	530.0	+5.0	716.0	513.0	380
Dec	532.0	543.0	529.0	540.0	+6.0	735.0	523.0	8,680
Fb88	540.0	550.0	539.0	548.5	+6.0	694.0	535.0	226
Apr	..	..	..	557.0	+6.0	685.0	545.0	116
June	568.0	570.0	565.0	565.5	+6.0	686.0	553.0	138

Est vol 500; vol Wed 894; open int 9,631, -276

Alternatively, another bank would be able to discount Mobiterm's receivables — Nokia had experience with this technique inside and outside Finland — although some of Intellivision's receivables were in DM and sterling. Metrobank had expressed an interest in discounting longer-term big-ticket trade receivables. Both approaches were excellent means of taking assets off the books of a company that had credit rating problems. Some investment bankers had even mentioned that they were working on a scheme to "securitize" such trade receivables and sell the paper to assorted widows and orphans.

Paula Perttunen had made a list of all these financing methods. However, she wondered, would top management live with the varying interest rates that these would entail? Perhaps just for the part that's financing our receivables or inventory? On the other hand, we should consider taking up Metrobank's suggestion that we create fixed-rate funds out of variable-rate financing by doing an interest rate swap. Let's see, how would that work? And what would it cost? She recalled a luncheon conversation at Ravintola Nevski with Timo Tyynela, the local rep of Metrobank.

Perttunen: Timo, if we drew down a Eurodollar loan at a spread over six-month LIBOR, how would you fix our cost of funds?

Tyynela: Well, in a floating-fixed interest rate swap, we would pay LIBOR to Nokia every six months, which you could then use to service your floating interest payments. In return, Nokia would pay us a fixed rate set at, I would guess, 93 basis points above the seven-year U.S. Treasury bond rate. Yesterday, seven-year Treasuries were yielding 9.59 percent.

Perttunen: Any fees?

Tyynela: Up-front fees used to be usual, but for many years we have waived them for clients such as Nokia. We could do a seven-year deal as big as $250 million for Nokia. The only thing I would say is that you would have to do a minimum of $10 million to make it worthwhile. And, of course we would have to get credit approval.

Perttunen: I find it odd that you would need further credit approval given that you would be lending us over US$150 million in a LIBOR facility! Does that mean that we would use up additional credit lines? By the way, could you do these swaps in other currencies?

Tyynela: Yes, interest rate swaps are being done in most of the major European currencies, and yen, and a few others. I brought a rate sheet along, for indications only (see Exhibit 6).

Exhibit 6 *Swap indications at a glance*

	US$ Interest rate swaps		Currency swaps	
Years	**Treasury curve** Price/Yield	**Spread**	**DM/U.S.$**	**¥/U.S.$**
2	99.18/8.74	79–86	5.50–5.60	5.68–5.78
3	97.07/8.99	80–85	5.95–6.02	5.85–5.93
4	99.21/9.23	78–84	6.20–6.30	5.93–6.00
5	96.07/9.30	80–86	6.42–6.50	6.10–6.18
7	92.06/9.59	86–93	6.75–6.83	6.23–6.30
10	93.06/9.71	88–94	7.18–7.28	6.40–6.50

		Currency swaps		
Years	**Sfr/U.S.$**	**£/U.S.$**	**ECU/U.S.$**	**A$/U.S.$**
2	4.90–5.00	10.60–10.70	8.65–8.75	12.68–12.76
3	5.30–5.40	10.58–10.68	8.75–8.85	12.74–12.84
4	5.42–5.50	10.58–10.68	8.85–8.95	12.90–13.07
5	5.62–5.70	10.68–10.78	8.95–9.05	12.90–13.07
7	5.65–5.75	10.60–10.70	9.15–9.25	N/A
10	5.80–5.90	10.68–10.78	9.30–9.40	N/A

LIBOR six-month U.S.$: 8.75%

Source: *Business International Money Report*, October 12, 1987

Perttunen: How about Finnmarks?

Tyynela: Anything's possible . . . at a price. We could also give you a rate swap based not on LIBOR but on the A1/P1 commercial paper rate; in fact, that would knock about 40 basis points off the fixed rate you'd have to pay. In addition we could fix you up with a currency swap, in case you need dollars but feel you have an advantage in the D-Mark or Swiss franc market. These would be priced as an interest differential for fixed-rate funds in the two currencies. Take a dollar-mark swap. The indicative rate for a seven-year fixed US$ against fixed DM swap is 9.59 + 86/93 percent against 6.75/6.83 percent in DM. For Swissies it would be 9.59 + 86/93 percent against 5.65/5.75 percent. For example, if Nokia has DM debt on which you're paying 6.75 percent fixed, we would give you the 6.75 percent annually in marks and you would give us 10.52 percent annually in dollars. At maturity we would pay you the DM amount of your principal and you could pay us the same amount in